Communities
of Women

Communities
of Women

An Idea in Fiction

Nina Auerbach

HARVARD UNIVERSITY PRESS
CAMBRIDGE, MASSACHUSETTS
AND LONDON, ENGLAND
1978

Publication of this volume has been aided by a grant
from the Andrew W. Mellon Foundation

Library of Congress Cataloging in Publication Data

Auerbach, Nina, 1943-
    Communities of women.

    Includes bibliographical references and index.
        1. English fiction—History and criticism.   2. Women
in literature.   3. American fiction—19th century—
History and criticism.   I. Title.
PR830.W6A9   823'.009'352   77-21213
ISBN 0-674-15168-2

For the ongoing community of women

at the Radcliffe Institute

And for the larger, still-growing community of women

teaching and writing in America

Acknowledgments

Planning and writing this book created a community of women and men, to all of whom I am more grateful than I can say here. First I should like to thank the Ford Foundation, whose generous grant allowed me a year free from other academic duties in which to write, though for all opinions and any misconceptions that arose in that year, the responsibility is solely my own. I should also like to thank my colleagues in the English Department at the University of Pennsylvania, who endorsed this project from its inception and supported it with good faith and good ideas to its final incarnation. Special thanks must go to Joel Conarroe, whose habitual grace under pressure provided me with unwavering support; Stuart Curran and David DeLaura, who tirelessly reread and commented on the manuscript, improving it each time; and Robert Lucid, who remembered the Ford Foundation and remembered me.

I owe an incalculable debt to the Radcliffe Institute for their invitation to spend the year as one of their Fellows. In the gracious blend of sisterhood and seclusion shaped by Patricia Albjerg Graham and Hilda Kahne, I received not only space and support for my work, but a model community of women which gave a local habitation to the Utopias I read about. Many of my fellow Fellows generously provided me with material that enriched my research immeasurably, and I would especially like to thank Sylvia Brown, Gayle Hannah, Janet James, Carroll Smith-Rosenberg, Mary Walsh, and Joan Hoff Wilson, for bringing important sources to my attention. Beyond Radcliffe Yard, Judith Dye, Avrom Fleishman, Maurice Johnson, Marjorie Perloff, and Vivian Pollak also suggested what seemed just the right books; and my friends Sharon Bassett, Saralyn Daly, and Victoria Kirkham provided their own varieties of an unchartered personal community of women that is still best and brightest in the world out of books.

I should like to thank Jerome H. Buckley for his extraordinarily thorough and helpful comments about an early version of this study, which introduced me to a wealth of new things to think about and new ways in which to see the material; and Carl Woodring, whose learned and incisive suggestions about my manuscript were only one example of his kindness and patient help over the years, teaching me again that I am as much, and as gratefully, his student as I was when he directed my dissertation at Columbia University.

Carolyn Heilbrun provided more than assistance to this project: she presided over it. From her hint for a topic at the beginning to the constructive criticism and sage counsel she gave throughout the book's course, she is so indelible a part of my community of women that it could not exist without her.

Lauren Bedau and Julie Tonkin typed various incarnations of the manuscript with indestructible fingers and an indestructible good faith for which I thank them even more.

An abridged version of Chapter 2 appeared in *Novel: A Form in Fiction* (Fall 1976); an abridged version of Chapter 3 appeared in *Modern Language Quarterly* (September 1977). I should like to thank the editors of both journals for permission to reproduce the material here.

N.A.

Philadelphia
September 1977

Contents

Introduction:
The Communal Eye

Lekythos. Drawing: *Battle of Greeks and Amazons*
Courtesy, Museum of Fine Arts, Boston. Catherine Page Perkins Fund

1

Initiation into a band of brothers is a traditional privilege symbolized by uniforms, rituals, and fiercely shared loyalties; but sisterhood, the subject of this book, looks often like a blank exclusion. A community of women may suggest less the honor of fellowship than an antisociety, an austere banishment from both social power and biological rewards. Yet the novels this study will examine grant these communities a subtle, unexpected power.

The Graie are three mythical sisters who are isolated from time: Hesiod's *Theogeny* states baldly that they were born old. In the "now" of myth, they have a single eye between them, which is passed unfailingly from sister to sister. They spend their lives endowing each other with vision: apparently it has never occurred to any one sister to keep the eye and run away. That is the hero's job. Perseus steals the eye, forcing them to reveal the whereabouts of their other triad of sisters, the irresistibly hideous Gorgons. Once the Graie are dispossessed of their eye, the Gorgons are doomed: Perseus triumphantly wears Medusa's fanged, snaky head as his second shield, whose magnetic ugliness turns his enemies to stone. Sisterhood seems powerless against the hero's theft of the communal eye.

The warrior Amazons suggest a less vulnerable community of mythic women. Today, "Amazonian" suggests female impregnability: on the state seal of Virginia, an Amazon personifying Virtue tramples down a male warrior personifying Tyranny. But in Greek folk etymology, the community's name immortalizes its defect, not its strength: with more meaning than accuracy, common tradition gives the derivation $\dot{a}^+\mu a \zeta \acute{o} \varsigma$, "without a breast," reminding us that these mythic warriors sliced off their right breasts in order to shoot more effectively. But despite this self-mutilation in the service of victory, the Amazons are routed over and over. The heroism of Priam, Bellerophon, Heracles, Theseus, and even Dionysus, is defined in part by their common ability to invade and disperse the Amazons. The elaborate discipline whereby their army is trained and replenished exists only as raw material, from which a solitary adventurer will chisel his heroism.

The endless age of the Graie and the indomitable vigor of the Amazons are opposites that meet at important points. Both are communities of women without men, and, as such, they are seen immediately as mutilated: the only eye possessed by the Graie is that of sisterhood, and the Amazons' name defines the sphere of erotic and maternal softness they are barred from. Both groups are outcast. Exiled from time, the ageless Graie live away from nature in its seasonal rotation and change, in a land literally out of sight. The far-off homeland of the Amazons is by definition beyond the frontier of civilization. Another possible derivation of their name was ἀ⁺μᾶζα, "without barley-cake," suggesting that they feasted barbarically on a nature wild and raw. Not only do they lack womanly biology; they lack the womanly skills that transform nature into sustenance. In Herodotus' *The Persian Wars,* an Amazon says defiantly: "To draw the bow, to hurl the javelin, to bestride the horse, these are our arts—of womanly employments we know nothing."[1]

Their inability to mold civilization from the land allies the Amazons to the barbaric and the savage, leaving them prey to the more sophisticated weapons and tactics of the monster-slayers who subdue them. In their manless persistence, they are aligned in Greek sculpture with the half-brute Centaurs whose nonhuman incursions are a touchstone for civilized prowess: "Often, as on the Parthenon metopes, an amazonomachy is paired with a sculptural representation of a battle of Greeks against centaurs."[2] But though they are implacably remote from everything that normally constitutes the human condition, the communities of the Graie and the Amazons nevertheless survive the depredations of the solitary hero, the Amazons by an elaborately ritualized group mating season, the Graie by their sheer eternality of grayness. Subsisting precariously at or beyond the boundaries of the reproductive cycle, these groups manage nevertheless to pull life out of death and to endure.

The dark power of these female communities in Greek mythology is not dissolved by the struggle of the hero to dispel it: these castaway worlds, subsisting beyond the recognizable, find their counterparts at the heart of experience. The nine Muses, Zeus's daughters, possess absolute control over that part of the human imagination which endures: memory and the arts. To possess human memory is to achieve power not merely over the past, but over immortality in the future the poet creates. Finally, control of memory is equivalent to the creation of life itself: "Oblivion or Silence is at one with the power of death, which is armed against the power of life—Memory, mother of the Muses. Underlying Praise and Blame, the fundamental opposition [in Greek culture] is between Mnemosyne and Lethe. The warrior's life is played out between these two poles."[3]

As the Muses determine a hero's ultimate survival through their control of the mind, another group of sisters determines the pattern of his life: the three Fates run human and divine destiny through their fingers, at one with an unspecified power Zeus cannot controvert. In this vision of the world, solitary women together are both beyond the pale of human experience and at the heart of it. Their exclusion from civilization seems at one with their control of mind, life, and immortality. A triad of sisters begins as an image of maimed and outcast pathos and ends as a unity of force neither god nor hero dare invade.

This corporate and contradictory vision of a unit that is simultaneously defective and transcendent forms part of all the novels this study will examine. As a recurrent literary image, a community of women is a rebuke to the conventional ideal of a solitary woman living for and through men, attaining citizenship in the community of adulthood through masculine approval alone. The communities of women which have haunted our literary imagination from the beginning are emblems of female self-sufficiency which create their own corporate reality, evoking both wishes and fears.

As a literary idea, a community of women feeds dreams of a world beyond the normal. This book is about the journey of that idea through almost two centuries of imaginative literature, exposing the potency of its impact on the novel and on the cultures novels reflect and create, and reminding us that female self-sufficiency is not a postulate of this or that generation of feminists, but an inherent and powerful component of our shared cultural vision.

But the image changes as cultural perspectives do; and as cultural imagination begins to intersect with official historical reality, the communities of women examined appropriate more and more of the era in which they are apparent anomalies. We begin with a British and an American portrait of a family of women. Both Jane Austen's irony and Louisa May Alcott's sentiment evoke the momentum of a matriarchal family and the point at which this momentum must withdraw before that large body of ungovernable men who compose the world beyond the hearth. In mid-Victorian England, Charlotte Brontë and Elizabeth Gaskell venture into an unchartered world in their delineations of governing women whose self-definitions come from their freedom from family. At the turn of the century, Henry James and George Gissing—two men with chivalry on their minds and some fear in their hearts—initiate their female communities into the sanctum of masculine history. Today, the communities of Muriel Spark and her contemporaries are bastions of military and metaphysical potency, the image having broadened its base from that of Austen's marriage-possessed mother to Spark's history-possessed Mother Superior, dreaming of dominion. Though history itself has only grudgingly accommodated the aspirations of women, literary history has moved through a series of emancipations and expanding fields of conquest.

Communities of women growing in time constitute a drama of widening cultural consciousness, finally taking shape as an evolving literary myth that sweeps across official cultural images of female submission, subservience, and fulfillment in a bounded world. As this myth takes shape as part of our imaginative inheritance, so does the fictional reality of women's autonomy: for though the communities gain substance and stature as we proceed, their isolation has had from the first the self-sustaining power to repel or incorporate the male-defined reality that excludes them.

In literature, at any rate, this power must be searched out and insisted upon, because even to sympathetic observers female communities still tend to evoke the maimed, outcast image of the Graie—a collective amputee by definition. A few years ago Charlotte Wolff, a feminist psychiatrist, observed bleakly: "The effect produced by a group of women alone is different from that of a group of men alone. Women by themselves appear to be incomplete, as if a limb were missing. They do not come into their proper place and function without the male."[4] Though "effect" and "appear" admit uncertainly that this mutilation may be in the eye of the beholder, for Wolff only a lesbian community has the integrity of "a group of men alone": by herself, a heterosexual woman can constitute only a sexual plea. Yet though lesbianism is a silent possibility in two or three of the novels discussed, in no case is it an accomplished fact bestowing on these communities extrinsic power. Their strength is inherent, though rarely initially apparent.

This distinction is echoed in literature: however overweening or debased they may become, all-male communities usually possess indisputable magnitude and significance. The reader of Tennyson's *Idylls of the King* never doubts Arthur's vision as he laments his lost fellowship: "A glorious company, the flower of men, To serve as model for the mighty world, And be the fair beginning of a time" ("Guinevere," 11. 461-463). For Sir Bedivere the Round Table looms even more suggestively as "an image of this mighty world." From the world's inspiriter and prime mover, Camelot has become the symbolic crystallization of the world's unity and power. But *The Princess* describes the still-unfallen might of Ida's Amazonian College for Women only as the strength of separation: "Each [handmaid] was like a Druid rock; Or like a spire of land that stands apart Cleft from the main, and wali'd about with mews" (IV, 261-263). In this vision, though no man is an island, it seems every woman is one. Even an imperfect kingdom of men is the main from which a nation of women is cleft.

The immediate authority generated by literary communities of men comes not merely from their possession of universal symbols of power, the resonance of "King," "Captain," and "Master"; as in the *Idylls,* it springs too from the powerful motion of the quest which so often gives them their structure. In the most memorable male quest novels the quest is for the primary reality of "this mighty world" which the community itself embodies: *Moby-Dick's* "ungraspable phantom of life," the pursuit of which is itself the savage and elusive truth of things. If notable treasure hunts like *Heart of Darkness, Treasure Island,* and *The Treasure of the Sierra Madre* perceive the treasure as the "ungraspable phantom," the hunt becomes "an image of this mighty world" that destroys the communities it immortalizes. In such variants of the quest novel as *Billy Budd* and *The Caine Mutiny,* the male community turns inward to explore the most precious treasure of all: the nature of its own authority, which in each novel emerges insane but intact. But whether these communities are destroyed or reasserted, they retain their magnitude as vessels of significance which such well-intentioned female outlanders as Starbuck's wife and Kurtz's Intended can never share.

The female communities examined here are endowed with no majestic titles, but must create their own, somewhat quirky and grotesque authority in the names of "Mother Bhaer," "Miss Jean Brodie," or the ambiguous "Madame" of *Villette.* In almost all instances, the male quest is exchanged for rootedness—a school, a village, a city of their own; while the treasure is the invisible and often partial gain of a possession that is also self-possession. The titles of two contemporary novels about single-sex communities define the poles of these different sorts of power: James Jones's *From Here to Eternity* evokes the cosmic and interminable majesty of an endless army; while *In This House of Brede,* Rumer Godden's novel about nuns, is the story of a single building. But Brede is not a shelter; its potency is not that of Erik Erikson's womblike "inner space," but that of a communal self-creation and the integrity of adherence. If initially "women by themselves appear to be incomplete," the quest and the treasure of Godden's nuns is this symbol of their corporate completeness.

The bridge leading from male to female communities lies in the differing connotations of the word "code." All true communities are knit together by their codes, but a code can range from dogma to a flexible, private, and often semi-conscious set of beliefs. In literature at least, male communities tend to live by a code in its most explicit, formulated, and inspirational sense; while in female communities, the code seems a whispered and a fleeting thing, more a buried language than a rallying cry, whose invocations, like Cranford's reiterated "elegant economy" or the ostensible etiquette of Jean Brodie's "la crème de la crème," have more than a touch of the impalpable and the devious.

Two short works from the end of the nineteenth century may show us the explicit and the hidden codes. The first sentence of Rudyard Kipling's *The Man Who Would Be King* (1899) lays down the Masonic code from which the story is drawn: "Brother to a Prince and fellow to a beggar if he be found worthy."[5] As author and character, Kipling finds "Brother Peachey Carnehan" and "Brother Daniel Dravot" worthy to be both princes and beggars in their quest for the treasure of Kafiristan, an image of the mighty forces their fraternity exists to rule: "no one has gone there, and they fight" (p. 34). To prime themselves to conquer, Carnehan and Dravot supplement their code by a "contrack" whereby they will eschew liquor and women. As long as the code is maintained, the quest is fulfilled in their possession of kingship and treasure; but once Dravot breaks it to covet a wife, he and his brother are expelled, like Adam and King Arthur, from Paradise and dominion into death. The true avenging God of the tale is their brotherhood; when it is betrayed, rule is impossible and all must die.

The novella begins with the code, finds its apex in the penetration of the remote, and ends with expulsion when women intrude on brotherhood. But "Miss Tempy's Watchers" in Sarah Orne Jewett's story (1888) live already, like the Amazons and the natives of Kafiristan, beyond the horizon of civilization: "the place was a small farming town in New Hampshire, remote from any railroad."[6] Like the Graie, the three women who constitute the story's cast of characters live beyond the reproductive cycle as well: Temperance Dent has died a spinster, as will Sarah Ann Binson when her time comes, while Mrs. Crowe's marriage is hopelessly childless. But instead of asserting ringing solidarity in gorgeous Masonic trappings, Miss Binson and Mrs. Crowe begin their final night's vigil over Tempy's corpse with a small sigh of pathos: "Poor Miss Tempy!"

But in the course of the watching, the memory of "poor Miss Tempy" expands again into magnanimous life, uniting the house of death in a sympathetic bond between the "vague" and wealthy married woman, the "sharp-set" impecunious spinster, and the quiet corpse. The isolation death brings warms into silent companionship: "These words were spoken as if there were a third person listening; somebody beside Mrs. Crowe. The watchers could not rid their minds of the feeling that they were being watched themselves. The spring wind whistled in the window crack, now and then, and buffeted the little house in a gusty way that had a sort of companionable effect" (p. 235). Though no bond is asserted, the "gusty" and threatening are translated into community. Finally, the two women fall asleep to partake of a momentary and miraculous interpenetration between wakers and sleepers, living and dead, watchers and watched: "Overhead, the pale shape of Tempy Dent, the outworn body of that generous, loving-hearted, simple soul, slept on also in its white raiment. Perhaps Tempy herself stood near, and saw her own life and its surroundings with new understanding. Perhaps she herself was the only watcher" (p. 243). Only the narrator is awake to suggest the momentary and miraculous sisterhood that is formed when "poor Miss Tempy" gains the power to embrace life and death together.

This community of women that exists for a night at the margins of the social and natural world attains an almost magical affinity with the sources of transformation and rebirth. But no "contrack" codifies it: it is defined only suggestively and obliquely through Mrs. Crowe's story of Tempy's psychic grasp of trees, of which the two survivors partake through their sympathetic perception in another spiral of communion between the watchers and the watched: "Now, she had only that one old quince-tree down in the far corner of the piece, but she'd go out in the spring and tend to it, and look at it so pleasant, and kind of expect the old thorny thing into bloomin' " (p. 241).

In the course of the story, Miss Binson and Mrs. Crowe do for Tempy's "outworn body" as Tempy has done for the tree: they "kind of expect the old thorny thing into bloomin'," and bloom she does, for them and for us. Like the communities of Greek women, the women of "Miss Tempy's Watchers" possess a power of quasi-magical self-sustainment that blooms out of apparent death. The bonds of hospitality and sympathy between women that pervade the isolated landscapes in Jewett's volume are more potent than men's railroad tracks in keeping alive the human world and knitting it together. The empire-building of Kipling's Masons is defined by the sanctioned heroism whose limitations are formulated in its code and its contract; but the community Miss Tempy and her watchers create is the quiet fruition of its own completeness, which incorporates apparent death into its life.

The unformulated miracle of the community of women is its ability to create itself. Much has been written recently deploring the reduction of women in literature to the "relative creatures" advocated by Sarah Stickney Ellis' Victorian conduct books, whose identities lie in the roles of daughter, wife, and mother men impose on them.[7] Such complaints neglect a tradition in the novel that does allow women an independent life beyond the saga of courtship and the settlement of marriage. "We women are, no less than men, each of us a distinct existence":[8] Dinah Mulock Craik's is a Victorian voice like Sarah Ellis', but one belonging to an absolute being, not a relative creature.

Women in literature who evade the aegis of men also evade traditional categories of definition. Since a community of women is a furtive, unofficial, often underground entity, it can be defined by the complex, shifting, often contradictory attitudes it evokes. Each community defines itself as a "distinct existence," flourishing outside familiar categories and calling for a plurality of perspectives and judgments. Thus, my own eclectic literary method might seem to resemble the whispered, unformulated female code in Sarah Orne Jewett's stories, but many perspectives are possible because communities of women have no one official banner to wave. At times, then, my approach is cross-cultural, as in my juxtaposition of Austen and Alcott. Or, sometimes, I stay within the confines of a single text, like *Cranford*, in order to redeem it from familiar critical assumptions about women without men. Or, again, as with James's *The Bostonians*, I use a single work to illuminate the totality of an artist's vision. But I have tried to be questioning throughout, to show the many possibilities in a rich idea that awakens deep and conflicting emotions in writers and readers. The strongest community we can conceive is one with many voices, and in defining a plurality of perspectives in a variety of ways, I hope to restore to a half-perceived literary image its integrity and its complex completeness. The intense debate the idea aroused, and still arouses, is its greatest strength, as a wealth of journalism and nonfictional prose reveals. Studying these shifting but always passionately held perspectives may reveal what has been enticing and threatening in the strength of this idea, to the Victorian world and to our own.

In defining the stereotype of female, along with homosexual, communities, Elizabeth Janeway seems to succumb to a traditional taboo: "Locked out of the larger community of a man's world, women and homosexuals develop profoundly ambiguous feelings about any sort of community they may set up themselves. Both groups are notorious for tight but short-lived cliques and bitter personal rivalries. Cattiness and disloyalty are expected, and cattiness and disloyalty are found among all those who regard part of themselves as unacceptable."[9] Though Janeway's analysis of female self-rejection is sympathetic, one wishes she had analyzed the assumptions which gave rise to this stereotype of the female community as being in the true sense nonexistent. This stereotype continues to thrive, as we can see by the continuing life of Clare Booth Luce's popular play *The Women* (1937), in which the shadowy men who never appear onstage are scrambled over by a ghetto of wealthy wives intriguing against each other to keep a husband or acquire somebody else's. Even the docile, virtuous wife who is at the center of the play's intrigues must jump into the jungle of a woman's world in order to win back her husband and the position he symbolizes. And the audience applauds her belated initiation into female bitchery as the rite of passage of the good wife.

If a woman's world is not always jungle red, people have believed that it was until recently. For Janeway, the law of mutual female betrayal is a logical outgrowth of inculcated self-shame; but the law itself remains a given. Yet her next book resurrects a joyful new ideal, transforming cultural fears into wish. *Between Myth and Morning* (1975) begins with a celebration of women's new "coming together with other women as friends and sharers of life instead of as rivals for approval by men." But perhaps the author's vision has changed more drastically than life has. Scholars in all areas are discovering not a new sisterhood, but sisterhood as a newly perceived fact of life. Patricia Meyer Spacks posits in *The Female Imagination*, "a special female self-awareness" that makes of every woman writer in every age a member of an unconscious sisterhood. And in *Literary Women* Ellen Moers reveals a self-conscious literary tradition among women that is secretly inoculated against male norms. What was once the stigma of a female community is now seen as a proud hidden profession.

In life as in literature, scholars are uncovering unperceived Utopias. "The Female World of Love and Ritual" takes its tone from its title, as Carroll Smith-Rosenberg defines the intensity of shared emotions and attachments between nineteenth-century American women not as an aberration from a norm or a sublimation of a norm gone wrong, but as a natural growth and a source of strength. Most radically, Yolanda and Robert Murphy's *Women of the Forest* laments the erosion of the highly sex-segregated society of the Mundurucú Indians. As the men move out of the men's house and try to make homes with their wives, who were previously united in an emotional community of resigned scorn for their strutting husbands, family intimacy is gained at the expense of sisterhood. Where the wives themselves find progress, the anthropologists who define them find only defeat, as the nostalgia of the book's title makes clear. For the Murphys, this resentfully segregated community of wives is not a bulwark against social and emotional deprivation: it has become the primary social and emotional fact, from which divergence is a falling-off. The search for the sisterhood that recently was shunned can go no further.[10]

Like our own, Victorian commentaries on sisterhood tended to veer between extremes of horror and hope. These polarized assumptions combined with the sanctity of the home to make of women's sphere the solitary confinement it so often became. In Victorian England, for example, one of the many impediments to female education seems to have been the reluctance of all parties to bring girls into too close contact with each other. Here is an extreme opinion on the subject from the *Imperial Review*: "We need not shrink from saying that the congregating of young girls of a certain age, either in boarding schools, true Colleges, or any other gregarious establishment . . . is a downright forcing of minds which ought, for the moment, to be kept as dormant as possible. By minds we do not mean intellects; we mean what everybody who is acquainted with human nature will understand. It is on this account, and on this alone, that female boarding-schools are so unspeakably pernicious."[11]

By "minds," the author clearly means "bodies." The effect of young women on each other must invariably be a subtle sexual contagion which gives their conjunction the status of a profound taboo. Such a community can only arouse the "dormant" horror of female sexuality: depths of sleeping perversion blossom in its inhabitants, and so, perhaps, do embarrassing memories of the bordello in the man who contemplates it. It is easy to dismiss such a statement as a choice slice of Victorian misogyny, but it is odd to find that the words of a foe of female education echo those of Mary Wollstonecraft, one of its first and truest friends:

women from necessity, because their minds are not cultivated, have recourse very often to what I familiarly term bodily wit; and their intimacies are of the same kind. In short, with respect to both mind and body, they are too intimate . . . On this account also, I object to many females being shut up together in nurseries, schools, or convents. I cannot recollect without indignation the jokes and hoiden tricks, which knots of young women indulge themselves in, when in my youth accident threw me, an awkward rustic, in their way. They were almost on a par with the double meanings which shake the convivial table when the glass has circulated freely.[12]

Like Elizabeth Janeway in her contemporary vindication of the rights of women, Mary Wollstonecraft adds the necessary saving clause: women ignite each others' grossness only because they are not trained to self-respect. In her late unfinished novel, *Maria or The Wrongs of Woman*, once Maria and Jemima have awakened to resist the degradation men and their laws impose, the novel can suggest that they will combine to raise and educate Maria's malleable little daughter. But such a community remains a postulate, a tentative sketch for an ending in a better world and a purer level of consciousness. In the society Wollstonecraft observes and denounces, the shared grossness, the "unspeakably pernicious" aura of "knots of young women" remains.

Notice how the terms have shifted in our own day. For Mary Wollstonecraft and for the writer in the *Imperial Review*, women together are repellent because they are "too intimate": they are an embarrassing reminder of the observer's own sexuality, a violation of the right to private distance. But for our contemporaries Elizabeth Janeway and, by implication, Clare Booth Luce, female communities are unnatural in their inevitable betrayal, their lack of intimacy and trust. For one group, they violate the laws of isolation and self-containment, and for the other, the norm of need. Though the nature of the threat shifts, the idea remains of contagion by values that are contrary to the best and proudest instincts of humanity. This sense of contagion remains even in a balanced and moderate Victorian essay by Elizabeth C. Wolstenholme, "The Education of Girls, its Present and its Future" (1869).[13] Though Wolstenholme deplores the scrappiness and amateurishness of the home-education that was traditional for girls, and of the small schools that purported to be ladylike approximations thereof, she repudiates the Rugby ideal for females: the students at her hypothetical school will not board together at school, but separately, with ladies "of education and refinement" in the town, despite the unreliability and inefficiency of such an arrangement. Even to a strong-minded follower of the crusader Josephine Butler, the education of females cannot be jeopardized by their contaminating contact with each other.

Tom Brown's Schooldays (1857), Thomas Hughes's account of a boy's crucial coming of age in a salutary microcosm of men and manly boys, begins with a quotation from the *Rugby Magazine* which assures the reader of the value of this little community: "As on the one hand it should ever be remembered that we are boys, and boys at school, so on the other hand we must bear in mind that we form a complete social body . . . a society, in which, by the nature of the case, we must not only learn, but act and live; and act and live not only as boys, but as boys who will be men." The portent of the little world as it imperceptibly becomes the great one underlies the public flair with which the Cambridge Apostles and the Oxford Movement triumphantly produce for the commonwealth a Tennyson and a Newman.

There are no majestic names for the deep quiet of Charlotte Brontë's communal apprenticeship. In a letter to Elizabeth Gaskell, Mary Taylor claimed to have made this gloomy remark about the solitary children in their early schooldays: "This habit of 'making out' interests for themselves, that most children get who have none in actual life, was very strong in [Charlotte]. The whole family used to 'make out' histories, and invent characters and events. I told her sometimes they were like growing potatoes in a cellar. She said, sadly, 'Yes! I know we are!' "[14] For Taylor, the gestation of the young artist is not a public trust, as it was for the Apostles, but a monstrous burial alive.

In conventional Victorian opinion, a girl educated with boys runs the risk of becoming "unsexed"; yet according to such antagonists as the writer for the *Imperial Review*, such a mutilation is trivial compared to the unwholesome lesson she will learn if she goes to school with other girls. The human and shared nature of the educational process only drives the young girl between the Scylla of asexuality and the Charybdis of sexual immersion.

But this shameful taboo attached to "knots of young women" is not the whole story. The fear is attached to a wish, and in *The Women of England*, Mrs. Ellis herself waxes visionary about just such a society:

> Let us imagine a little community of young women, among whom, to do an act of disinterested kindness should be an object of the highest ambition, and where to do any act of pure selfishness, tending, however remotely, to the injury of another, should be regarded as the deepest disgrace; where they should be accustomed to consider their time not as their own, but lent them solely for the purpose of benefiting their fellow-creatures; and where those who were known to exercise the greatest charity and forbearance, should be looked upon as the most exalted individuals in the whole community. Would these girls be weary? Would they be discontented, listless, and inanimate? The experiment remains to be tried.[15]

Here is a diminutive female Utopia worthy of J. M. Barrie's Never-Never Land. But where the contentedly lost boys will live for adventure, Mrs. Ellis' model citizens live for mutual service. Clearly, once that abrasive commodity, the female self, is transcended, a female state is a microcosm of a well-run paradise. Yet the basis of this Platonic vision of community does not rest upon the Victorian sentimental cliché that since little girls are made of "sugar 'n' spice 'n' everything nice," pure womanhood compounded will purge society of the bestial human ego. In her analysis of the sororal bond, Mrs. Ellis defines sisterhood less as selfless goodness than as shared pain: "[Unlike men], women *do* know what their sex is formed to suffer; and for this very reason, there is sometimes a bond existing between sisters, the most endearing, the most pure and disinterested of any description of affection which this world affords . . . [This bond] arises chiefly out of their mutual knowledge of each other's capacity of receiving pain" (pp. 68-69). In fact, the female bond is capable of transcendence only because it arises out of tacit self-awareness. The shared selfhood which is "too intimate" for Mary Wollstonecraft is for Sarah Ellis a wordless understanding which passes beyond duty into communion.

Mrs. Ellis' vision of a paradisal female community founded on a sisterhood of shared pain takes definite form as a pervasive motif in the writing of the period: there is a reiterated dream of institutionalizing Anglo-Catholic sisterhoods, whose impassioned persistence is remarkable in the face of official anti-Catholicism. What is a nightmare to Mary Wollstonecraft and a dream to Sarah Ellis becomes a social panacea for many writers of the 1850s and 1860s, when the number of unmarried nubile women rose alarmingly[16] and the "redundant woman" became a social headache almost as great as that of the ubiquitous "deserving poor." Dora Greenwell begins her article "Our Single Women" with the obligatory sigh of pathos: "A single woman! Is there not something plaintive in the two words standing together?" But when she postulates their organization into Protestant sisterhoods, her vision of social cleansing becomes almost mystical: "Such a Community, great, almost boundless as may be its resources, lives in the singleness, and moves with the freedom of individual life; it adapts itself to the varying hour, it extends itself to meet the fresh need. What centres of light and consolation such communities may yet prove to the many-peopled desolations of our mining districts, and manufacturing and seaport towns!" The pivot that transforms plaintiveness into power is, of course, community: "for how many are the objects now presenting themselves to Christian energy which cannot be accomplished, cannot even be attempted, without the aid of organization!"[17] Given the sanction of medieval trappings and an object other than itself on which to exert its collective goodness, Mrs. Ellis' exemplary community of unselfish girls is envisioned as a sweeping social force—one not far removed from that secular Protestant sisterhood, the feminist movement, which also learned that its strength lay in organization as it worked to purify society by freeing itself.

The added note is the idea of power. Organized female sisterhoods remain in large part a dream—almost twenty years
later, "the experiment remains to be tried"—but now it is a
dream of power more than it is one of consolation or seclusion,
grotesque though this power may seem to some observers. In
her famous attack on "The Shrieking Sisterhood," Eliza Lynn
Linton's burlesque sweeps beyond Josephine Butler's crusade
against the Contagious Diseases Acts, its ostensible target, to
encompass this very idea of collective female power: "One
woman alone, quietly taking her life in her own hands and
working out the great problem of self-help and independence
practically, not merely stating it theoretically, is worth a score
of shrieking sisters frantically calling on men and gods to see
them make an effort to stand upright without support, with
interludes of reproach to men for the want of help in their attempt."[18] The shrieking sisters become sirens turned hideous,
trying to lure the brave solitary soul off her course; for Eliza
Lynn Linton, as for Mary Wollstonecraft, female communities
embody a whirlpool of subhuman chaos which can only sap
strength. In a letter to Oscar Wilde, Dinah Mulock Craik represents herself as Linton's triumphant "woman alone," the
source of whose strength is her avoidance of community: "For
myself, whatever influence I have is, I believe, because I have
always kept aloof from any clique. I care little for Female Suffrage. I have given the widest berth to that set of women who
are called, not unfairly, the shrieking sisterhood."[19] For both
Linton and Craik, a female community threatens the integrity
of power of the solitary woman who is their stalwart ideal:
Mrs. Ellis' "relative creature," with no sanctioned existence
apart from her relationships with men, has become inverted.
She will now exist relative to nothing, and in the very absolute-
ness of her isolation, she becomes a late Victorian culture
heroine.

In Craik's books, there is a repeated insistence on the nobility of total solitude and the avoidance of corrupt female claims.
A Woman's Thoughts about Women is intended as a sort of
handbook for spinsters "[i]n this curious phase of social history, when marriage is apparently ceasing to become the common lot" (p. 37). But this laudable enterprise effectively for-

bids any substitution for the human joys of marriage, consoling the unmarried reader in mournful tones for her implacable solitude. In a chapter on "Female Friendships" ("pure" friendships with men are virtually impossible), she hesitatingly admits that some relationships between women can be noble (though never as noble as those between the noblest men), but usually on the condition of "a difference—of strong or weak, gay or grave, brilliant or solid—answering in some measure to the difference of sex. Otherwise, a close all-engrossing friendship between two women would seldom last long; or if it did, by their mutual feminine weaknesses acting and reacting upon one another, would most likely narrow the sympathies and deteriorate the character of both" (p. 163). Men are off limits and women corrupt. In a world shorn of relationships, death can be only

> A finished life—a life which has made the best of all the materials granted to it, and through which, be its web dark or bright, its pattern clear or clouded, can now be traced plainly the hand of the Great Designer; surely this is worth living for? And though at its end it may be somewhat lonely; though a servant's and not a daughter's arm may guide the failing step; though most likely it will be strangers only who come about the dying bed, close the eyes that no husband ever kissed, and draw the shroud kindly over the poor withered breast where no child's head has ever lain; still, such a life is not to be pitied, for it is a completed life.   (p. 308)

In a life consisting of negations and presided over by "not" and "no," death alone brings the completeness worth living for. The qualifications and denials in which Craik shrouds this life suggest the force of the taboo she places on all relationships which are not those of husband, parent, child. No longer a relative creature, this abandoned corpse is an image of absolute desolation, admonishing the reader to count no single woman happy until she is dead, and then only because her loneliness is consummated. But the intensity of solitude this "finished life" represents has its counterweight in Craik's later essay, "On Sisterhood," about her mixed reactions to a friend who does become an Anglican sister: "It is a strange thing to say—yet I dare to say it, for I believe it to be true—that entering a Sisterhood, almost any sort of Sisterhood where there was work to do, authority to compel the doing of it, and companionship to sweeten the same, would have saved many a woman from a lunatic asylum."[20]

The largeness of this claim suggests the cost with which Craik has kept her "influence" by eschewing the "shrieking sisterhood." The uncharacteristic syntactical stammer with which she makes the admission reflects the power she attributes to sisterhoods: such colonies can drain one's potency through their invocation of "mutual feminine weaknesses" and presumably undermine one's influence because men don't listen to them—or they can save a soul. She goes on to say that the best course is still "to live and work alone," but subservience, natural or acquired, shackles women's capacity to do this. If they have read Craik's own description of "a finished life," one can hardly blame them. Thus, for some women at least, the sisterhood need no longer be shrieking, except in response to the intensity of a need. Mrs. Craik's ambivalent life manages to encompass Mary Wollstonecraft's fear of invasion by "knots of women," licentious and primitive, and Mrs. Ellis' beatific vision of their collective saving power.

But, as Dora Greenwell made explicit the idea of power in Ellis' dreamt-of holy community, so Craik quietly transforms its sweet mutual service into fulfillment of the profound and pervasive thirst for work that recurs insistently in the women's literature of the Victorian age.[21] A community of women freely offers the work that must be wrenched grudgingly out of the "real" world of Victorian patriarchy. In Edith Simcox's description of "Eight Years of Co-operative Shirtmaking," the salvation offered by her female community is not spiritual and attenuated, but economic and professional: "Our dream was of a strictly self-supporting clothes-making factory, where women should do all the work, and divide the profits among them." As she describes the realization of this dream, there was a period when a collective female Utopia was not merely a postulate.

The principle of this cooperative shirtmaking venture was the common identity of workers and employers. Even when the organization was running at a loss, wages were paid and no one was laid off; the risks all belonged to the partners. Moreover, they resisted the temptation to plunge into the game of laissez-faire and undersell their rivals. The note of cooperation was its essential disinterestedness: "when we found that we were in some cases dividing amongst them more farthings and halfpence for making a particular shirt than our employers paid us for it, the ladies in parliament assembled voted the necessary redistribution and reduction of prices, without, so far as we could judge, thinking us at all to blame for the unamiable limitations of arithmetical possibilities."[22]

The "experiment" of the Ellis female community, run on principles of "disinterested kindness," has been tried, and it succeeds. The venture flourishes, moves to larger quarters, a virtuous socialist enclave of "industrial cooperation" in the cutthroat marketplace. Perhaps Simcox elides some procedures that were less than beautiful; nevertheless, her essay stands as a monument to reality—the tangibility of a female community's shared profits—in a welter of hopes and fears.

Edith Simcox was in love with George Eliot, who in the matriarchy of her imagination played the role of Mother-God. In her Autobiography entry of 9 November 1877, she notes a rather tortured conversation between the two of them which dramatizes the difficulties with which relationships between women were, and are, fraught:

> She said perhaps [a kind letter from a young Cambridge man] would make me more charitable to men-folk. I protested I wasn't otherwise and she said she had always owed me a grudge for not being grateful enough to the Italian officer who was kind to me when the train was snowed up beyond Foggia. She said unlike most people she believed I should have thought more of the adventure if a woman had been kind to me. I said I might have if I had had the opportunity of being kind to a woman, but that I had no prejudice whatever against man. He and she said . . . they have [noticed] before that among chance acquaintances men are more appreciative and courteous to

her than women. I said that I had found women kinder than men, which she was "glad to hear," as showing they could be kind to each other—and I didn't explain either that I had always taken their kindness as a sign that I was half a man—and they knew it; or that I thought it rather hard she should visit, as a fault, my constitutional want of charm for men.[23]

Much of this conversation probably involves feints on George Eliot's part to discourage Simcox's wooing. Nevertheless, she protests too much, as she often does,[24] about the invariable kindness of men and faithlessness of women. If, as she says, women rarely extend a hand to each other, Edith would have been quite right to think more of a woman's assistance on a snowbound train than of a conventionally gallant man's. Moreover, her own life was studded with women who had been kind to her, while she had been repudiated by a fair share of men, including her father and brother. Most revealing, though, is the halfheartedness of Simcox's defense of women. At a time when the venture in cooperative shirtmaking, which she describes with such Utopian verve, was just beginning, she attributes women's kindness to her to the fact that in her soul she is a man and not a sexual rival. In short, were she a "constitutional" woman, community would be impossible. Although her ambivalence about female communities is less dramatically extreme than Craik's, it suggests that the title of her "Autobiography of a Shirt Maker" may dramatize a self-chosen identity that is more of a wish than a fact. But despite the doubts and depressions that accompanied it, Mrs. Ellis' experiment had at last been tried.

In nineteenth-century America, that country of colonies, the idea of female communities seems to have been more amorphously glorious, less potentially threatening, than it was in England. In what can be taken as a fairly typical example of the pulpit wisdom out of which women were supposed to shape their lives, George W. Burnap, Pastor of the First Independent Church of Baltimore, defines both their corrupting and their salutary incarnations with no apparent sense of contradiction. First, he says, men and women elevate each other through blessed ignorance of each other's fallen nature. Thus, single-sex communities are corrupt because of the self-aware intimacy on which they rest:

> This is a fact, which I have never seen noticed by any writer on the moral constitution of man, the instinctive reverence which the two sexes have for each other above and beyond that which they cherish for their own. It is a sort of human religion. The human soul, made after the similitude of God, has ever a sort of Divinity about it. The presence of one of our own sex is a quickener of the conscience, is a moral restraint, and is so far a perpetual discipline to the conduct. But with this reverence there is toward the other sex an instinctive desire to please. There then is a two-fold power. No man ever felt in the presence of a man the same awe and restraint that he feels in the presence of a woman; and no woman is ever so much put on her good behaviour before one of her own sex as she is in the presence of a man. Here then is an immense moral influence which the sexes are perpetually exerting upon each other, and in the aggregate its effects must be beyond all estimate. Nothing can be wiser then, than that arrangement of society, which God has established, where the sexes associate freely together. Hence also the deterioration of every form of society which separates either into a community by themselves.

Compared to British repugnance toward the shrieking sisterhood, this is a mild, egalitarian denunciation. In a later chapter Burnap gives the familiar, well-intentioned nineteenth-century defense of old maids: their position is honorable and not ridiculous, provided that they are never happy in it.[25] A *Woman's Thoughts about Women* makes the same contention, but Burnap's instinctive collectivism is quite unlike the implacable isolation Craik insists upon:

> [Unmarried women] seem to constitute in the designs of Providence a sort of corps de reserve. As no wise general brings all his forces into the field at once, but keeps back a part to supply deficiencies, to remedy accidents, to throw in their aid at emergencies; so are unmarried women stationed up and down in life to aid the weak, to take the

place of those who are cloven down in battle, or of those who refuse to do their duty. So far from meriting the reproaches of the married portion of mankind, they have their full share of the labors of life with fewer of its rewards. So far from being drones in the hive, their lives are especially set apart to good works. Being less closely connected with the world, their labors are more disinterested. Is any one in trouble, the resort is immediately to them. *They are in fact the sisters of charity to the whole species.* While the thoughts of others are shut up in themselves and their families, theirs go abroad to seek out the helpless and unfortunate; and the destitute and forgotten find in them an advocate and a friend when otherwise there would be none to care for their relief. It will be found that among them all benevolent enterprises find their most efficient support. And when the young, the gay, and the prosperous are pursuing their pleasure, are glittering in splendid balls, or treading the mazes of the dance, those faithful souls are toiling over those household duties which the gay and thoughtless have forgotten, or are watching by the bed side of pain and death.[26]

In England the old maid is generally the "odd woman," eccentric and alone. For Mrs. Craik, her perpetually untouched corpse is an emblem of a desolation beyond marriage touching that of such nineteenth-century monsters as Frankenstein's, who, denied a mate, finally hurls himself beyond the horizon on his ice-raft. For Dora Greenwell, the organization of these solitaries is a remote and cloudy dream; but for Burnap, writing earlier, it is already a fact. Old maids are *now* a collective body, a "corps de reserve," and "the sisters of charity to the whole species." The "experiment [that] remains to be tried" in England is seen in America as a providential sororal reality.

In Margaret Fuller's vision, the Burnap corps de reserve moves up to the front lines, losing in the process its mandatory grimness. Despite the vast differences of tone and intention, there is a connection between the prompt corporate efficacy of his respectably self-effacing sisterhood and the earthly salvation Fuller finds in a collective release of the self-sustaining female soul, washing over the world to transfigure it: "We would have every path laid open to Woman as freely as to

Man. Were this done, and a slight temporary fermentation allowed to subside, we should see crystallizations more pure and of more various beauty. We believe the divine energy would pervade nature to a degree unknown in the history of former ages, and that no discordant collision, but a ravishing harmony of the spheres, would result."

But the power inherent in such an explosion of female energy is vaguely defined. "The electrical, the magnetic element" which is Fuller's untrammeled womanhood proves more of a metaphysical arsenal than a social one:

> It is not money, nor notoriety, nor the badges of authority which men have appropriated to themselves [that women want]. If demands, made in their behalf, lay stress on any of these particulars, those who make them have not searched deeply into the need. The want is for that which at once includes these and precludes them; which would not be forbidden power, lest there be temptation to steal and misuse it; which would not have the mind perverted by flattery from a worthiness of esteem; it is that which is the birthright of every being capable of receiving it,—the freedom, the religious, the intelligent freedom of the universe to use its means, to learn its secret, as far as Nature has enabled them, with God alone for their guide and their judge.[27]

Freedom for women is freedom in the sphere of the soul, not society; freedom is attaining access to the heavens, not the professions. In Victorian England communities of women are seen as modified and purified versions of traditional religious and social institutions: an Anglo-Catholic sisterhood is an English, and therefore acceptable, variant of a time-hallowed body, and cooperative shirtmaking transforms an old and familiar activity only to make it nobler. But in Victorian America the aim is to transcend all known quantities and flood nature with divine female energy "to a degree unknown in the history of former ages." Women in union may bring no less than a third covenant.

Thus, in 1848, the year of revolutions, Queen's College was

founded in England by Charles Kingsley and F. D. Maurice; while in America, women convened at Seneca Falls and heard Elizabeth Cady Stanton say: "woman herself must do this work; for woman alone can understand the height, the depth, the length and the breadth of her degradation."[28] The aim and effect of Queen's College was local and practical: it offered women professional training under the aegis of professional men, instead of benevolent ladylike dithering at instruction. Many gladly accepted the chance to hone themselves for the marketplace. More capable governesses became in time more capable teachers and administrators of secondary schools, and, eventually, of women's colleges. Queen's College bore its most dramatic fruit in Emily Davies' singleminded campaign to admit women to the great male universities on strictly masculine terms, and in 1873, a small band of young girls fiercely rang the firebell when, having proved themselves prepared, they were permitted to take the Cambridge Tripos.[29] But the concrete political results of the Seneca Falls Convention were secondary to the emotional and theatrical impact of so many women gathered together at once, talking and listening to each other for what felt like the first time. In the one event, women are permitted to take the hand of history as it was patriarchally defined; in the other, they find the force to cut across it. Later, Jane Addams' vision cuts across history in a similar way, feeling her Hull House can transcend through sympathy the existing economic structure of the state: "As an organizing force in politics, they would moralize and socialize a state which Jane Addams recognized was at present organized to protect and promote the interests of businessmen. Of even greater importance, women would be able to solve the problems of city government because the efficient management of urban affairs involved generalizing the skills of housekeeping which were exclusively feminine skills."[30] George Burnap's corps de reserve takes on the momentum of Margaret Fuller's electrical, magnetic element to become an irresistible cyclonic force carrying no coloration of the system it sets out to purify.

But such insistently nonintegrated energy can easily become a mere wail for a magic escape, as it does in this letter from one "kindred spirit" to another, whose combined intensity and whimsy is a far cry from Edith Simcox's constrained, self-accusatory dialogue with George Eliot:

> Nevertheless, I cannot but often dream of hours like these —they seem so soft, and sweet, and unalloyed—so like a fairy life, in which, invisible dwellers in Nature's holy sanctuaries, we should quietly work unseen blessings for the race of man, and bless ourselves in our deeds. You see how *self* predominates in these dreams, how I would draw you from all your domestic ties, and make you a very girl with myself. I am very foolish, I know—a perfect *natural*, for in my baby-days I had the same wild fantasies floating in my brain, and the same dreamy desires for gipsy freedom.[31]

All socially beneficial pretext trails away: "blessings for the race of man" fade into the self-blessing of "gipsy freedom." Women, too, were calling to each other to join the expanding world of Huck and Jim, but few were able to do so. Perhaps because they were cast immutably as grim-faced "sivilization" on the shore, the dream of sorority was so powerful in America that it tended to choke on its own energy. The women's clubs that grew out of the early feminist movement soon proliferated away from their initial purpose into a formlessness resembling Sarah Edgarton's "gipsy freedom," though it went under the more respectable name of "self-culture." In 1898 a female reporter disgustedly defined the women's club as "a body of women banded together for the purpose of meeting together."[32] Too pure to accommodate itself to the surrounding medium, the group loses any clearly defined purpose except the crucially important one of community. Stripped of a high-minded rationale, cultivated American women are revealed in the unexcused simplicity of their wish to meet.

Dr. Mary Walker's projected "Adamless Eden" is an extreme embodiment of the groping contradictions inherent in the hope of a female community. After her dramatic Civil War service and the petering-out of her campaigns for dress reform and female suffrage, Dr. Walker settled down, still in male attire, to become a local character on the family farm in Oswego, New York. On October 19, 1895, the *Oswego Times* reported that "Dr. Walker planned an Adamless Eden on a 135-acre tract. It was to be a colony for young women who would pledge themselves to single blessedness. They would work and study, and eventually go forth as examples of the new womanhood." This was followed by an elaborate burlesque by Bill Nye in the manner of Tennyson's *The Princess,* replete with funny woebegone men peering in at the funny ladies in their exotic costumes.

Two months later a British newspaper ran a serious interview with Mary Walker, presenting what her biographer considers "a fair and sympathetic recital of her plans." Dr. Walker explains herself like this: " 'Every woman must do something to be somebody. Girls who intend to marry must learn what housekeeping and household duties mean. This is especially true of women who are to become farmers' wives. My intention is to make my place a sort of training school for these women, and when desired, practical instruction in actual field work.' She denied the report that bloomers were required. Girls might choose their own apparel. It would not be a 'new woman's colony, but a new wives' training school.' "[33]

Here, as in so many examples we have looked at, the vision of a female colony is stronger than a sense of its meaning, nature, or purpose. Mary Walker's virtuously conventional statement to the press omits the fact that she herself knew nothing whatever about running a farm, leaving its boring but essential upkeep to her domestic sister. Her own incompetence and indifference would probably not have prevented her from teaching farm administration to anyone who would listen, but it does suggest that her first interest was not likely to have been the training of young wives in the arts of rural housekeeping. Most likely, had the colony taken root, it too would have been "a body of women banded together for the purpose of meeting together." But once this purpose is called upon to justify itself, the conflict remains, still unresolved: a new woman's colony or a new wives' training school? The shrieking sisterhood or the holy sisters? A corrupt knot of inferior creatures or a charmed circle of selfless purity? How can the observer define and justify the power of women's incomprehensible desire to "meet together"? The novels we will look at present a series of imaginative answers.

The "Adamless Eden" was never formed, which technically makes of it a truer Utopia than the cooperative community in which Edith Simcox produced real shirts for eight years; as solitary an Eden as Thoreau's Walden, the farm in Oswego remained "Dr. Mary Walker's colony of one." But the shifting idea of female communities survives beyond its problematical realization, and as art gives it body, it becomes part of the history it opposes and improves.

The novels chosen to illustrate the growth of this idea may seem as bizarre a conjunction as a community of women. In British idiom, a manless woman is by definition an "odd woman," her oddity matching the paradoxical dislocation of time and nature inherent in our "old maid." My community of novels is an appropriate oddity, yoking childhood and age, the banal and the unique, as does the phrase "old maid" itself. *Pride and Prejudice* is paired with *Little Women* to show two kinds of female families that share more than they seem to, though Jane Austen is a darling of the select and Louisa May Alcott, of the popular consciousness. Moving beyond the family into the state, Elizabeth Gaskell's mellow idyll *Cranford* seems strangely paired with Charlotte Brontë's dissonant, dismal *Villette*. Once communities of women coalesce from hidden force into public movement, the men who treat feminism's burgeoning power seem an equally odd couple, Henry James's apparent travesty of his *Bostonians* weaving a dangerous irony around Gissing's earnest endorsement of his *Odd Women*. Finally, Muriel Spark seems to stand alone as an architect of communities of women today. Our only female contemporary to explore communities of women as fact and idea, she keeps aloof from the pieties and conventions that have evolved in recent feminist literature. One statement attributed to her— "Derek, don't you love authority?"[34] —might seem to remove her forever from the self-sustaining women in this study; but only she has the audacity to yoke her communities to the abso-

lutes of history, myth, and divinity, their stubborn conjunction
of authority and deceit making her a fitting initiate to this odd
fellowship.

Perhaps so many women are odd because we lack an agreed
-upon common denominator of womanhood; hence the dispar-
ity of tone and mode found in these writers, and the gulf between their implied audiences as well. The nineteenth century
claimed to know exactly what it meant by "boyhood," an absolute condition diagnosed solemnly in Kipling's *Stalky & Co.*:
" 'It's not brutality,' murmured little Hartopp, as though answering a question no one had asked. 'It's boy; only boy.' " [35]
But commonality is less widely spread in girlhood. In *Tom
Brown at Oxford*, though Thomas Hughes expansively assumes
a delicious sharing among his masculine readers, the possibility of such universality among "lady readers" remains a wavering enigma:

> Who amongst you, dear readers, can appreciate the in-
> tense delight of grassing your first big fish after a nine
> months' fast? All first sensations have their special plea-
> sure; but none can be named, in a small way, to beat this
> of the first fish of the season. The first clean leg-hit for
> four in your first match at Lord's—the grating of the bows
> of your racing-boat against the stern of the boat ahead in
> your first race—the first half-mile of a burst from the
> cover side in November, when the hounds in the field
> ahead may be covered with a tablecloth, and no one but
> the huntsman and a top-sawyer or two lies between you
> and them—the first brief after your call to the bar, if it
> comes within the year—the sensations produced by these
> are the same in kind; but cricket, boating, getting briefs,
> even hunting, lose their edge as time goes on. As to lady
> readers, it is impossible, probably, to give them an idea of
> the sensation in question. Perhaps some may have experi-
> enced something of the kind at their first balls, when they
> heard whispers and saw all eyes turning their way, and
> knew that their dresses and gloves fitted perfectly. But
> this joy can be felt but once in a life, and the first fish
> comes back as fresh as ever, or ought to come, if all men
> had their rights, once in a season. [36]

Though boyhood was depicted in novels as a universal known, there is no better indication of the fact that the "woman question" remained open than the reminder that one of the most beloved beginnings in literature, the first half of *Little Women*, seemed disappointingly dull to Louisa May Alcott's editor, Thomas Niles. The equivocal limbo of a shared female world may account for the diversity of appeal these novels claim. It might also justify Alcott in naming her powerful March household the "pathetic family" in its first, sketchy incarnation.

This remoteness from a common audience defines the isolation these communities share, for on the surface their settings are the known world. Though we may accept Tennyson's metaphor and feel we are traveling to a group of islands, we will find no literal islands to match those microcosms on which Robert Louis Stevenson's or William Golding's males are stranded; there are no ships, battlefields, or hallowed schools, which despite their self-enclosure form "a complete social body" like that of Tom Brown's Rugby. The isolation explored here is one of experience and consciousness within the larger body of commonality that is given the name "reality." In *Pride and Prejudice*, *Little Women*, *The Bostonians*, and *The Prime of Miss Jean Brodie* the reality of the masculine world beyond the island of consciousness is that of war. *Cranford*, *Villette*, and *The Odd Women* depict exotic enclaves within the known—"our" obsolete village society in an embattled marketplace of false currency, the alienness of Gallic priestcraft to a staunch English Protestant norm, the arcane sociology of poverty within the workshop of the world. Unlike those of male communities, their autonomy and their solitude are not institutionalized, but inward and unexpressed.

Our female communities are united by their necessary oddity as well as by their corporate strength. Together they form a tradition within the British and American novel that gains in power and magnitude as we move from the nineteenth century to our own and from communities that are represented as strangely powerful pockets of history to potent representations of history itself, as they abandon the family to invade that larger reality which is both war and the target of warriors.

Waiting Together:
Two Families

Edgar Degas. *The Bellelli Family*
Musée du Louvre, Jeu de Paume

The family is the first community we know, and it takes the shape of Mother. The government of the mother over her family is an uncomfortable reality that has been exalted to celestial proportions, denounced as the source of all psychic ill, and explained away. In "The Paterfamilias of the Victorian Governing Classes," David Roberts dilutes the administrative power of so many Victorian mothers by locating its true source in the absent, omnipotent father, whose maternal delegate is merely provisional and thus easily removed. But Isabella Beeton's *Book of Household Management* assures its enormous Victorian audience that the rule of "the mistress" is absolute and her presence more insistently pervasive than God's:

> Her spirit will be seen through the whole establishment. . . She ought always to remember that she is the first and the last, the Alpha and the Omega in the government of her establishment; and that it is by her conduct that its whole internal policy is regulated. She is, therefore, a person of far more importance in a community than she usually thinks she is. On her pattern her daughters model themselves; by her counsels they are directed; through her virtues all are honoured;—"Her children rise up and call her blessed; her husband also, and he praiseth her." [1]

In a family of daughters, at any rate, the mother's power is seen as all-suffusing; this indomitable community of women aligns father with children as a ritual praiser, rather than sharer, of her reign. Mrs. Beeton's blueprint of power finds its way into two novels that have become different sorts of classics. Jane Austen's *Pride and Prejudice* (1813) is the English novel's paradigmatic courtship romance, memorable in that it celebrates "the positive advantages of maturity over childishness"[2] and allows us, as a successful courtship romance must do, to believe in marriage as an emblem of adulthood achieved. Louisa May Alcott's *Little Women* (1868-69) is one of America's

most loved celebrations of childhood, whose rather perfunctory concluding marriages give a twilight flavor to the enforced
passage into womanhood. But the darting adult wit of the one
and the contagious nostalgia of the other treat a similar
process: the passage of a bevy of sisters from the collective
colony of a woman's world presided over by their mother to the
official authority of masculine protection.

The families of both novels are explicitly matriarchal, and in
both the mother is indefatigably committed to the administrative "business" of marrying her clamorously alive but economically superfluous daughters; it is she who forges the family's
liaison with the outside world of marriage, morals, and money
that eligible men embody. Mr. Bennet begins *Pride and Prejudice* by calling on Bingley because his wife has, as usual,
nagged him into submission; and it is she who throws open the
hospitality of Longbourn (such as it is) to all eligible comers. In
Little Women, princely Laurie's grandfather makes a friendly
gesture toward the March family because he remembers the
genteel father of Mrs. March; and it is she who quietly estab-
lishes Jo's connection at the New York boardinghouse where
she meets her future husband.

While the mother builds connections, the father retreats
from the business of marriage to his library, adapting to himself the remote privacy of ideal Victorian womanhood. Though
both novels are set in wartime, the absence of the father is less
physical than psychic: we scarcely know when Mr. March
returns from the Civil War, so absorbed is he by his invalidism
and his Plato. The father lives in a ghostly haven of "philosophy," while the mother thrives as an administrator; in order to
survive economically and emotionally, the girls must scatter
themselves in marriage. In each novel the favored girl, the surrogate son who is allowed into the private sanctuary of the
library, marries a man who embodies all the administrative
power her father lacks. In the marriages that conclude the
novels, the father's philosophic detachment is honored as a
distant beacon, but the mother's executive ability survives to
be transmitted.

Each matriarchy, then, is a school for wives, and each is the only school allowed. Lady Catherine de Bourgh is horrified that the Bennet girls have had no governess, only undirected access to their father's books. Plain, platitudinous Mary Bennet, with her indefatigable extracts, lacks even the inconsequential schooling the feather-headed orphan Harriet Smith in *Emma* will have: Longbourn has no Mrs. Goddard's, only anxious mothers waiting for the men to come in. In *Little Women* the frosty Englishwoman Kate Vaughn is as shocked as Lady Catherine that the March girls have had no governess. Only vain little Amy goes to school, spending most of her time there worrying about her clothes; and when she is publicly punished, she is quickly snatched back to the home sanctuary, where she and Beth do vague and apparently unsupervised "lessons" together. For the real lessons these girls must learn come from their mothers, and they are lessons about a woman's life.

As both groups of sisters are schooled only in womanhood, neither is permitted the solitary childhood world of fantasy so dear to the nineteenth century. Austen defines the Bennet sisters as hardheadedly as Mrs. Bennet does, by assessing their chances on the marriage market without reference to the childhood they have presumably left behind. Despite its incessant games, Alcott's novel begins with the end of the girls' secure childhood: the family fortunes have been lost and the sisters are young adolescents, forced into self-denial. As they grow into womanhood and the alternatives of marriage or death, womanly Meg, literary tomboy Jo, frail angelic Beth, and worldly Amy must leave behind a household that has a value beyond that of a dollhouse. For, despite its reputation as a sugary children's classic, *Little Women's* implicit paradigm is not an escape to childhood innocence, but the formation of a reigning feminist sisterhood whose exemplary unity will heal a fractured society. Both novels are belied by their familial settings in that they are concerned less with girlhood joys than with the difficult adjustments of women to an adult society that supersedes the reality of their world.

Pride and Prejudice

> Anxious and uneasy, the period which passed in
> the drawing-room, before the gentlemen came,
> was wearisome and dull to a degree, that almost
> made her uncivil. She looked forward to their en-
> trance, as the point on which all her chance of
> pleasure for the evening must depend.[3]

Since Elizabeth Bennet has passed her life in a world of waiting women, and we have passed it with her for much of the
previous two volumes of the novel, this passage need describe
such a world only as a temptation to lose one's temper. The
story, the glow, will begin with the opening of the door.

In an earlier description of a similar situation we are given a
chance, not so much to hear what women say to each other
during this excruciating period, as to have our attention called
to the distrust and emotional pressure that forbid their saying
anything:

> Elizabeth soon saw that she was herself closely watched
> by Miss Bingley, and that she could not speak a word, es-
> pecially to Miss Darcy, without calling her attention. This
> observation would not have prevented her from trying to
> talk to the latter, had they not been seated at an inconven-
> ient distance; but she was not sorry to be spared the
> necessity of saying much. Her own thoughts were employ-
> ing her. She expected every moment that some of the gen-
> tlemen would enter the room. She wished, she feared that
> the master of the house might be amongst them; and
> whether she wished or feared it most, she could scarcely
> determine.   (p. 268)

Darcy has gently commanded that Elizabeth and his sister like
each other, but his absent presence is the only emotional point
of reference for all three women. Waiting for the entrance of
the gentlemen, their shared world is a limbo of suspension and
suspense, which cannot take shape until it is given one by the
opening of the door.

The unexpressed intensity of this collective waiting for the door to open and a Pygmalion to bring life into limbo defines the female world of *Pride and Prejudice*; its agonized restraint is reflected microcosmically in the smaller community of the Bennet family, and macrocosmically in the larger community of England itself. With a nod to Pritchett, Jane Austen's most recent biographer allows her to touch British history in a manner that most admirers of her self-enclosed miniatures have forbidden: "In his *George Meredith and English Comedy*, V. S. Pritchett has a challenging aside in which he describes Jane Austen as a war novelist, pointing out that the facts of the long war are basic to all her books. She knew all about the shortage of men, the high cost of living, and . . . about the vital part played by the Navy."[4] In presenting these drawing rooms full of women watching the door and watching each other, Jane Austen tells us what an observant, genteel woman has to tell about the Napoleonic Wars: she writes novels about waiting.

As her England is in large part a country of women whose business it is to wait for the return of the men who have married them or may do so, so her heroine's family has occupied much of its history in waiting, with increasing hopelessness, for a male to enter it:

> When first Mr. Bennet had married, economy was held to be perfectly useless; for, of course, they were to have a son. This son was to join in cutting off the entail, as soon as he should be of age, and the widow and younger children would by that means be provided for. Five daughters successively entered the world, but yet the son was to come; and Mrs. Bennet, for many years after Lydia's birth, had been certain that he would. This event had at last been despaired of, but it was then too late to be saving. Mrs. Bennet had no turn for economy, and her husband's love of independence had alone prevented their exceeding their income. (p. 308)

In the family microcosm, the male whom all await can alone bring substance: by inheriting the estate, he will ensure the family the solidity and continuity of income and land. Without him, their emotional and financial resources, and ultimately the family itself, can only evaporate. The quality of the Bennet household is determined by the Beckett-like realization that the period of protracted waiting is not a probationary interim before life begins: waiting for a male is life itself.

The Bennet home, as its name indicates, is not an autonomous, self-sustaining entity: unlike Lucas Lodge, the home of their neighbors, Longbourn House bears the name of the village in which it is set, although a son might have changed its name to his own. This interchangeability of name between village and home suggests the primacy of "the neighborhood" in *Pride and Prejudice,* a primacy which nobody questions. The walls of the family are made of brittle glass: when Longbourn House receives a piece of news, its inhabitants do not gather together to savor it as the March family will do; they disperse it instantly to the neighborhood, which makes of it what malicious use it may. Elizabeth Bennet accepts this primacy, though like her father, she makes conversational capital out of its absurdity: "If he means to be but little at Netherfield, it would be better for the neighborhood that he should give up the place entirely, for then we might possibly get a settled family there. But perhaps Mr. Bingley did not take the house so much for the convenience of the neighborhood as for his own, and we must expect him to keep or quit it on the same principle" (p. 178). The family exists to feed the neighborhood, and not the other way round. The reductio ad absurdum of this priority is Mr. Bennet's mordant: "For what do we live, but to make sport for our neighbors, and laugh at them in our turn?" (p. 364). Although the habitual Bennet note of self-mockery makes these speeches slippery as statements of belief, "we" clearly cannot live for families who are so nearly interchangeable with neighbors; and in fact, when Elizabeth and Jane marry Darcy and Bingley, we learn of their activities in their new neighborhood of Derbyshire rather than of the new families they start. This is a world far from Jo March's euphoric cry at the conclusion of *Little Women:* "I do think that families are the most beautiful things in all the world!"[5] In *Pride and Preju-* *dice* they are the most beautiful things in all the world to leave: "There was novelty in the scheme [of Elizabeth's journey to Hunsford], and as, with such a mother and such uncompanionable sisters, home could not be faultless, a little change was not unwelcome for its own sake" (p. 151).

The two evasive double negatives that suggest Elizabeth's nonfeeling for her nonfamily suggest also the most striking characteristic of the Bennet ménage: its nonexistence. Austen boasted to her sister of the success with which she had "lop't and crop't" the manuscript of *Pride and Prejudice,* and I suspect that it was the scenes among the Bennets that were lop't and crop't, for the version we have contains scarcely any fully-developed sequence in which the family are alone together. It is true that in the second chapter, "the girls" all flock around Mr. Bennet in rapture at his having paid a call on Bingley, but this is the last time they act in concert. After their first shared joy at this possible escape from home—the March girls are equally joyful at a letter from their father admonishing them to conquer, not hypothetical suitors, but themselves—the unity between the sisters fractures, the two younger raucously pursuing officers in Meryton and the two elder more decorously pursuing gentility at Netherfield, while plain Mary disappears at home into being a mouthpiece of platitudes. The groupings between the sisters are rigidly separate and hierarchical. During her brief infatuation with Wickham, Elizabeth steps across a wide gulf as she moves from Jane's camp into Lydia's and, when her vision clears, shifts with mortification back into Jane's. There is none of the emotional fluidity that exists among the March sisters, with each older girl mothering a younger one, the one most different from herself: the passionate tomboy Jo appropriates saintly Beth, while gentle, domestic Meg nurtures vain, ambitious Amy. In *Pride and Prejudice* this cross-fertilization and balance of opposing temperaments would threaten to complete a circle that by definition can never be complete, as long as a "single man in possession of a good fortune" exists who is "in want of a wife"—or is wanted by one. For, according to the mother-evolved dictum of the famous first sentence, such a quintessence of eligibility *must be* both wanting and wanted. These two words take us out of the novelistic sphere of contingent, palpable reality into a world of wish and vision, somewhere between injunction and hope, command

and prayer. Its replacement of "is" by "must be" lifts us from the empirical to the absolute, in a false, feminine similitude of logical necessity whose note of wishful command gives the texture of a world ruled by women but possessed by men.

We are not allowed to see Longbourn House until a man does; for the reader as for its inhabitants, it is an insubstantial place that exists to be left. Though Jane Austen's descriptions never number the streaks of the tulip, she is almost always precise; but Longbourn is so impalpable that even such a precisionist as R. W. Chapman must search for a misprint to explain its shifting design.[6] When the unregenerate Lydia returns to make everybody miserable as the family's first bride, and looks "eagerly round the room, [takes] notice of some little alteration in it, and observe[s], with a laugh, that it [is] a great while since she [has] been there" (p. 315), it matters to nobody what the little alteration might be. Details of Longbourn are not "known, and *loved* because they are known," as George Eliot will put it in *The Mill on The Floss*: here and elsewhere, notice of the house evokes the joy of absence from it, not presence in it. Lydia's wedding parties crystallize the role of the household in the novel as a whole: "These parties were acceptable to all; to avoid a family circle was even more desirable to such as did think, than such as did not" (p. 318). Meg, the eldest and so the natural first bride of the March household, will turn longingly back to the circle immediately after her wedding ceremony, crying, "The first kiss for Marmee!" But Lydia, the youngest and her mother's favorite, leaves with never a backward glance a family we have never seen together, a house with wavering contours and rooms we cannot visualize. The near-invisibility of Longbourn and the collective life of the Bennets within it is at one with its economic invisibility under an entail which denies a family of women legal existence. Mrs. Bennet is a constant shrill reminder of the entail's overweening power over the family unit, and Jane Austen presents Longbourn House in part as Mrs. Bennet perceives it—as an inherently lost and already half-vanished mirage.

Further erosion of Longbourn's solidity comes from its lack

of a past. The inhabitant with whom we are most intimate is Elizabeth, and for her the house has none of the density and texture which a childhood in it would bring. Though she scrupulously watches and analyzes and talks, Elizabeth is beyond a certain point devoid of memory. "The *present* always occupies you in such scenes—does it?" says Darcy to her "with a look of doubt," and she answers half-consciously, "yes, always" (p. 93). Later he tries to lead her back into her past by saying, "*You* cannot have a right to such very strong local attachment. *You* cannot have been always at Longbourn." We never know the answer. Elizabeth merely "look[s] surprised" and is silent (p. 179). Elizabeth Bennet is the only one of Austen's heroines who is deprived of a childhood and a setting for her childhood. Marianne Dashwood's rhapsody to the "dear, dear Norland" she is forced out of would have some resonance for all the rest. Only Elizabeth shares none of Maggie Tulliver's later panic at childhood dislodged: "The end of our life will have nothing in it like the beginning." With her home a vacuum and her memory a blank, such an end can only be Elizabeth's dearest wish.

After the engagement, when she is coming sufficiently close to Darcy to begin to educate him, one of her first pedagogical gifts is her cool repudiation of memory: "You must learn some of my philosophy. Think only of the past as its remembrance gives you pleasure" (pp. 368-369). Darcy chivalrously denies such a philosophy in his "dearest, loveliest Elizabeth"; but shortly thereafter, in speaking of him to Jane, she uses this philosophy to obliterate a great part of Darcy: "You know nothing of [my dislike of him]. *That* is all to be forgot. Perhaps I did not always love him so well as I do now. But in such cases as these, a good memory is unpardonable. This is the last time I shall ever remember it myself" (p. 373). The novel's mode of perception suggests the seriousness of Elizabeth's jokes. If she shares nothing else with her mother, her faculty of nonremembrance confirms Mrs. Bennet's perception of the nonlife they have had together.

Oddly, it is men who bring domestic substance into the representation of this world. Dorothy Van Ghent writes beautifully about the physicality that somehow emerges from Jane

Austen's spare language: "Curiously and quite wonderfully, out of her restricted concern for the rational and social definition of the human performance there does arise a strong implication of the physical."[7] But men alone endow female existence with this physicality. Mrs. Bennet is perpetually begging any and all eligible males to come to a dinner we have never seen the family at Longbourn eat, as if only in their presence can nourishment present itself. The first male to grace their table is Mr. Collins, and in token of the reality of male appetite, Mrs. Bennet gives us the first domestic detail of Longbourn we have seen—a fish they do not have: "But—good lord! how unlucky! there is not a bit of fish to be got to-day. Lydia, my love, ring the bell. I must speak to Hill, this moment" (p. 61). Mr. Collins brings a sense of domestic reality to Longbourn by his interminable descriptions of the arrangements and situation of Hunsford; he even permits us to hear about "some shelves in the closets up stairs," which stand out vividly in a house that as far as we know has neither closets nor shelves. While the sonorous presentation of these details reminds us primarily of the weighty tedium of Mr. Collins' self-absorption, like Miss Bates's outpourings in *Emma* they also unobtrusively fill the world in a manner that looks forward to the opulently detailed presentation of Darcy's Pemberley.

Pemberley is Elizabeth's initiation into physicality, providing her with all the architectural solidity and domestic substance Longbourn lacks. It has real grounds, woods, paths, streams, rooms, furniture; real food is eaten there: "The next variation which their visit afforded was produced by the entrance of servants with cold meat, cake, and a variety of all the finest fruits in season; . . . though they could not all talk, they could all eat, and the beautiful pyramids of grapes, nectarines, and peaches, soon collected them round the table" (p. 268). The "pyramids" of fruit suggest both architectural and natural power, neither of which is available in the blank space of her mother's house. Surely, to be mistress of Pemberley is "something," in view of the imprisoning nothing of being mistress at Longbourn. But when Bingley and Darcy appear there for dinner at last, in all the glory of prospective husband-ness, food seems to spring into abundance for the first time: "The dinner was as well dressed as any I ever saw. The venison was roasted to a turn—and everybody said, they never saw so fat a haunch. The soup was fifty times better than we had at the Lucas's last week; and even Mr. Darcy acknowledged, that the partridges were remarkably well done; and I suppose he has two or three French cooks at least" (p. 342). For the first time, Mrs. Bennet applies the numbers with which she is obsessed, not to abstract and invisible sums of money, but to the immediately edible and nourishing. Contrary to sentimental myth, it is not women but available men whose presence makes a house a home.

If men can bring what seems a cornucopian abundance to the scanty Bennet dinner table, men also create whatever strength of sisterhood we see in the novel. If at times the fight for male approval prevents cooperation among women,[8] the mysterious power of a man can also draw women together under its aegis. During the many confidences we see between Elizabeth and Jane, they talk of nothing but Bingley and Darcy, speculating over their motives and characters with the relish of two collaborators working on a novel. Moreover, Lydia is never so much their sister as when she disgraces herself with Wickham and seems to spoil their chances of marriage as well: unwanted family solidarity is created by sexual disgrace as it is celebrated in sexual triumph. *The Watsons,* Austen's fragmentary beginning of a novel, defines more baldly the law that a family of women is never so much a family as when one member finds a man to remove her from it: "We must not all expect to be individually lucky replied Emma. The Luck of one member of a Family is Luck to all. —"[9] Not merely is the descriptive energy of the novel reserved for the homes the girls marry into: only the presence of suitors brings substance to the families they leave. The law governing the technique of *Pride and Prejudice* is at one with Mrs. Bennet's economic obsession: marriage and marriage alone gives the world contour.

The vaporousness of Longbourn, as a narrative center and as an empty reflection in memory, is surprising in view of the primacy of the family in Austen's other novels. Darcy will emphasize its role as moral shaper, second in significance only to his loving adult encounters with his "dearest, loveliest Elizabeth." In the other novels, no matter how distant family relationships might be, explusion thence is in some sense a loss of Eden; the family is enriched by its traditional incarnation as a microcosm of society, endowing the life within it with weight and purpose, if not the intimacy later writers learned to want.[10]

But when this weighty center of gravity becomes a household of women, its cultural resonance goes. While Sir Thomas Bertram governs there, the household of *Mansfield Park* has magnitude even in its errors; but when Sir Thomas withdraws to Antigua and Mrs. Norris presides over a bevy of women, Mansfield dissipates into a center of artifice and false faith. The passage of the household from moral crucible to sanctuary of unreality is suggested by the shift of its chief emblem from Fanny's nest in the little schoolroom, austere yet solidly comforting, to the opulent green baize curtain Aunt Norris makes for the aborted performance of *Lovers' Vows*. Symbolized in *Mansfield Park* by its ill-fated theatricals, a female household brings the family from center to shadow of cultural reality.

As Jane Austen presents a family of women, invisibility is its essence: economic invisibility infects the physical world. In *Sense and Sensibility*, dispossessed of their estate by another patriarchal entail, the four Dashwood women are systematically stripped of compensatory support by their mean-minded half-brother and his grasping wife, whose calculations reduce them to a nullity: "Altogether, they will have five hundred a-year amongst them, and what on earth can four women want for more than that?—They will live so cheap!" The married woman's attrition of the manless colony's needs is reminiscent of Regan's piercing "What need one?" to the dispossessed King Lear, who is all need. But Austen's unaccommodated women are more accommodating than Shakespeare's unaccommodated man; instead of hurling themselves into madness and storm for revenge, the mother and sisters settle into cramped Barton Cottage, on which no descriptive detail is

lavished until the dashing Willoughby brings it to romantic life:
" 'To me it is faultless. Nay, more, I consider it as the only
form of building in which happiness is attainable, and were I
rich enough, I would instantly pull Combe down, and build it
up again in the exact plan of this cottage.' 'With dark narrow
stairs, and a kitchen that smokes, I suppose,' said Elinor." [11]
The oppressive becomes the idyllic only to a man who is to be
mistrusted, and it is vaguely insulting when Willoughby goes
on to rhapsodize about Barton's "dear parlour" and the dese-
cration of any "improvements" on it. *Little Women* will create
a world where Laurie's exuberant affection for the cramped
cottage of the March women shows the soundness of his heart
and values; but Willoughby's effusions about such straitened
surroundings render him emotionally suspect and deflected
from what Elizabeth Bennet terms "a proper way of thinking."
There is a similar aura of hovering insult in *The Watsons,*
when Lord Osborne and Tom Musgrave abruptly deign to pay
a formal call on the stinted family of sisters. But in this more
assertive and self-aware ambience food does not obligingly
spring into being upon the entrance of men; the men are driven
away by the family's preparations for its unfashionably early
dinner. This unwelcoming imminence of food hints that a
woman's primary hunger is the need to feed herself rather
than a man. The novel was never finished, so the implications
of this gesture toward self-sustainment were never explored.

Throughout Austen's completed novels, women lead a pur-
gatorial existence together. When Maria Bertram is banished
to the ministrations of Mrs. Norris in *Mansfield Park,* we feel
that such a colony of two is a fate worse than the death or
transportation that are the usual recourses of the fallen
woman; and in *Emma,* living with Miss Bates and her mother
can only be a mortifying exacerbation of Jane Fairfax's refined
nerves. In fact, Jane Fairfax uses the female collectivity of the
convent as a metaphor for her life's utter deprived negation:
"She had long resolved that one-and-twenty should be the
period. With the fortitude of a devoted noviciate, she had resolved at one-and-twenty to complete the sacrifice, and retire
from all the pleasures of life, of rational intercourse, peace

and hope, to penance and mortification for ever."[12] The "penance and mortification" endured by women living together does not spring from their contaminating sexual degradation, as it does for Jane Austen's contemporary Mary Wollstonecraft;[13] worse than contaminated, their lives are presented through an avoidance of detailed presentation as unshaped, unreal, a limbo.

The lack of texture in Austen's delineation of a family of women is the more surprising in that during her major creative period she lived in one. The household at Chawton in which she lived between 1809 and her death in 1817 consisted of herself, her sister Cassandra, their widowed mother, their unmarried friend Martha Lloyd, and sometimes brother James' daughter Cassy, lacking even the token nonauthoritative male the novels provide to give the little community official identity. In fact, Mrs. Austen chose the cottage that was as far as possible from the parent estate of Godmersham, where her son and patron, Edward Austen Knight, resided. Just before the move, Jane Austen wrote a jaunty doggerel poem whose conclusion is the foundation for something of a "Chawton myth" on the part of her biographers: "You'll find us very snug next year."[14]

And so commentators have found them, particularly with sundry nieces and nephews always coming to stay and be amused. The usual impression of life at Chawton is expressed in the phrase Frank Churchill finds so oddly euphonious in *Emma*: "a crowd in a little room." Jane Aiken Hodge creates an almost Orwellian Chawton—"The two letters Jane Austen wrote to Fanny that autumn . . . give one a frightening picture of the total lack of privacy in her life"—on which Brigid Brophy elaborates: "[Q]uite apart from servants, the regular complement of the house was four adult females and one child. A visit to Chawton makes it clear in turn that that *must* have been cramped—not intolerably so, and not, indeed, in comparison with the living quarters of most English people at that time, but in comparison with the milieux of Jane Austen's novels and with what, it can be legitimately guessed, Jane Austen herself had originally expected of life . . . [I]tem after item in Jane Austen's letters seems to anticipate [the] horror of a transposition from grandeur to poverty."[15] Brophy's essay creates a vivid enclave of "distressed aristocracy" among which the proud Jane lived as deposed queen.

Except in the independent and possibly defensive orbit between Jane and Cassandra, this community of four manless women is never depicted as intimate, but always as encroaching and intruding. Yet the Jane Austen we still want to know about was born there; it was at Chawton that she finally outgrew the role of family court jester and came to see herself as a serious writer, her books as alive. It is significant that her first serious projects there were almost certainly the recasting of *Sense and Sensibility* and *Pride and Prejudice*, both of which deal extensively with the vacuum that is the lives of "superfluous" women. If these novels were originally epistolary, as some critics suggest, her recasting from letters into dramatized narrative would throw the sisters into a proximity impossible in the old form, which may reflect the intimacy of the new female world in which she lived.[16] Though she may have been inspired by a sense of her new life's vacuity, inspired she was, and the Chawton community, almost always deplored as an impediment, must be given credit for some of the same generative power that living with George Henry Lewes possessed for George Eliot.

Some of the strength of Chawton's productive impetus may have come from the fact that, as with Longbourn House, its existence as a family was indistinguishable from its life as a neighborhood. Not only did it function as a clearinghouse for the next generation of Austens and their social lives, but the house itself was caught between its private and public characters: according to the *Memoir* written by Jane Austen's nephew, it was originally built as an inn and after 1845 was divided into "tenements for labourers," retaining some of its original collective function.[17] "Very snug" they might have been at Chawton, but the outside world poured through it, and the pressure of people fed into the pressure of art, endowing a real female community with a power for which we must be grateful.

But it is on this very issue of direct female power that Jane Austen's novels are most equivocal. Beginning with such trivial incidents as the married Lydia's displacement of her older and more level-headed sister Jane at the head of the table, or the married Mrs. Elton taking precedence over the elegant Emma at a ball, there is an unnervingly arbitrary and grotesque quality to the assumption of power by women. If flabby fathers are to be deplored in the novels, strong mothers or mother-substitutes like Lady Susan, Mrs. Norris, and Lady Russell are almost always pernicious in their authority: female power is effectively synonymous with power abused.[18] Mrs. Bennet's desire to establish Jane at Netherfield is depicted only as a series of murderous attacks upon the pliant girl, despite the fact that in the end, Jane's illness at Netherfield does further her marriage as Mrs. Bennet had planned, leading Elizabeth toward glory as well. Like Chawton, Mrs. Bennet is given credit only for obstructing; as one critic says well, "Mrs. Bennet moves in an atmosphere of repugnance that is scarcely explained."[19]

It was Mrs. Bennet's grotesque specter that led the Victorian feminist Harriet Martineau to back into an oblique apology for the little authority Englishwomen were allowed: "I was asked whether it was possible that the Bennet family would act as they are represented in 'Pride and Prejudice': whether a foolish mother, with grown up daughters, would be allowed to spoil the two youngest, instead of the sensible daughters taking the case into their own hands. It is certainly true that in America the superior minds of the family would take the lead; while in England, however the domestic affairs might gradually arrange themselves, no person would be found breathing the suggestion of superseding the mother's authority."[20] Given such meager-minded despotism, Martineau might have better understood why men looked with trepidation on the idea of female participation in the government of their countries; but despite Mrs. Bennet's aura of awfulness, she is in league with her creator as she drives her daughters out of a nonhome into the establishments they deserve. "The business of her life [is] to get her daughters married," in fact as well as obsessed fantasy; though in the case of the three most nubile, the end crowns the whole, her government is shown to be at one with the usurpation that is the paramount characteristic of Mrs. Bennet's counterpart in the larger social world—the overpowering Lady Catherine de Bourgh.[21]

Wickham's anticipatory description of Lady Catherine defines the woman we eventually meet as most of his characterizations do not: "She has the reputation of being remarkably sensible and clever; but I rather believe she derives part of her abilities from her rank and fortune, part from her authoritative manner, and the rest from the pride of her nephew, who chuses that every one connected with him should have an understanding of the first class" (p. 84). In other words, Lady Catherine's authority is not inherent, but derived in arbitrary and misplaced fashion from accidents and contrivances outside herself; she is a pastiche of external pretensions, an embodiment of that power without selfhood that threatens to make all authority ridiculous. This monster of misgovernment is the only character other than Mrs. Bennet to deplore the exclusively male right of inheritance, which the sprightly, iconoclastic Elizabeth seems to accept as a matter of course: "I am glad of it; but otherwise I see no occasion for entailing estates from the female line.—It was not thought necessary in Sir Lewis de Bourgh's family" (p. 164). This interesting fact makes clear one role that Lady Catherine plays in the novel: she functions as an image of the overweening matriarchate that would result could widow and daughters inherit the estate Mrs. Bennet craves. In her futile confrontation with Elizabeth, Lady Catherine makes clear that her private great society runs on matriarchal principles:

> "I will not be interrupted. Hear me in silence. My daughter and my nephew are formed for each other. They are descended on the maternal side, from the same noble line; and, on the father's, from respectable, honourable, and ancient, though untitled families." [After this condescending inclusion of the lesser paternal line, Lady Catherine goes on to warn Elizabeth not to "quit the sphere" in which she was brought up.]

"In marrying your nephew, I should not consider myself as quitting that sphere. He is a gentleman; I am a gentleman's daughter; so far we are equal."

"True. You *are* a gentleman's daughter. But who was your mother?" (p. 356).

This bit of dialogue, particularly Lady Catherine's final challenge, throws Elizabeth back on the female, matriarchal dream world she is trying to escape. In asserting the primary reality of men and patrilineal inheritance, she comes close to denying that she is her mother's daughter. In the context of the novel's artistic methods and its social scheme, the male principle Elizabeth invokes is the invincible "reality" that counters Lady Catherine's fantasy of matriarchal omnipotence, whose visionary impossibility is reflected even in its syntax: "While in their cradles, we planned the union" (p. 355). Given the real, masculine center of power in the novel, Lady Catherine's trumpeting of her divine omnipresence is as hollow a delusion as she is herself: "Do not deceive yourself into a belief that I will ever recede" (p. 356), she says, receding. Lady Catherine's withdrawal, and the reassuringly ardent Darcy's quick appearance in her place, suggests the salutary recession of the usurped power of all mothers before the meaning and form only men can bestow.

The acknowledged center of power in the novel is the shadowy Darcy. "As a brother, a landlord, a master, she considered how many people's happiness were in his guardianship!—How much of pleasure or pain it was in his power to bestow!—How much of good or evil must be done by him!" (pp. 250-251). Looking at Darcy as his portrait immortalizes him, Elizabeth is overcome by a kind of social vitalism: she is drawn not to the benignity and wisdom of Darcy's power, but to its sheer extent as such, for evil as well as good. What compels her in the portrait is the awesomely institutionalized power of a man, a power that her own father has let fall and her mother, grotesquely usurped. Loathing the idea of any kinship to her mother, Elizabeth will doubtless be content not to have her own portrait displayed after her marriage, as Austen speculates: "I can only imagine that Mr. D. prizes any Picture of her too much to like it should be exposed to the public eye.—I can imagine he wd. have that sort of feeling—that mixture of Love, Pride & Delicacy."[22] After the clamorous anonymity of Longbourn, marriage waits for her as a hard-won release into a privacy only Darcy can bestow.

Underneath this pervasive largesse, Darcy has as shadowy a selfhood as his aunt, Lady Catherine. If Elizabeth's childhood is obliterated in memory, Darcy's is a muddled contradiction. The man who caught Elizabeth's eye before audibly insulting her was, according to his "intelligent" housekeeper, a fount of virtue from the beginning of his life. He was merely too modest to declare his goodness, and Elizabeth too prejudiced to see it: "I have never had a cross word from him in my life, and I have known him ever since he was four years old. . . I have always observed, that they who are good-natured when children, are good-natured when they grow up; and he was always the sweetest-tempered, most generous-hearted, boy in the world. . . . . Some people call him proud; but I am sure I never saw any thing of it. To my fancy, it is only because he does not rattle away like other young men" (pp. 248-249). A good deal of weight is put on this testimony, though it is oddly redolent of Mr. Collins extolling the condescension of Lady Catherine; also, it meshes neither with the reliable Mrs. Gardiner's "having heard Mr. Fitzwilliam Darcy formerly spoken of as a very proud, ill-natured boy" (p. 143), nor with Darcy's own meticulous diagnosis of his boyhood:

As a child I was taught what was *right*, but I was not taught to correct my temper. I was given good principles, but left to follow them in pride and conceit. Unfortunately an only son, (for many years an only *child*) I was spoilt by my parents, who though good themselves . . . allowed, encouraged, almost taught me to be selfish and overbearing, to care for none beyond my own family circle, to think meanly of all the rest of the world, to *wish* at least to think meanly of their sense and worth compared with my own. Such I was, from eight to eight and twenty; and such I might still have been but for you, dearest, loveliest Elizabeth! What do I not owe you! You taught me a lesson, hard indeed at first, but most advantageous. By you, I was properly humbled. (p. 369)

Darcy the man is as muddled a figure as Darcy the boy. Is he indeed converted into humanity by Elizabeth's spontaneity and spirit, or was he always the perfection that maturity allows her to see? Oddly, Elizabeth herself prefers the latter interpretation, which replaces her power over him with a reassuring silliness: "And yet I meant to be uncommonly clever in taking so decided a dislike to him, without any reason. It is such a spur to one's genius, such an opening for wit to have a dislike of that kind. One may be continually abusive without saying any thing just; but one cannot be always laughing at a man without now and then stumbling on something witty" (pp. 225-226). Elizabeth's selective memory serves her well here by erasing the fact that she had, and has, several good reasons for disliking Darcy; but she seems to need a sense of her own wrongness to justify the play of her mind. In choosing to emphasize her own prejudice over Darcy's most palpable pride, she can wonder freely at the power in his portrait while her own (if there is one) will be closeted away, invisible to all eyes but her husband's. Standing as a tourist before the solitary grandeur of his portrait, she recalls the young Jane Austen, a "partial, prejudiced, and ignorant Historian," willfully slicing off fragments from the magisterial pageant of Goldsmith's *History of England* in order to establish a private community of four between Mary Queen of Scots, "Mrs. Lefroy, Mrs. Knight and myself." [23] The power of silliness can yoke a country girl and a queen, but in the face of the magisterial and masculine parade of reality there is safety in imaginative appropriation only if one is "partial, prejudiced, and ignorant." Objectivity, impartiality, and knowledge might endanger the cloak of invisibility which is so intrinsic a part of Austen's perception of a woman's life. After the battle of Albuera, she wrote a partial, prejudiced, and ignorant comment about it to Cassandra: "How horrible it is to have so many people killed!—And what a blessing that one cares for none of them!" [24] It is more than an "opening for wit" to celebrate the rift that lies between one's own world and history; for Jane Austen this rift seems to have been the foundation of imagination, of art itself, and turned her exclusion into a blessing.

The sanctioned power of management with which she endows Darcy allows him to prove his heroism in the third volume by taking over the mother's role: like the shadowy "Duke of dark corners" in *Measure for Measure*, he moves behind the scenes and secretly arranges the marriages of the three Bennet girls. The end of the novel finds the neighborhood of families that centers around Pemberley busily improving Kitty for a good match, leaving only the lumpish Mary still at home to be displayed by her mother, their alliance a fitting penance for the pedantry of the one and the presumption of the other. The last page tells us incidentally that the war has ended, and, with Darcy's will to harmony, perhaps the waiting will as well. In becoming the novel's providential matchmaker, Darcy brings about the comic conclusion by an administrative activity for which Mrs. Bennet and Lady Catherine were, and Emma Woodhouse will be, severely condemned. In the end, the malevolent power of the mother is ennobled by being transferred to the hero,[25] and the female community of Longbourn, an oppressive blank in a dense society, is dispersed with relief in the solidity of marriage.

Little Women

> [P]ublishers are very perverse & wont let authors
> have their way so my little women must grow up &
> be married off in a very stupid style.[26]

In *Pride and Prejudice* a world without men is empty of effects. Lacking an inheritance, the Bennet girls are only theoretically impecunious—unlike the March girls, they have nothing to do with the kitchen, and clothes available for any ball—but physically as well as psychically they live in an empty world. The world of the March girls is rich enough to complete itself, and in this richness lies the tension of *Little Women* and its two sequels.

" 'Christmas won't be Christmas without any presents,' grumble[s] Jo, lying on the rug" (*LW*, p. 2), to start the series off with a spiritual absurdity that will be contradicted by the almost immediate entrance of all-dispensing Marmee—unlike the mother-generated absurdity that opens *Pride and Prejudice,* which has no higher authority to contradict it. The Christmas gift Marmee seems tenderly to offer her girls is hunger. First, each decides to give up her one precious dollar to buy a Christmas gift for their mother instead of a loved item for herself; Marmee then enters with a letter from Father, who is nobly serving as a chaplain in the Civil War, admonishing the girls to "conquer themselves . . . beautifully" and making them all feel deliciously guilty. On Christmas Day, in response to their sacrificial gifts, she makes her climactic request that the girls give up their holiday breakfast to a starving family. They go trooping through the snow, with full hands and empty stomachs, "funny angels in hoods and mittens" who have learned that it is better to renounce than receive. And the book succeeds in making us believe that this hungry day is "A Merry Christmas."

When Ebenezer Scrooge gives Bob Cratchit a Christmas turkey as a token of fellowship, we easily but rather abstractly accept the bird as a metaphor of Scrooge's change of heart; but we know that Scrooge could buy a wilderness of turkeys for himself, had not his nephew Fred joyfully invited him to dinner. The March girls, whom no one invites, are made of sterner stuff. Their pilgrimage to the poor quarter of town is significant only because they themselves are hungry, and the food that Marmee gently requests they renounce is vividly appetizing. I surmise that their vanished buckwheat cakes, bread, cream, and muffins have been longed for by more female readers than the cold meat, cake, and pyramids "of the finest fruits in season" that Elizabeth Bennet was served when she finally entered Pemberley. The largesse is Darcy's; the renunciation is the March girls' own, and their concert in performing it, *after* the narrative has established them as selfish and turbulent, wanting all sorts of things they won't be permitted to have, is the sisterhood the novel is about. Longbourn was a hungry world because an empty one; the hungry

March cottage is full of things, each of which is both fact and spiritual emblem.

In the richness of that uneaten breakfast it is easy to forget that the March girls are rewarded for their generosity by masculine largesse. As Meg has said, "although [or because?] we do have to work, we make fun for ourselves" (p. 5), and that evening they put on a play Jo has written, which is described in extended detail. After it is over, all find waiting a splendid supper sent over by wealthy Mr. Laurence next door, in appreciation of their good deed. The supper is less important in itself than as a liaison established between the two houses that makes possible the friendship between the four girls and his grandson, rich, spirited Laurie. Laurie plays the role of Bingley in *Pride and Prejudice:* he is not only marriageable in himself, but the cause of marriage in other men. Introduction to him indirectly makes possible the marriages of all the girls: Meg marries his tutor; Jo goes to New York to escape his importunity and meets Professor Bhaer there; and he himself finally marries Amy. Like Darcy, Laurie has "good match" emblazoned all over him. The morning's renunciation ultimately aligns the March girls with the spirit of marriage, and Christmas is Christmas indeed.

The treatment of this simultaneous savior and intruder is quite different in the American story. In *Pride and Prejudice* the sisters acted in joyous concert only at Mr. Bennet's wry announcement that he had paid a formal call on Bingley. In *Little Women* the sisters act in concert with no reference to Laurie, and in deference to its beauty he solicits access to their harmony with only partial success. Instead of calculating the value of his establishment, Marmee perceives his need: "He looked so wistful as he went away, hearing the frolic, and evidently having none of his own" (p. 27). Her assessment turns out to be as compassionately knowing as Mrs. Bennet's was financially knowing:

> Laurie colored up, but answered frankly, "Why, you see, I often hear you calling to one another, and when I'm alone up here, I can't help looking over at your house, you always seem to be having such good times. I beg your pardon for being so rude, but sometimes you forget to put

down the curtain at the window where the flowers are; and when the lamps are lighted, it's like looking at a picture to see the fire, and you all round the table with your mother; her face is right opposite, and it looks so sweet behind the flowers, I can't help watching it. I haven't got any mother, you know"; and Laurie poked the fire to hide a little twitching of the lips that he could not control.

The solitary, hungry look in his eyes went straight to Jo's warm heart. She had been so simply taught that there was no nonsense in her head, and at fifteen she was as innocent and frank as any child. Laurie was sick and lonely; and, feeling how rich she was in home love and happiness, she gladly tried to share it with him.   (p.57)

The balance of *Pride and Prejudice* is inverted. The hero now peers wistfully in at the female family, "like looking at a picture," as Elizabeth did at Pemberley. Plenitude belongs to the community of women, hunger to the solitary man. When Elizabeth's family inadvertently exposed itself to Darcy by a parade of vulgarities at the Netherfield ball, he could only flee in horror with Bingley; but when the March family inadvertently exposes itself by leaving up the shade, Laurie glimpses a carefully poised fullness that draws him to its perfect self. He solicits entree to a sometimes reluctant circle in similar fashion throughout the first half of the novel, hiding in a closet while the girls debate his admission to their Pickwick Club, whose rituals and jokes are described in the same extensive detail as the Christmas play. He is even more importunate when he stumbles on their Busy Bee Society, which he again perceives as a carefully grouped and self-complete work of art:

It *was* rather a pretty little picture, for the sisters sat together in the shady nook, with sun and shadow flickering over them, the aromatic wind lifting their hair and cooling their hot cheeks, and all the little wood people going on with their affairs as if these were no strangers but old friends. Meg sat upon her cushion, sewing daintily with her white hands, and looking as fresh and sweet as a rose, in her pink dress, among the green. Beth was sorting the cones that lay thick under the hemlock near by, for she made pretty things of them. Amy was sketching a group of ferns, and Jo was knitting as she read aloud. A shadow passed over the boy's face as he watched them, feeling that he ought to go away, because uninvited; yet lingering because home seemed very lonely, and this quiet party in the woods most attractive to his restless spirit. He stood so still that a squirrel, busy with its harvesting, ran down a pine close beside him, saw him suddenly and skipped back, scolding so shrilly that Beth looked up, espied the wistful face behind the birches, and beckoned with a reassuring smile.

"May I come in, please? Or shall I be a bother?" he asked, advancing slowly.   (pp. 155-156)

The March girls offer Laurie all the richness of interchange between art, taste, and nature that Pemberley held out to Elizabeth Bennet. Even when he is not present, the girls are almost always described as a balanced tableau. With characteristic abundance of detail, the author sees it as her artistic duty to give us, not the income, but the appearance of the March girls as soon as possible: "As young readers like to know 'how people look,' we will take this moment to give them a little sketch of the four sisters, who sat knitting away in the twilight, while the December snow fell quietly without, and the fire crackled cheerfully within" (p. 6). After an intimate survey of hair, coloring, carriage, and so on, the author archly concludes with a mystery which is no mystery at all: "What the characters of the four sisters were we will leave to be found out" (p. 7). We have already found their characters in their appearance; raised among disembodied sages in Transcendentalist Concord, Louisa May Alcott clings stubbornly throughout her novels to the primary reality of physical things.[27] In her world people can decipher character and mood instantly by subtle shifts in faces, bearing, eyebrows, clothes. Mr. Laurence's kindness speaks to Jo out of his portrait before they meet; when Jo becomes a writer her jaunty cap communicates instantly to the peeping family the degree to which genius is burning. When the physical body is so insistently alive and expressive there are no barriers to intimacy but time and death; this accessible and familial world, where character is a language all can read, contains no Austenian "intricate characters" who deceive by their appearance.

Alcott trusts what she can see, and nowhere is her reliance on the life in things more vividly apparent than in her delineation of the March haven: the expressive rattle of Jo's knitting needles; the high-heeled boots which crush Meg's feet; Beth's divine piano; Amy's plaster casts and the delicate "things" she dramatically sweeps off the bazaar table; Marmee's crooned-over slippers. Throughout the novel the March women are defined in their primary relationship to the "things" that display their characters. The physicality of their community is not bestowed, but inherent and overflowing. Clothes in *Pride and Prejudice* were vaguely mentioned, usually in terms of some inane question from Mrs. Bennet about "style" which was cut short by her contemptuous husband. But Alcott slips her views about dress reform into the novel by forcing the female reader to feel Meg's agony when she is pinched and squeezed in her attempts at elegance. Letters in *Pride and Prejudice* were sparsely used and significant; either they were severe tests of character, like those of Mr. Collins and Darcy, or they conveyed necessary information, like Jane's and Mr. Gardiner's about Lydia's elopement. But *Little Women* spills over with letters that are given to us simply for the purpose of relishing their writers: "As one of these packets contained characteristic notes from the party, we will rob an imaginary mail, and read them" (p. 186). We learn nothing from these letters but the fact that Meg is Meg, Jo, Jo, Beth, Beth, and Amy, Amy, which has already been amply demonstrated; but if we are engulfed in their lives as a fifth sister, it is enough. The abundance in which we perceive the life of the circle dramatizes its message of the richness of poverty when Marmee's and Alcott's moralizing makes us wince. Despite the girls' mechanical grumbling, it is difficult for the reader to believe in what they have given up when she finds herself surrounded with what they have.

In *Pride and Prejudice* the family fed itself to the omnipresent neighborhood, but in *Little Women* it is the heart of its world. Though Jo tells Laurie, "we have got acquainted with all our neighbors but you" (p. 58), Laurie and his grandfather are for most of the book the only neighbors we see, and they exist more as honorary family than as neighbors proper. When the girls get older, the Chesters and the Lambs and the rest exist for Jo and Amy to call on, but they function only as obstacles in the girls' perpetual Pilgrims' Progress game, as tests of character for the sisters rather than as an independent social context to which they must belong. The primacy of the female family, both as moral-emotional magnet and as work of art, is indicated by the quality of their appeal to Laurie: though he thinks he loves Jo best, his true role is that of son-brother-squire to the family unit as he is mulled over by each of the girls in turn. In the beginning of the book, the sophisticated Moffats and Jo herself link him to Meg, who is scornful about being matched to a mere "boy." Later comes Jo's rejection of him, which, despite Alcott's indifference to her obligatory marriage plots, remains the most talked-about part of the book from its day to ours;[28] and Jo's private hope that a match with Beth will soften him and cure her lingering illness. Beth amazedly disabuses her, her characteristic "trouble" being that she must die and leave the family circle, with never a thought of love or Laurie. So Jo brusquely and pragmatically consigns him to the match he does eventually make: " 'Why, Jo, how could I, when he was so fond of you?' asked Beth, as innocently as a child. 'I do love him dearly; he is so good to me, how can I help it? But he never could be anything to me but my brother. I hope he truly will be, sometime.' 'Not through me,' said Jo decidedly. 'Amy is left for him, and they would suit excellently; but I have no heart for such things, now ' " (p. 416). Thus, before romance blooms for him, Laurie is rejected by each of the girls in turn. It is impossible to imagine romantic heroes like Darcy, or even Bingley, being so bandied around the Bennet circle before settling on the one sister who is "left for him." Even in designing his marriage to Amy, Alcott seems to smooth poor Laurie's path by making Amy shed her artistic ambitions in favor of being "an ornament to society"—as Louisa's singleminded sister May never did—and by Amy's homesick vulnerability abroad after learning that Beth has died without her. With all his winsomeness, love, and money, Laurie's attempts to enter the charmed circle are continually frustrated until death makes a place for him.

Amy's is not the only March marriage to take place under the shadow of death. Womanly Meg's love match to poor-but-honest John Brooke is colored for us by Jo's tragic sense that the wrench to the family it entails is more of an ending than a beginning: "I knew there was mischief brewing! I felt it; and now it's worse than I imagined. I just wish I could marry Meg myself, and keep her safe in the family" (p. 224). Though Jane Bennet was Elizabeth's only female companion in the family, as Meg is not Jo's, Elizabeth's desire to consign her to Netherfield and Bingley was wholehearted and intense: her rage at Darcy for attempting to separate them is at one with Jo's rage against Laurie for furthering her sister's love affair. Jo's equation of all life with the family circle echoes Louisa's own mournful love letter upon her older sister's wedding: "After the bridal train had departed, the mourners withdrew to their respective homes; and the bereaved family solaced their woe by washing dishes for two hours and bolting the remains of the funeral baked meats."[29]

Gawky, unawakened Jo is not alone in seeing Meg's marriage as a precious death; the structure of the novel reinforces this mournful tone. Even Marmee seems to view it with resigned acquiescence rather than joy, and their father's voice breaks as he performs the ceremony as it will at Beth and John's funerals. Despite the apparent severity of her regime, [30] Mrs. March allows her girls a great freedom that may explain why the book has been so unreasonably beloved for over a century: the freedom to remain children and, for a woman, the more precious freedom *not* to fall in love: "Right, Jo; better be happy old maids than unhappy wives, or unmaidenly girls running about to find husbands . . . One thing remember, my girls: mother is always ready to be your confidante, father to be your friend; and both of us trust and hope that our daughters, whether married or single, will be the pride and comfort of our lives" (p. 110). The solemnity of the moment when Mrs. March oracularly reveals her "plans" endows the sisters with an independent selfhood which is a rare dowry in any century, and draws the circle even more tightly together.

Meg's marriage is placed alongside a series of calamities that darken it irreparably: Mr. March's illness, Marmee's hurried departure for Washington, Beth's near-fatal illness, and father's return as a befuddledly noble center of reverence that deflects family intimacy.[31] The inclusion of young love among these upheavals implicitly defines it as more of a destroyer of sisterhood than an emotional progression beyond it; and the equation between the departures of marriage and of death continues in the last half of the book, where Beth's wasting illness and death run parallel to the marriages of the rest of the sisters. Both stress the loss of the childhood circle rather than the coming into an inheritance of fulfillment.

The intense bond between Jo and Beth is puzzling at first; the logical unit would seem to be Jo and Amy, the two most artistic and aspiring, whose relationship throughout is at best a tender truce. But in their desire for perpetual sisterhood Jo and Beth are at the heart of the novel. Jane Bennet's illness was a result of the exposure into which her mother flung her, precipitating herself and Elizabeth into success on the marriage market. Beth's long wasting is the waning of childhood and the collective death of the sisters; in a sense, she dies so that the others can marry. Beth is usually recalled as a tranquil domestic angel, but the intensity of her yearning for home recalls that of Emily Brontë's heretical Catherine Linton: "I'm not like the rest of you; I never made any plans about what I'd do when I grew up; I never thought of being married, as you all did.[32] I couldn't seem to imagine myself anything but stupid little Beth, trotting about at home, of no use anywhere but there. I never wanted to go away and the hard part now is the leaving you all. I'm not afraid, but it seems as if I should be homesick for you even in heaven" (p. 417). The spirit of home, Beth dies when it does. In her last illness Beth has a dying room into which are brought all the favored relics of the family. For as long as she can hold a needle she makes "little things for the school children passing to and fro," which she throws out the window like utilitarian manna from Heaven. She dies when she relinquishes her hold on these "things" that are the quintessence of the family; the necessity of the parting is the necessity of growing away from home completion and of living despite the splitting of the circle.

Alcott's other writing shows more directly what the circle of women meant to her than we can find in a moral tale for girls which she felt compelled by her publisher to write. Had she written the *Little Women* she envisioned, Beth might have survived to preside over a self-sustaining sisterhood: "Girls write to ask who the little women marry, as if that was the only end and aim of a woman's life. I *won't* marry Jo to Laurie to please any one," she wrote after the appearance of the first half.[33] In fact, she did write a piece about nondiminutive women, at the same time that she began the book we know. In her article "Happy Women"[34] "she gratified her love of single life by describing the delightful spinsters of her acquaintance. Her sketches are all taken from life, and are not too highly colored. The Physician, the Artist, the Philanthropist, the Actress, the Lawyer, are easily recognizable. They were a 'glorious phalanx of old maids,' as Theodore Parker called the single women of his Society, which aided him so much in his work."[35] Here is the idyll lying behind Marmee's new wives' training school: a community of new women, whose sisterhood is not an apprenticeship making them worthy of appropriation by father-husbands, but a bond whose value is itself. Jane Austen may have been too close to Chawton to write about it, but for Alcott, the communal cottage itself, and not the roads out of it, was the palace of art that made her ideal subject.

An Old-Fashioned Girl (1870) stops suddenly at a chapter called "The Sunny Side," in which the eponymous Polly introduces her weary society friend to the life and jollity of a community of women artists who find their meaning and inspiration in helping each other. The collectivity of the March girls is moving from the involuntary sphere of the family into professional organization:

Fanny had been to many elegant lunches, but never enjoyed one more than that droll picnic in the studio; for there was a freedom about it that was charming, an artistic flavor to everything, and such a spirit of good-will and gayety, that she felt at home at once. As they ate, the others talked and she listened, finding it as interesting as any romance to hear these young women discuss their plans, ambitions, successes, and defeats. It was a new world to her, and they seemed a different race of creatures from the girls whose lives were spent in dress, gossip, pleasure, or *ennui*. They were girls still, full of spirit, fun, and youth; but below the light-heartedness each cherished a purpose, which seemed to ennoble her womanhood, to give her a certain power, a sustaining satisfaction, a daily stimulus, that led her on to daily effort, and in time to some success in circumstance or character, which was worth all the patience, hope, and labor of her life.

The collective spirit of the group is enshrined in a half-created, rather agitprop statue of the noble woman of the future standing monumental and alone, with a ballot box for her emblem but no husband or baby. Though Polly finally marries appropriately, and we hear no more of this group of women, or of the Amazonian statue that is their collective daughter, the narrator spends the final chapter grumbling about the need to marry off the heroine and compensates by telling the romantic reader that Fanny's little sister "did *not* marry Will, but remained a busy, lively spinster all her days."[36] Taking shape as a professional and political entity, the spirit of the March girls is implicitly aligned against the patriarchal family it claims to revere.

The conjunction between art, politics, spinsterhood, and the female community is made explicit in an untitled fragment of a novel that was never published.[37] Its four chapters are obviously based on Louisa's relationship with her sister May, who spent the better part of her adult life studying art abroad; the second chapter is an almost exact transcription of May's letters, and the intensity of her devotion to her work makes an instructive contrast to Amy March's flighty, flirty letters home. In a work which never saw the light, Louisa allows Persis-May to define even more clearly her corporate dream in the following description of a group of militant woman artists crusading for the right to draw from nude models:

As for "the women who unsex themselves by going to J's studio," where alone they could get the teaching they needed, we think it a thing to heartily respect them for, as one respects those who study anatomy in order to be surgeons. That little band of dignified and earnest women so far from unsexing themselves were treated with the utmost respect at J's, and very soon made by their mere presence a purer atmosphere around them. Courage is honored every where, and this terrible effort to get the same advantages as men in the same profession at any cost, won for them a place at once in the regard of all real art students. I had rather the French judged us by these brave, right-minded women than by the frivolous creatures who bring discredit on the name of American girls by their wild pranks and empty heads.

This is the female studio of *An Old-Fashioned Girl*, but they have stopped eating and laughing and begun to march. The March girls had to relinquish the art they all aspired toward; though we learn in *Jo's Boys* that even placid Meg once pined to be an actress, Jo acts for all of them when she commemorates her latent love for "her Professor" by burning all her published stories. In Alcott's imagination, art, militancy, and sisterhood seem to be one. Had she allowed the girls to embrace such a triad, her "little women" might, like the statue in *An Old-Fashioned Girl*, have grown beyond control.

This fragment of a novel is the story of the conflict between sisterhood, art, and marriage.[38] In the first chapter Persis vows to obey Diana's injunctions as if she were indeed a goddess: "Do not look for [meaning] in marriage, that is too costly an experiment for us. Flee from temptation and do not dream of spoiling your life by any commonplace romance." In the last, however, Diana is visiting Persis, her husband, and baby, and despite her friend's obvious happiness and her husband's orotund feminist pronouncements, there is a layer of dust in her studio and the paint on her palette has gone dry. The fragment ends in this failure of fellowship. In making explicit the subversive undercurrents of the female community, Alcott has evoked a conflict she cannot resolve.

Work: A Story of Experience (1873), an autobiographical

adult novel on which Alcott worked for twelve years before publishing it, attempts another solution to the conflict between the surging emotion and creativity of the female community and the "normal" tenderness and sacrifice of patriarchal marriage by reversing the order of the phases of Little Women. The novel's structure is the working-out of strong-willed Christie's opening "declaration of independence." Determined to support herself as a man does, Christie moves from profession to profession—including a successful stint as an actress which begins with her playing an Amazon Queen—and thus from life to life. The novel is a kind of domestic picaresque, to which the Pilgrim's Progress metaphor is more immediately appropriate than it is in the static setting of Little Women: Christie is our constant, but her settings are ever-changing. After a series of trials and some serious defeats, her "progress" brings her to marriage with the Thoreauvian David Sterling; but no sooner are they pledged to each other than the Civil War begins.

Christie does not linger in a woman's world. As Jo March wanted to do and as Louisa May Alcott accomplished, she marches off with her new husband to new triumphs as a nurse, an activity which is described less in womanly and nurturing terms than in combative and soldierly ones. From the beginning, the two are less husband and wife than comrades-in-arms: "Then shoulder to shoulder, as if already mustered in, these faithful comrades marched to and fro, planning their campaign."[39] She feels no sense of loss in the war's disruption of their life together: "I like it, David; it's a grand time to live, a splendid chance to do and suffer; and I want to be in it heart and soul, and earn a little of the glory or the martyrdom that will come in the end" (p. 376). The triumph of her war work comes when David (as well as a rejected suitor who is brought in maimed) lies dying under her hands, and she ushers him efficiently and skillfully into death. Her marriage has begun and ended with the Civil War, leaving her with memories of death and a daughter.

At the end of the novel, like most picaresque protagonists, Christie finds permanence: through her new vocation as a public speaker at feminist rallies, she brings together leisured and working women in political and loving sisterhood. Her private life has become the sisterhood she works to perpetuate historically: she and her daughter live in a cooperative commune with David's mother and sister, whose shared profits her capitalist Uncle Enos sneers at somewhat enviously: " 'That ain't a fair bargain if you do all the work.' 'Ah, but we don't make bargains, sir: we work for one another and share everything together.' 'So like women,' grumbled Uncle Enos" (p. 419).[40] By the end of the novel the private and the public communities are moving into a single unit that transcends barriers of class, age, and race: "With an impulsive gesture Christie stretched her hands to the friends about her, and with one accord they laid theirs on hers, a loving league of sisters, old and young, black and white, rich and poor, each ready to do her part to hasten the coming of the happy end" (p. 442). In *Little Women* sisterhood was dissolved by marriage. Here, marriage is an interim episode at one with war, valuable in that it helps to create the crowning community of women whose cooperative blend of private and public life heals the divisions the Civil War embodied. Moreover, marriage produced Christie's all-important daughter Pansy, whose future in the brave new world her community of mothers awaits with hope and awe. The novel's climax comes when Pansy puts her hand on the circle and says, "me too." As in Henry James's *Portrait of a Lady*, the hope at the end of *Work* rests on the little Pansy the book has helped grow.

In the saga of the March family this militant vision of permanent sisterhood is a felt dream rather than a concrete possibility. Like all good art, Alcott's most famous trilogy represents a conscious compromise with her deepest fantasies. The most autobiographical of writers, she seems to have chosen the girls' name in deference to the maiden name of her mother, Abigail *May*: by naming her sisters after another month beginning with "M," she secretly makes them the mother's entirely, with nothing in them of the father—which would have warmed Lady Catherine's matriarchal heart. Along with its adherence to the mother, March also suggests militancy, as when Louisa departed for the Civil War more as soldier than as healer: "I was ready, and when my commander said 'March!' I marched."[41] But with all this, the month of March is an undeveloped anomaly, waiting for its consummation in summer: the suggestion is that the March girls will bloom only when they have lost their name in the warmth of a man's, as all but Beth eventually do. In the loss of this sisterhood, the three remaining girls establish a matriarchy under Jo's aegis at Plumfield.

Jo inherits Plumfield from her tyrannical Aunt March, who in *Little Women* plays the Lady Catherine role, even to precipitating Meg's marriage by her snobbish opposition to it. But while Lady Catherine existed to be escaped from, Aunt March is transmitted in the inheritance of her estate: unlike Elizabeth, Jo is delighted to inherit from a woman and promptly moves "her" movable professor there to teach "a wilderness of boys" and (rather improbably) farm the land. By the time we meet her *Little Men*, Jo has attained the position of Marmee, but her title is more formidable than that comfortable, clinging name: the power of Plumfield is known grandly as "Mother Bhaer," the Goldilocks-like joke containing a tinge of maternal threat. At times she is simple "Mrs. Jo," an image of self-sufficient maternal power; at other times she and her husband are raised Germanically to the status of cosmic powers: "the mother," "the father."[42] In the course of the sequel, all the sisters' children come to Plumfield to be educated; there will be no more cozy family enclaves like the one in which they grew up. Instead, Marmee's power is institutionalized and the lessons of their girlhood made into a "method" by which to form the little men who may become the men in power.

Only in the sequel does Jo's refusal to marry Laurie become comprehensible. (The reasons given in *Little Women* seem more rationalization than explanation.) True, Marmee has said both are too strong-willed and fond of freedom to be happy together; but as Jo has already reconciled Laurie to his authoritarian grandfather instead of running off to Washington with him, she obviously understands quite well her role as a "miserable girl" who softens men's wildness rather than sharing it. In the proposal scene itself, she blurts out desperately, "you'd hate my scribbling, and I couldn't get on without it" (p. 406). Though this is a good strong-minded reason,

Laurie, far more than her sisters, has been Jo's ally in scribbling, the sharer of her secret when she publishes her first newspaper story and her collaborator in Plumfield theatricals, Throughout the series Laurie is excited about her writing; it is Bhaer's disapproval that makes her burn it. But while wealthy Laurie can make his comrade a lady, marriage to Professor Bhaer, an educator, makes her a cosmic mother—the greatest power available in her domestic world. Poor Laurie, pushed into the background as "Lord" to Amy's "Lady," spends the rest of the series compensating for his discontent in business by endowing all Jo's projects as her little empire spreads and spreads.[43]

Like that of *Work*, the real impetus of the saga focuses on the next generation. Planted and harvested at Plumfield like crops, according to principles of cooperation and mutual help, the children belong both to a "great family" and a "small world."[44] Raucous and cozy, conceived by women and on women's ground, Plumfield is the comic dream of Jo, though her portly husband brings to it a Teutonic intellectual weight. Yet as headmaster, he is an institutionalized denial of his own authority: when called upon to perform that great nineteenth-century ritual of flogging, so dear to boarding-school literature, Bhaer presents his big hand and orders the shocked, weeping boy to flog *him*. In presenting recreants with this token of his own vulnerability, Bhaer inflicts a greater punishment than the iron men of unshakable authority apotheosized in *Tom Brown's Schooldays* and its progeny, who are most cleanly defined in the poem that begins Kipling's *Stalky & Co.*:

> There we met with famous men
> Set in office o'er us.
> And they beat us on with rods—
> Faithfully with many rods—
> Daily beat on us with rods—
> For the love they bore us!

But Kipling's "famous men" were conscientiously training leaders of empire, who had to learn to obey in order to command. Bhaer, who is not famous and whose boys are not likely to rule, holds out his naked hand to a young liar; but Mrs. Jo, who will become famous in the third book, is fiendishly inventive in her punishments, the most Kiplingesque of which is to tie up hotheaded Nan like a dog for running away. For post-Abolitionist New England, this violation of liberty was a more radical affront than a flogging; but Nan, who may be a leader of women, needs severe discipline by wise Mrs. Jo, who sits laughing, unflogged and intact.

She rather than her husband assumes the authoritarian role of ingenious and judicious punisher of select students who may have battles to win. Beyond sisterhood, Mother Bhaer presides over a Utopian community of cooperation among and between the sexes, whose influence as it follows sailor Emil, musician Nat, and pioneer-jailbird Dan, spreads into the capitals and the wasteplaces of the world. Though stormy Jo now functions more as beacon than pilgrim—"I am not as aspiring as I once was" (*LM*, p. 367)—her influence penetrates the future. The school she shapes at Plumfield, which is also family, farm, and cosmos, bears a faint resemblance to the Shaker community which thrived in opposition to her father's own short-lived Fruitlands in Harvard, Massachusetts. Essentially matriarchal in its worship of its founder, Mother Ann Lee, the celibate Shakers lived according to principles of sexual equality and cooperation; like that of the March family and Plumfield, their greatest spiritual release was the ritual of confession. The Harvard society had an unusually large percentage of women who worked and governed equally with men, while in Bronson's neighboring Fruitlands, the men tended to do the thinking and the Alcott women, the work.[45] If Louisa could not desert her father in fact, she did in art; in her later works, she seems quite deliberately to shape her father's Utopian vision to the dimensions of her stoical mother, and of the rival paradise that destroyed his own.

In establishing Jo's matriarchal reign, Alcott has not forgotten her early dream of sisterhood. *Jo's Boys* sees a diminished reunion of the original circle, as Amy and Laurie and the widowed Meg move to the grounds of Plumfield, where the campus of Laurence College now stands in virtuous opposition to nearby Harvard, Jo's dumping ground for her "failures." If she can, Jo will train good sons rather than good governors. Hopes are higher for the female students, whom the sisters now direct in an institutionalized version of Marmee's old sewing circle: instead of repeating Marmee's lessons of suppression and self-conquest, hardly won out of her own experience, Mother Bhaer gives "little lessons on health, religion, politics, and the various questions in which all should be interested," [46] reading copious extracts from the growing body of feminist literature and instilling in her pupils a greater respect for work and independence than for marriage.

This little school within the school seems a greater success even than Plumfield: among the girls whose lives we follow, only "poky" domestic Daisy marries in the course of the novel. Meg's Josie and Amy's Bess go on to attain artistic triumphs and "worthy mates," and "Naughty Nan" graduates under Jo's tutelage from hoyden to doctor: "Nan remained a busy, cheerful, independent spinster, and dedicated her life to her suffering sisters and their children, in which true woman's work she found abiding happiness" (*JB*, p. 338). Though the March girls themselves must compromise, they can at least create free women.

Though "Naughty Nan" grows up to create a healing sisterhood, only "A Firebrand" can institutionalize one: dangerous Dan, the black sheep of Jo's flock whom she loves most, the only one who might become a hero and leader. He grows up to rove the untamed West, and in *Jo's Boys* dreams briefly of founding "Dansville" there, a new town run along the cooperative lines of Plumfield which would accommodate and enfranchise all dispossessed social groups: "You shall vote as much as you like in our new town, Nan; be mayor and alderman, and run the whole concern. It's going to be free as air, or I can't live in it" (*JB*, p. 71). But the town that can be run by women never takes political shape: life tames Dan to self-sacrifice rather than self-perpetuation. He spends a year in prison for killing a rogue, has his legs crushed in a heroic mine rescue, falls hopelessly in love with Amy's daughter, a Hawthornesque snow maiden, and sacrifices his broken life defending the Indians. Jo's long relationship with him, half-envious and half-erotic, shows the irresolution behind the triumph of "the mother." The trilogy's final sight of her is of a wistful woman, "still clinging fast to her black sheep although a whole flock of white ones trotted happily before her" (*JB*, p. 337). She has achieved her position of matriarch, but the roads are closed to the offices of "mayor and alderman." The family has been stretched to its limit.

The families of women created by Jane Austen and Louisa May Alcott have arrived at the same impasse before history and public life. The household of the one is invisible and that of the other aggressively visible; one is both economic nullity and social embarrassment, while the other finds no greater happiness than its own being and power, transcending poverty in the creation of a community that is the most potent reality of its society. Yet the March sisters too are finally forced into a posture of waiting, less for the entrance of the men than for "the coming of the happy end" which is the coming of the children: new little women, who are allowed to be angry, study art, marry and create simultaneously, embrace spinsterhood; and the little men, who may build towns for them to govern.

Elizabeth Bennet's sense of herself as a "partial, prejudiced, and ignorant historian" as she stands before Darcy's formal portrait is rewarded by her incorporation into his estate and by her family's happy absorption into the outside world of men, power, and history which gives it substance. But Jo March stands before Mr. Laurence's imposing portrait and declares "decidedly": "He isn't as handsome as *my* grandfather, but I like him" (*LW*, p. 60). She is rewarded for this impertinence by an empire, on her own grounds, which incorporates school, college, and family, if not town. Instead of scattering for survival, the March girls are finally able to take almost everything to themselves; everything except the final amalgamation of their matriarchate with the history it tries to subdue. For this "happy end" the family is not enough. Though with love or coercion it can train its daughters in the art of waiting, history remains where we found it at the beginning of *Little Women*: "far away, where the fighting was."

Beyond the Family:
Idyll and Inferno

Fresco. *La Passione—La Resurrezione.* Villa of Dionysiac Mysteries, Pompeii
Anderson-Art Reference Bureau

Louisa May Alcott's Dansville was, like Mary Walker's Adamless Eden, an American dream renounced: there can be no town governed by and for women to bridge the gap between the family and the large, embattled world outside. A conservative American periodical presents history to proper young ladies accordingly, as a remote compound of artifice and dust: "History has often been compared to an old almanac—in my estimation it bears a greater resemblance to an old play-bill. The names of the actors are there, and the names of the performances; with a puff preliminary about unexampled success, and shouts of admiration; but the life and lineaments are absent—the green curtain down, the lights extinguished, and the audience dispersed."[1] In England, Thackeray will denounce in just such images the pageant of Vanity Fair, whose empty fluctuations and plots rob the family of its emotional grandeur and history of its epic dignity. Despite Thackeray's thunder, a recent monograph has seen the rituals, exclusions, and metamorphoses of this very Society he deplores as a female-run political machine, providing women with an achieved version of Alcott's aborted Dansville: "a linking factor *between* the family and political and economic institutions."[2] Despite their enclosure in the sanctuary of Home, many women in England thus lived the inherently political life that took forbidden Utopian shapes in the American dream.

Perhaps for this reason, the boundaries of the family melt down in two popular midcentury English novels: Elizabeth Gaskell's *Cranford* (1851-1853) and Charlotte Brontë's *Villette* (1853) depict communities of women that have moved from the sphere of household management into that of government. Cranford is a town; Villette, despite its diminutive and feminine name, is a capital city; both are feminine entities, governed by tightly-knit circles of women.

Gaskell's homely little village could only be a native growth, a sadly withering root of English kindness and community;

while Brontë's far-off frightening city is an image of perpetual strangeness. Together they show the two faces of female communities as they were envisioned at that time, the welcoming and the fierce, one a dream of rest and return and the other a nightmare of weird intrigue which (for Lucy Snowe at least) banishes integrity and murders sleep.

The polarized reactions these novels evoke have obscured the imaginative vision they share, a vision that generated an intense, ambivalent response in Victorian England. To its first readers *Cranford* was genial and humorous and instantly beloved, the only work of Gaskell's early phase that was immune from angry controversy.[3] But *Villette* seemed obsessive and disturbing, the few readers who were sensitive to its power finding in it only the "hunger, rebellion and rage" that distressed Matthew Arnold.[4] Yet to one shrewd critic, a woman, who was perhaps more familiar than Arnold with the subtle modulations of female rebellion and rage, the novels of Elizabeth Gaskell and Charlotte Brontë were equally "a . . . boiling over of the political cauldron . . . Here is your true revolution. France is but one of the Western Powers; woman is the half of the world. Talk of a balance of power which may be adjusted by taking a Crimea, or fighting a dozen battles—here is a battle which must always be going forward—a balance of power only to be decided by single combat, deadly and uncompromising, where the combatants, so far from being guided by the old punctilios of the duello, make no secret of their ferocity, but throw sly javelins at each other, instead of shaking hands before they begin."[5] Margaret Oliphant begins her attack by placing Gaskell and Brontë, the charming hostess and the stormy spinster, in league with each other as militant female warriors in humanity's only profound and eternal war. For an embattled opponent on the other side, the novels of both these women are in possession of the Amazons.

Cranford

But, to be sure, what a town Cranford is for kindness![6]

Cranford beams with kindness; "Cranford is in possession of the Amazons" (p. 1). These paradoxes define Elizabeth Gaskell's rural idyll of a village inhabited by widows and aging spinsters whose fussy gentility has somehow tucked itself away from the harsh industrial world of her other novels. Cranford seems initially so pacific as it bustles lovably through its tea parties and inconsequential gossip that the appellation "Amazons" seems simply to chuck these sweet ladies under the chin; but the Amazons bob up repeatedly in Victorian writing, usually to be banished as soon as evoked.

Mrs. Oliphant hurled the label at her two seditious competitors; later, John Stuart Mill evokes the Amazons and lets them stand as models of possible female independence.[7] Tennyson's Princess Ida erects them as models for her pupils in her combination of college and battlecamp, but the Amazonian shadow dissolves when the school is transformed into a hospital and Ida melts into her proper role of nursing her antagonist rather than killing him. In *Villette*, just as Lucy is gaining strength and courage (and, unknown to the reader, Madame Beck is grouping her forces to attack), we are treated to the spectacle of M. Paul routing an Amazon from the faculty in the form of Madame Panache, "bellicose as a Penthesilea," bristling with erudition and confidence. And Charlotte Brontë herself wrote demurely to Sydney Dobell: "I am no 'young Penthesilea *mediis in millibus*,' but a plain country parson's daughter."[8] The Amazon is repeatedly summoned only, it seems, to be repeatedly banished; but once having come, she leaves her specter behind.

Gaskell's Amazons have a more durable power than Brontë's Madame Panache: "Cranford is in possession of the Amazons; all the holders of houses above a certain rent are women" (p. 1). As in the first sentence of *Pride and Prejudice,* the emphasis is on possession; but these women are beyond the years of waiting. The hunt has failed, their mothers are dead, and they are in possession themselves, reminding us of the stability and strength that accompany Cranford's genteel destitution: if the lives of single women in Victorian England were socially and economically marginal, they were legally endowed with the unique power of property-owning. In 1856,

Gaskell signed a petition endorsing the Married Woman's Property Act, though with some doubt of its power to put a married woman truly "in possession" as "the holder of a house."[9] Beneath its idyllic veneer, the interest of *Cranford* comes from the tension between power and deprivation in its analysis of the etiquette of penury in this town of redundant women.[10]

A family of women like that of the Bennets exists to disperse itself in the world outside; but the essence of Cranford, "Our Society" as the narrator jealously dubs it, is its cohesion against that world; we have moved from economic to literal and geographic isolation. Clinging to itself, maintaining a genteel silence about its diminishing resources, free from the upheavals of birth, death, marriage, and moving, Cranford seems at first to share the solitude of the mad astronomer in *Rasselas,* who denies that the heavenly bodies move independently of his will: "Oh, the busy work Miss Matty and I had in chasing the sunbeams, as they fell in an afternoon right down on this carpet through the blindless window! We spread newspapers over the places and sat down to our book or our work; and, lo! in a quarter of an hour the sun had moved, and was blazing away on a fresh spot; and down again we went on our knees to alter the position of the newspapers" (p. 20). Though this ritual fails to halt the sun at a spot convenient to Deborah's carpet, Matty's mind remains undaunted: "in a private and confidential conversation, she had told me she never could believe that the earth was moving constantly, and that she would not believe it if she could, it made her feel so tired and dizzy whenever she thought about it" (p. 121). A world in motion is a world Cranford denies. In its stasis, its seclusion, its protective resistance to the rhythms of the universe, Cranford would have been defined by Deborah's beloved Dr. Johnson as insane.

Matty's solicitude about the purity of her formidable sister's carpet defines the relation between them, and thus the heart of the Cranford community. For though the officious Mrs. Jamieson keeps snatching at the reins, Cranford's unofficial queens are the Jenkyns sisters, whose contrasting natures

might have posed for the awful Red Queen and the fluttery
White Queen in Lewis Carroll's *Through the Looking-Glass and
What Alice Found There* (1871). Miss Deborah rules with an
iron hand in the opening chapters, unyieldingly invoking the
spirit of her stern, revered father, while timid Matty radiates
tenderness and self-mistrust. Deborah's sudden death shortly
after the novel has begun, and Matty's consequent elevation to
the fearsome title and authority of "Miss Jenkyns," provide
some continuity to the apparently episodic narrative.

But from the opening pages, in which the outspoken Captain
Brown moves to Cranford with his daughter and outrages the
ladies' sensibilities, both the Jenkyns sisters are aligned with
incompetence and unreality. This erosion of their authority by
a bluff male intruder strategically intensifies the shock of the
Captain's death at the end of the first number, for he has
been established from the beginning as a norm of sense and
skill, honesty and power. His literary battle with the reaction-
ary Deborah, in which his Dickensians mock her Johnsonians, is
loaded from the start, as the Dr. Johnson she champions is
made to seem the epitome of outdated pomposity in the face of
The Inimitable Boz—in whose *Household Words*, moreover,
Cranford originally appeared. Yet with all apparent human
and literary right on his side, Captain Brown is struck by a
train, as the villain Carker had providentially been in Dickens'
own recent *Dombey and Son*. If the collective spirit of Cranford
cannot harness the sun, it can, it seems, harness the most un-
pastoral and ungenteel railroad, which would seem more appropriate to its antagonist, the masculine and mechanized city
of Drumble. The railroad makes a single obliging appearance
to kill off Captain Brown and then fades out of this happy rural
seat forever.

The episode of Captain Brown illustrates not only Cranford's
unsettling power to obliterate men, but its corresponding gift
of producing them at need. When the Captain's self-sacrificing
daughter is left alone and unable to support herself after the
death of her sister, a former suitor with a good estate in Scot-
land obligingly appears, with Deborah's thorough approval, to
give a home to Miss Jessie and a use to her dimples. The advo-

cate of the misogynist Pickwick Club, whose benign male fellowship thwarts its desperate caricatured spinsters, is not allowed to survive, but a patient and polite provider is a welcome intruder.

Throughout the novel, Cranford veers in this way between being a sanctuary of unreality—during a mass burglar panic Matty erects an elaborate device intended to summon imaginary men to her aid against imaginary men—and a repository of sudden, quasi-magical power that destroys or appropriates the reality it excludes. "The Last Generation in England," Gaskell's suggestive title for the first sketch of the novel which appeared in Philadelphia's *Sartain's Union Magazine* in July 1849, pulls together the varying definitions Cranford takes on in the course of its story. With her interest in dialect, Gaskell may have used "generation" in its obsolete sense of "family, breed, race; class, kind, or 'set' of persons," whose last appearance is dated 1727 in the *OED*. Such an obsolete and rarefied social meaning is at one with the ladies' sense of themselves as the last well-bred gasp in the face of vulgarity, men, and machinery. Our broader, more familiar use of the word is faintly apocalyptic here: the death of the ladies of Cranford will not extinguish a pocket of England, but will constitute the end of England itself before the alien and the new; the hidden, obscure nation is the true one. But particularly in its nineteenth-century connotation, "generation" means also "procreation," suggesting perhaps the power of a new and unexpected national birth out of women whom many dismiss as "self-deceiving, frustrated spinsters."[11] The pathos of the little community is at one with its promise.

The death of Deborah Jenkyns, and with it the waning of Cranford's strict code of gentility, has been seen as the healthy demise of the town's female militancy.[12] It is more plausibly the end of the severe patriarchal code which Deborah inherits from her remote, adored father and enshrines throughout her life. With her death, leadership passes to the feminine, fluttery Miss Matty, "meek and undecided to a fault," whom nobody can remember to call "Miss Matilda." With Matty's ascension, the town becomes feminine as well as female; but if it loses its

Amazonian veneer, the essence remains. Sentimental, self-hating, child-loving, beloved, Miss Matty is the biblically appropriate follower of her sister, whom their father named after Deborah, the Hebrew prophetess. In *Judges*, Deborah prophesies in ringing tones, but it is the womanly, domestic Jael who slaughters the male enemy after meekly feeding and serving him: "He asked water, and she gave him milk; she brought forth butter in a lordly dish. She put her hand to the nail, and her right hand to the workman's hammer; and with the hammer she smote Sisera, she smote off his head, when she had pierced and stricken through his temples. At her feet he bowed, he fell, he lay down: at her feet he bowed, he fell: where he bowed, there he fell down dead" (*Judges* 5:25-27). "Peace to Cranford," the last chapter of the novel, echoes the conclusion of Deborah's song of triumph: "And the land had rest forty years" (*Judges* 5:31). Matty's succession has a biblical ring which insists upon the savage mission within her meekly feminine domesticity. By the book's definitions, the more womanly sister is also the more Amazonian.

Miss Matty's career in the novel is a series of quiet, unconscious, yet Jael-like triumphs over blustering men who intimidate her. Shortly after Deborah's death, her beloved Mr. Holbrook, whom Deborah's snobbishness had prevented her from marrying, returns to her life. With his honesty, appetite, loud voice, and love of books, he seems a resurrection of the hearty Captain Brown. At a visit to his house, his blithe unconsciousness of gentility reduces the ladies to helplessness when he offers them two-pronged forks with which to eat their peas: "I looked at my host: the peas were going wholesale into his capacious mouth, shovelled up by his large round-ended knife. I saw, I imitated, I survived! My friends, in spite of my precedent, could not muster up courage enough to do an ungenteel thing; and, if Mr. Holbrook had not been so heartily hungry, he would probably have seen that the good peas went away almost untouched" (p. 50).

As with Captain Brown, our affections are thrown on the superior survival power of hearty hunger; but these lusty assurances are displaced when Mr. Holbrook is dead a few days later, leaving Matty mourning his loss and her own docility. While Miss Pole insists that Paris has killed him, Matty trembles violently and the reader remains to wonder about the impact of their reunion on this striding, distanced man who has gone the way of Captain Brown. Like her sister, Matty replaces the openhearted dead with a proxy mate: Martha, her servant, is allowed a follower, the honest Jem Hearn, who, on the failure of Matty's investments, will obligingly marry his sweetheart to provide her mistress with a home and will father a daughter perpetuating Matty's name. With the abrupt death of the unexpectedly mortal Holbrook, "she submit[s] to Fate and Love" in the lower classes and will recoup her home and her name thereby.[13]

When Signor Brunoni, the conjuror, sweeps into Cranford, the town is confronted with all the autocracy and mysterious skill the male seems to embody. Like Captain Brown and Holbrook, he enters with a burst of power, transforming the Assembly Room which was the theater of their girlhood triumphs into an arena of self-display. Matty is denied the sea-green turban she covets, emblem of masculine power as well as style, but the Signor wears a resplendent one which leads Miss Pole, half-sarcastic and half-awed, to dub him "The Grand Turk." The aura of foreignness that surrounds all the men in the novel crystallizes around the exotic Brunoni, reminding us of a less parodic Grand Turk: Charlotte Brontë's overweening and irresistible Rochester.[14]

Like that of Rochester, as well as Brown and Holbrook, Brunoni's power is more theatrical than real: the cynosure who makes them tremble is brought low in an accident which renders him helpless, while the little ladies survive to pity and nurse him. The facade of the Grand Turk Brunoni crumbles into the reality of the broken and pliable Samuel Brown, linked by name and destiny to the jolly, vulnerable Captain before him with his literary alter egos, Samuel Pickwick and "Samivel" Weller. Of all the novel's intruding males, only Hoggins the doctor safely defies Cranford's magic circle to marry Lady Glenmire, the sole nobility "our society" boasts, and he never enters the action directly: we are allowed only witty glimpses of his embarrassingly flaunted knees. Moreover, Lady Glenmire is an acquisition of Cranford, not a native, her rank isolating her from the tattered gentility which is the badge of the authentic Cranfordian. Her true alliance is not with this rooted corporate world, but with Martha, the maid, for whom life's only substantial aristocracy is its race of brides.

If Matty's lethal influence over the Grand Turk resembles that of an unconscious little Jael, her final triumph over the superior survival power of masculine reality is a triumph of community rather than slaughter. The failure of the Town and Country Bank, in which Deborah had insisted that they invest their small competency, is less an illustration of Deborah's "feminine" incompetence than it is of her misplaced trust in the masculine omnipotence her father embodied. Matty's response to the failure of the bank is (by the book's definition) feminine and corporate: "I don't pretend to understand business; I only know that if it is going to fail, and if honest people are to lose their money because they have taken our notes—I can't explain myself . . . only I would rather exchange my gold for the note, if you please" (pp. 188-189). "Our society" has become "our notes": rather than seeing herself as a helpless victim of the masculine "system," as Dickens' equally self-depreciating Esther Summerson does, Matty firmly identifies herself with it. Apparently tucked away from reality, Cranford's closely knit self-sustainment leads its representative to conceive herself instantly as part of a whole. The solitude of this feeble, deprived, far-from-stoical heroine is worlds away from the layers of bleakness in the lives of Miss Mann and Miss Ainley, the grimly spotless spinsters in Charlotte Brontë's *Shirley*, who perform innumerable and unyielding good works but seem never to approach each other. Tender as they are, the ladies of Cranford are too involved with each other to interest themselves in their larger charitable mission. Their corporate clinging might have arisen from Emily Winkworth and Elizabeth Gaskell's own horror at Charlotte Brontë's isolation, which the sisterhood of the Winkworth correspondence reveals in its starkest tones:

Thanks for Mrs. Gaskell's. Poor Miss Brontë, I cannot get the look of the grey, square, cold, dead-coloured house out of my head. One feels as if one ought to go to her at once, and do something for her. She has friends though now, surely? I wonder whether she has any unmarried ones; people who could go and look after her a little if she were ill. Oh dear, if the single sisters in this world were but banded together a little, so that they could help each other out as well as other people, and know how important they were, and what a quantity of work lies ready for them! One feels that her life at least *almost* makes one like her books, though one does not want there to be any more Miss Brontës.[15]

Miss Matty and her neighbors do know "how important they are," and this banded knowledge is their Pickwickian triumph over the failure of economic and masculine reality outside.

Cranford's motto of "elegant economy" becomes more than a demure euphemism by which it disguises its sexual and financial poverty from itself: its stinting is a whispered reproof to the man's world outside that seems so attractive and powerful with its big boots, but which is so consistently perishable. Unlike those of the banks, "on Mondays [Miss Matty's] accounts were always made straight—not a penny owing from the week before" (p. 110). Matty's greatest act of innocence is to invest laissez-faire reality with her own communality, as she had previously invested Signor Brunoni and the nonexistent burglars with her own aura of magical power: "She almost made me angry by dividing her sympathy between these directors (whom she imagined overwhelmed by self-reproach for the mismanagement of other people's affairs) and those who were suffering like her. Indeed, of the two, she seemed to think poverty a lighter burden than self-reproach; but I privately doubted if the directors would agree with her" (p. 213). The atomized city of Drumble lacks the power that makes Matty's teashop thrive on love and incompetence and the silent cooperative gifts of "our society": "she did not dislike the employment, which brought her into kindly intercourse with many of the people round about. If she gave them good weight, they, in their turn, brought many a little country present to the 'old rector's daughter'; a cream cheese, a few new-laid eggs, a little ripe fruit, a bunch of flowers. The counter was quite loaded with these offerings sometimes, as she told me" (p. 226).

Matty's innocent generosity which invokes its own return is her last Jael-like triumph over the enemy of her people. The narrator's intimidating father from Drumble, reverently presented to us only as "my father," embodies the incomprehensible omnipotence of all the novel's patriarchs. In view of the unthinking tyranny of Matty's own grandfather and father, and the alacrity with which her mother withered out of life in the manner of *Shirley's* Mrs. Helstone, Miss Pole's laugh line sufficiently explains Cranford's crushed shrinking away from men: "My father was a man, and I know the sex pretty well" (p. 145). Though the men we meet in the novel are always kind, by the Cranford code "they are very incomprehensible, certainly." Only once are the hieroglyphics of their world brought into direct contact with the touchstone of Cranford community, and the result of this confrontation is the patriarchy's failure on its own terms: "But my father says 'such simplicity might be very well in Cranford, but would never do in the world.' And I fancy the world must be very bad, for with all my father's suspicion of every one with whom he has dealings, and in spite of all his many precautions, he lost upwards of a thousand pounds by roguery only last year" (p. 221). In the verbal and commercial battle of nineteenth-century England, the cooperative female community defeats the warrior world that proclaims itself the real one.

Part of its artillery is the power of deceit.[16] After the bank failure, Matty is preserved by a series of Cranford conspiracies on her behalf, "a few evasions of truth and white lies (all of which I think very wrong indeed—in theory—and would rather not put them in practice)" (p. 222). Throughout the novel, Cranford threads its monotonous life with what Charlotte Brontë called "the strange, necromantic joys of fancy," peopling its world with self-created magic burglars, ghosts, spies, Frenchmen, and witches, placing the latter on a footing with Brunoni himself: "My dear Mrs. Forrester, conjuring and witchcraft is a mere affair of the alphabet," Miss Pole insists

(p. 128). But the final solidification of the community comes only when Matty's brother Peter returns from the East and institutionalizes lies.

According to Miss Deborah and her father, "poor Peter" shamed the Jenkyns family irrevocably in his youth by dressing in Deborah's clothes and crooning over a mock-baby, thus abdicating his manhood and aligning himself with the tender femininity of Matty and their frail mother. Though his father's rage drives him out of Cranford to make his fortune in the mysterious East, his transvestism has forecast Cranford's ultimate possession by the Amazons. Having risen from "poor Peter" to the "Aga Jenkyns," he can return grandly home now that the patriarchal family is banished from his birthplace. Now "so very Oriental," Peter is a domestication of the Grand Turk to the dimensions of the community. There is some apprehension that he will restore families to Cranford by marrying Mrs. Jamieson, but instead of proposing to the widow, he shows his loyalty to the Amazons by enthralling her with a spirited account of shooting a cherub. Marriage succumbs to a wonderful lie, and Cranford is at one with itself: "I want everybody to be friends, for it harrasses Matty so much to hear of these quarrels" (p. 244).

Though Peter seems to enter as a providential savior, Matty does not need him to make of Cranford a holy community, for she has already transmuted it herself: "It was really very pleasant to see how her unselfishness and simple sense of justice called out the same good qualities in others" (pp. 220-221). At the end of the novel the natives of Cranford have achieved beatitude under her aegis without the usual novelistic sacrament of marriage, and the financial, skilled, and procreative power of the Grand Turk has been harnessed to the perpetuation of the little world. Unlikely as it seemed at the beginning, Matty has captured the sun after all. Entertained without terror by a restored Signor Brunoni, supported by Peter, and carried into the next generation by honest Jem, she can rest in an alliance between the kindness of gentility and the fertility of its servants that excludes both patriarchal marriage and the industrial and speculative rogueries of "my father":

This day to which I refer, Miss Matty had seemed more than usually feeble and languid, and only revived when the sun went down, and her sofa was wheeled to the open window, through which, although it looked into the principal street of Cranford, the fragrant smell of the neighbouring hay-fields came in every now and then, borne by the soft breezes that stirred the dull air of the summer twilight, and then died away. The silence of the sultry atmosphere was lost in the murmuring noises which came in from many an open window and door; even the children were abroad in the street, late as it was (between ten and eleven), enjoying the game of play for which they had not spirits during the heat of the day. It was a source of satisfaction to Miss Matty to see how few candles were lighted, even in the apartments of those houses from which issued the greatest signs of life.   (pp. 236-237)

Destitute of the props and dimensions of the Victorian woman's life, the relationships of daughter, mother, and wife, Matty is restored as she presides over an organic community rooted in the past and containing the future. If its triumph is aligned with the female error of discreet falsity, the code that is secret message rather than ethical imperative, its sustained existence celebrates the heretical accomplishment of shooting a cherub with elegant economy.

The ceremonial "Peace to Cranford" with which the novel closes is an index of the Amazons' victory, in the economic war outside and in the more fundamental war between the sexes Margaret Oliphant defined as eternal. Cranford's "peace" is its quiet code for "victory" in a contest its native gentility need never acknowledge. The female war that must call itself peace was defined as early as Aristophanes' *Lysistrata* (413 *B.C.*), whose "convention of wives" paradoxically is forced to declare a biological war to end a territorial one. Stung by the reluctance of her troops to deny their husbands' lovemaking, Lysistrata excoriates the bodily debris under which a woman's selfhood is buried: "Lewd to the least drop in the tiniest vein, Our sex is fitly food for Tragic Poets, Our whole life's but a pile of kisses and babies."[17] But this "lewd," slovenly eroticism is the wives' only artillery. By contrast, the Victorian Matty's strength is her timid eschewal of this biological debris, evident as she tidily and tearfully burns her mother's love letters. Her triumph is not Lysistrata's brief appropriation of the men's monument, but the possession of a living society on her own terrain whose integrity feeds on the defeat or the collaboration of its invaders.

The solidity of Cranford can be defined by a comparison with its American cousin, Sarah Orne Jewett's "The Dulham Ladies" (1886). "Miss Dobin and Miss Lucinda Dobin" seem direct descendants of Deborah and Matty Jenkyns,[18] but these superannuated "ladies" are vulnerable anomalies in mocking Dulham, which has reduced their patronymic from "D'Aubigne" to "Dobin" to the ignominious "Dobbin." Isolated from their setting, from "the cruel thievery of time," and from their own pasts—lacking Matty's evergreen memory, they feel their mother has been dead a hundred years—the Dulham ladies are not perpetuated by a child, but stabbed by one into humiliating awareness of their thinning hair: " 'Do Miss Dobinses wear them great caps because their heads is cold?' the little beast had said; and everybody was startled and dismayed."

In abashed obedience to "the little beast," the sisters adorn their ample foreheads with hideous "frizzes," which only entertain their neighbors further. Helpless to prevent derision, the solicitous servant can only take on the role of chorus, not that of savior and preserver into the future: " 'Oh, my sakes alive!' the troubled handmaiden groaned. 'Going to the circle, be they, to be snickered at! Well, the Dobbin girls they was born, and the Dobbin girls they will remain till they die; but if they ain't innocent Christian babes to those that knows 'em well, mark me down for an idjit myself! They believe them front-pieces has set the clock back forty years or more, but if they're pleased to think so, let 'em!' "[19] Basking in unreality, the Dulham ladies conquer society and time by ignoring them; they are transcendentalists survived into an age of scrutiny. Cranford lights no candles in deference to Matty's dread of waste, and it survives to embrace the future with the past by taking what it needs of masculine reality and defeating what remains with its communal faith. But the isolated Dobins, like the March sisters in *Little Women*, stubbornly cling to a perishable world of their own and find a certain ironic immortality by remaining girls till time devours them. Gaskell's Amazons absorb a society, while Jewett's sisters spin one for themselves unsustained.

Cranford's durability as a community springs from an unlikely alliance: memory's transfiguration of Elizabeth Gaskell's own halcyon days in Knutsford before her marriage; and her powerful obsession with the Brontë sisters as they appeared in her imagination. When she met Charlotte Brontë, in August 1850, Emily and Anne had been dead more than a year, and *Cranford*, which first appeared in December 1851, was presumably in unconscious gestation. From the beginning, she was inflamed by the story of the beleaguered sisters,[20] a good deal of which seeped into and animated the genteel exclusiveness of Cranford before a biography proper seemed conceivable.

Though the soft-spoken Miss Matty might seem to us an odd portrait of the messianic Charlotte Brontë, to the assured literary circles into which she was inaugurated, Charlotte emerged primarily as timid and tiny, leagues away from the coarseness and insurrection her books were said to harbor. In the *Life*, Gaskell emphasizes (somewhat disingenuously) Charlotte's Cranfordian ignorance of the world of men: "From these many-sided sons [of Joshua Taylor], I suspect, she drew all that there was of truth in the characters of the heroes in her first two works. They, indeed, were almost the only young men she knew intimately, besides her brother" (p. 379). Matty's squeamish palate is a similar legacy from Charlotte: both women quail at the evils of green tea, though the nervous reaction Charlotte feared for herself the solicitous Matty fears for others.[21] The economy of both takes the form of candle-hoarding, so that each is surrounded by an aura of twilit dimness, although the darkness that is gently protective of Miss Matty is the prison of the Brontë sisters: "They put away their work, and began to pace the room backwards and forwards, up and down,—as often with the candles extinguished, for economy's sake, as not—their figures glancing into the fire-light, and out into the shadow, perpetually" (p. 166). Matty is also endowed with Charlotte Brontë's tremor, frequent attacks of incessant trembling which Elizabeth Gaskell must have interpreted as aftershocks of the stoical burial of emotion defined by Lucy Snowe's plaintive: "But if I feel, may I *never* express?" Similarly, after the death of Holbrook, "[Miss Matty's] effort at concealment was the beginning of the tremulous motion of head and hands which I have seen ever since" (p. 59). No wonder Charlotte ignored *Cranford's* charm and cut through to what was "graphic, pithy, penetrating, shrewd"!

Charlotte's docility in the face of Emily's precipitous investment of their small capital in railway shares—"I feel as if I would rather run the risk of loss than hurt Emily's feelings by acting in direct opposition to her opinion" (p. 289)—takes the shape of Matty's disastrous fidelity to Deborah's investment in the Town and Country Bank. Apparently to Gaskell the forbidding Emily, whose memory Charlotte worshiped and whom she had never met, was an appropriate model for the unimaginative dragon Miss Deborah. Both the Brontë and the Jenkyns households have a robust young servant named Martha, who tries to cushion the blows laid on her betters. *Cranford's* irrepressible Peter may be a wish-transfigured, comic reincarnation of Branwell; but he reminds one more of William Weightman, Mr. Brontë's delightful curate whose flirtatious antics thawed even the suspicious knot of sisters, though before admitting him into the circle they metamorphosed him (as *Cranford* does Peter in his transvestite youth) into "Celia Amelia." Though Weightman is tactfully omitted from Gaskell's biography, Charlotte may well have told stories about him during the composition of *Cranford*. Matty's reading of her mother's love letters prior to burning them is taken from Charlotte's reading of similar letters from the mother she barely knew.[22] The foreboding ironic awareness of the living girl rushing to the man who will crush her and blight her children must remain implicit in the biography, though it is spelled out sufficiently in *Cranford*; in both, this contrast between marital hope and its wasted fruition takes the shape of a shared tremor, penury, and pathos, surmounted only by the community of women.

The image of the Brontë sisters that haunted Gaskell appeared disguised in her idyll before it was commemorated in her biography, adding to Cranford a strain of duplicitous power over the Grand Turk and bestowing on the Yorkshire parsonage an aura of retrospective sanctity: the sweetness of lies becomes the evasion of art.

Like Cranford, the Yorkshire parsonage in Gaskell's *The Life of Charlotte Brontë* has a Sleeping Beauty halo in the inhospitable landscape with its feuding residents: "Everything about the place tells of the most dainty order, the most exquisite cleanliness. The doorsteps are spotless; the small old-fashioned window-panes glitter like looking-glass. Inside and outside of that house cleanliness goes up into its essence, purity" (p. 56). As the biography is constructed, the outside world of masculinity, reality, and combat, which remains a distanced and mysterious antagonist of little Cranford, becomes an actively savage invader, snatching at and decimating the clinging circle of Brontë women. Gaskell's incomprehensibly vengeful Mr. Brontë, shattering the quiet with pistol shots and burning the treasured gown of his dying wife, fades into the power-hungry William Carus Wilson, whose sadistic ministrations at Cowan Bridge School kill the two oldest sisters and send Charlotte and Emily home blighted.

According to Gaskell, "the affection among [the three remaining sisters] was stronger than either death or life" (p. 178). "There is little record remaining of the manner in which the first news of [*Jane Eyre's*] wonderful success reached and affected the one heart of the three sisters" (p. 324). To her, the sisters' dream of founding a school for girls is less an escape from dependence and disdain than a means of consecrating their unity by living together. In their essence, Currer, Ellis, and Acton Bell *were* one person to Elizabeth Gaskell, and the lash that drives them apart is treated with all the outrage of a broken convenant.

The trapped circle of sisters, pacing and plotting by the light of the fire, is defined by its remoteness from the lordly and self-generated dissipation of Branwell. Gaskell's double-edged apology for the family's ravaged scion makes quite clear the distance between the absolute male self and the female unit:

> At this time, the young man seemed to have his fate in his own hands. . . His aunt especially made him her great favourite. There are always peculiar trials in the life of an only boy in a family of girls. He is expected to act a part in life; to *do*, while they are only to *be*; and the necessity of their giving way to him in some things, is too often exaggerated into their giving way to him in all, and thus rendering him utterly selfish. In the family about whom I am writing, while the rest were almost ascetic in their habits, Branwell was allowed to grow up self-indulgent; but, in early youth, his power of attracting and attaching people was so great, that few came in contact with him who were not so much dazzled by him as to be desirous of gratifying whatever wishes he expressed. Of course, he was careful enough not to reveal anything before his father and sisters of the pleasures he indulged in; but his tone of thought and conversation became gradually coarser, and, for a time, his sisters tried to persuade themselves that such coarseness was a part of manliness, and to blind themselves by love to the fact that Branwell was worse than other young men. At present, though he had, they were aware, fallen into some errors, the exact nature of which they avoided knowing, still he was their hope and their darling; their pride, who should some time bring great joy to the name of Brontë. (p. 197)

As he is presented here, Branwell siphons off all the incipient riot and abuse of power of the female circle: he alone possesses the coarseness with which Charlotte's work had been impugned. Later biographers insist that the Brontë children lived more in Angria and Gondal, the imaginary countries they created as children, than they did in Yorkshire, Angria's "burning clime" creating a quasi-incestuous meeting ground between Charlotte and Branwell that never existed in Victorian society. In her emendation of Gaskell's biography, Margaret Lane brings together Charlotte's Angrian and Branwell's opium addiction and names a significant chapter "Charlotte and Branwell in Love"—containing the buried suggestion, "with each other."[23] Winifred Gérin suggests a sharing in deeper and more mysterious regions when she titles her chapter on Branwell's deterioration, "The Alter Ego."[24]

Gaskell's union of sisters has no place for Charlotte and Branwell's shared world. For Gérin, and for Margot Peters after her, Charlotte was driven to her sisters and their shared literary assault only when Branwell had wasted beyond her reach. Locked in their obsession with Gondal, Emily and Anne let her manage them, but never included her, and finally evaded her altogether by dying. Though Gaskell wisely did not spend much time deciphering the turgid little notebooks of Brontë juvenilia, she knew of Charlotte's overriding bond with Branwell, but suppressed it in favor of the besieged yet eternal band of sisters. Her biography prints only impersonal extracts from a letter to Branwell which in fact began: "As usual I address my weekly letter to you, because to you I find the most to say."[25] Admitting this sentence and its implications into the biography would not merely have tarred Charlotte with the disgraced Branwell's brush; it would have thrown off the allegiances whose shifting balance of power constitutes the book's sense of Charlotte Brontë's story.

Gaskell reminds us early of a fact that later critics have unfortunately forgotten[26] —that the collective Brontë vision was political in its inception: "Politics were evidently their grand interest; the Duke of Wellington their demi-god" (p. 120). The Brontë family is subtly presented accordingly, as a political seesaw that begins with Napoleonic male invasions on the circle of women and finds its triumph in juxtaposing female ascension with the males' decay—just as the far-off fragmentation of Drumble had solidified Cranford into true community. The end of the first and the beginning of the second volumes of *The Life of Charlotte Brontë* consist of cross-cutting between Mr. Brontë, majestic and helpless in his blindness, the flamboyantly ruined Branwell, and the tight secret enterprise of the sisters whose result is their escape via their books to London and public life. Gaskell's cinematic juxtaposition makes its point more insistently, and perhaps more persuasively, than the pseudo-scientific diagnoses of some modern biographers: "It is not inappropriate that this woman, whose masochistic dependence and passivity had evolved within the strictures of a patriarchal Victorian family, should find the sources of freedom in the moral and physical disintegration of her brother and in the growing blindness of her father."[27] The clarity of Gaskell's organization and the power of her sympathy have already defined this sexual war for all subsequent writers about the Brontës, as at one point she excoriates Mrs. Robinson in an invocation whereby Charlotte, Emily, and Anne, Maria and Elizabeth, seem to rise into mythic life, scourging by implication persons more powerful than Branwell's weak-hearted seducer: "The Eumenides, I suppose, went out of existence at the time when the wail was heard, 'Great Pan is dead.' I think we could better have spared him than those awful Sisters who sting dead conscience into life" (p. 353). At the book's apex, the "almost ascetic" deprivation of the community of sisters is raised to the power of avenging divinity.

Emily's and Anne's plunges into death and Charlotte's ensuing desolation invert the survival of Cranford as an organic whole in the face of assaults on its integrity. The glum tableau at the end of the book replaces "the one heart of the three sisters" with a community worthy of those in Wuthering Heights, which might have inspired it: "Early on Saturday morning, March 31st, the solemn tolling of Haworth church-bell spoke forth the fact of her death to the villagers who had known her from a child, and whose hearts shivered within them as they thought of the two sitting desolate and alone in the old grey house" (p. 524). "The two" are Charlotte's grim father and (in Gaskell's opinion) her grimmer husband, radical antagonists, each implicitly accusing the other of killing the woman he possessed, and each doing so with right.[28] The death of the one remaining sister leaves the purity of the Parsonage in the hands of a stripped and smouldering pair of men, whose only communal activity is a shared Heathcliff-like wait to be haunted by the tiny departed—or perhaps by the larger community of "those awful Sisters." The structure of the book suggests that the triumph of male reality is at one with its doom.

The fluctuating balance of power in the Brontë parsonage

has continued to draw so many writers and readers that Emily Winkworth's remark that "her life at least *almost* makes one like her books" must still have adherents today. It was Gaskell who placed Haworth for us as the site of a microcosm, a literary but lethal battle of the sexes whose outcome she left open for us to discover as we discover ourselves. The assurance of Richard Chase's "there is no doubt that Haworth Parsonage was a man's society" is giving way before Elizabeth Hardwick's courteous: "The Brontë household was in fact a household of women, women living and dead."[29] Hardwick's emendation suggests that the Eumenides have risen, and if we now know that the sisters had three separate hearts which were often at variance, their community of art was knit by the gallantly taciturn understanding of battlefield fellowship: "Mine bonnie love . . . Corragio." "Take courage, Charlotte, take courage." "And now I must close, sending from far an exhortation, 'Courage, courage,' to exiled and harassed Anne, wishing she was here."[30]

Though some readers find her novels embarrassingly autobiographical, Charlotte never succumbed to her own family romance. Her true subject is the estrangement of orphanhood and exile: her novels never seem at ease with the necessities of intimacy. The bombastic declamatory dialogues between Caroline Helstone and Shirley Keeldar are her only attempt to approximate sisterhood, and these sound indeed as if their author had "long forfeited the society of her own sex."[31] In her one extended delineation of a community of women, Madame Beck's cloistered pensionnat in *Villette*, there are no shelterless sisters, "[clinging] to each other like tender vines";[32] stripped of Cranford's self-protective whimsy, the Pensionnat de Demoiselles is a study in the power of a female world that has left the family behind.

Villette

This was a strange house, where no corner was sacred from intrusion, where not a tear could be shed, nor a thought pondered, but a spy was at hand to note and to divine.[33]

Madame Beck's "demi-convent, secluded in the built-up core of a capital" (p. 92) seems at first as fitting a retreat as Cranford for the austere and lonely Lucy Snowe. But the haven of this decorous girls' boarding school is a mirage: at heart it is a nest of schemes and secrets. Instead of nurturing the wanderer, this woman's world swerves between intolerable extremes of intimacy and of solitude, in which confession and isolation are equally unrewarding: " 'This will not hold long,' I thought to myself; for I was not accustomed to find in women or girls any power of self-control, or strength of self-denial. As far as I knew them, the chance of a gossip about their usually trivial secrets, their often very washy and paltry feelings, was a treat not to be readily foregone" (p. 282). The women thrust their selves at each other, but to Lucy in her role as Diogenes, these selves are synthetic. In *The Professor*, Charlotte Brontë's early treatment of her Brussels experience, the supercilious male narrator muses at length on the difference between the ideal of a bevy of *jeunes filles* and its unwashed reality. In *Villette*, Lucy would be expected to harbor no such initial illusions, so Crimsworth's disenchantment is condensed into a single observation on the part of M. Paul, who has spent years spying on his students: "And my pupils, . . . those blondes jeunes filles—so mild and meek—I have seen the most reserved—romp like boys, the demurest—snatch grapes from the walls, shake pears from the trees" (p. 354).

Though Paul talks like Dante emerging from the Inferno, he has merely learned that when women are alone the bait of a passive female essence can be discarded. In *Pride and Prejudice* the energies of women without men were stretched in anticipation of their coming, and in *Cranford*, the spinsters evolved a separatist code that outfaced male acquisitiveness. But the seclusion of *Villette* gives the women an opportunity to set free their own "masculine" instincts of plunder and assault: "Yet, no sooner had we reached [the drawing-room], then [Ginevra] again became flat and listless: throwing herself on a couch, she denounced both the 'discours' and the dinner as stupid affairs, and inquired of her cousin how she could bear such a set of prosaic 'gros-bonnets' as her father gathered about him. The moment the gentlemen were heard to move, her railings ceased: she started up, flew to the piano, and dashed at it with spirit" (p. 305).

If one could find a core in the endlessly fabricated personality of Ginevra, it would lie in this abusive, non-piano-playing, couch-monopolizing self which the men's entrance banishes. The reality that emerges when women are together is their lack of discrete reality, of sanctified and special "inner space." Boys and girls, women and men, are alike in their desire to snatch grapes from the walls. These nunlike girls, "so mild and meek," partake of the governing male condition we have already seen defined in Kipling's *Stalky & Co.* as that exclusive absolute called "boy." As the distance between the sexes proves illusory, so, imperceptibly, does the distance between the "secluded" pensionnat and the theatrical, political life of Villette.

In this coming-together we find one of the most significant alterations from *The Professor*: the boys' school and the girls' school are collapsed into one. In the first novel William Crimsworth finds both sets of pupils equally repulsive and recalcitrant; for teaching in Charlotte Brontë's novels is almost always a psychodrama, in which the pupils are less sentient human beings than they are the teacher's own rebellious urges with cahiers before them, bobbing up to be crushed down. But there is a fundamental distinction between the organized bloc of the one and the anarchy of the other. The inert bulk of boys has all the massed brutality of statehood: "Had the abhorred effort been extorted from them by injudicious and arbitrary measures on the part of the Professor, they would have resisted as obstinately, as clamorously, as desperate swine; and though not brave singly, they were relentless acting *en masse* . . . Pelet's school was merely an epitome of the Belgian nation."

In the flower of its manhood, King Arthur's Round Table was, as we saw, "an image of this mighty world"; and in the potency of its stupidity, Pelet's school is an equally weighty epitome of its country. Though the girls are equally brutish, they are in a laissez-faire and atomized state which bears no microcosmic relation to the larger community outside: "In dress all were nearly similar, and in manners there was small difference; exceptions there were to the general rule, but the majority gave the tone to the establishment, and that tone was rough, boisterous, marked by a point-blank disregard of all forbearance towards each other or their teachers; an eager pursuit by each individual of her own interest and convenience; and a coarse indifference to the interest and convenience of every one else."[34]

Such flying, disordered aggression can never take political shape. *The Professor* adheres to the conventions of Victorian boarding-school literature, which make of the boys' school, no matter how corrupt, a seat of government, while the girls' school is a remote haven from the state. In Thackeray's *Vanity Fair*, for example, Miss Pinkerton's Academy is the only world in which clinging Amelia Sedley can succeed. Silly and pretentious though it is, this rosebud garden of girls is the sole alternative to the massed rapacity of the Napoleonic Wars, whose battles and whose treaties are equally devastating to Miss Pinkerton's prize pupil. In Brontë's own *Jane Eyre*, Lowood School is a retreat of a different sort, whose fierce restraint is contained in Helen Burns's "Hush, Jane! . . . you are too impulsive, too vehement." But this warning female whisper makes no impact on the impulsive vehemence of Rochester, the novel's Napoleonic embodiment of social and sexual power. In all three novels, a school for girls is a circle of anti-power, in which the characteristics cast off by outside political life hold limited sway.

Only *Villette* breaks through this duality, quietly endowing Madame Beck's pensionnat with the political resonance usually reserved for such male celebrations as the hymn to cricket that closes *Tom Brown's Schooldays*:

> "What a noble game it is too!"
> "Isn't it? But it's more than a game. It's an institution," said Tom.
> "Yes," said Arthur, "the birthright of British boys old and young, as *habeas corpus* and trial by jury are of British men." . . .

"And then the Captain of the eleven!" said the master, "what a post is his in our School-world! almost as hard as the Doctor's; requiring skill and gentleness and firmness, and I know not what other rare qualities."

"Which don't he wish he may get?" said Tom, laughing; "at any rate he hasn't got them yet, or he wouldn't have been such a flat to-night as to let Jack Raggles go in out of his turn."

"Ah! the Doctor never would have done that," said Arthur, demurely. "Tom, you've a great deal to learn yet in the art of ruling." . . .

"What a sight it is," broke in the master, "the Doctor as a ruler. Perhaps ours is the only little corner of the British Empire which is thoroughly, wisely, and strongly ruled just now. I'm more and more thankful every day of my life that I came here to be under him."[35]

No writer about girls could make so natural the passage from game to institution to the art of ruling to the greatness of the ruler, as the life of the school carries boys and reader unobtrusively into ever-larger circles of power. But though she discards masculine sportsmanship and gallantry, Madame Beck similarly unites her school into a political organ that achieves the status of a little nation. Lucy Snowe can define its political cohesion only through a hedge of qualifications: "I used to think sometimes (if such a comparison may be permitted), that the quiet, polished, tame first division, was to the robust, riotous, demonstrative second division, what the English House of Lords is to the House of Commons" (p. 73).

As ruler of this trim little state Madame Beck inhabits a strangely inhuman limbo between the Godlike perfect power of "the Doctor" of Rugby and the shrewd solicitude of "the Mother" of Plumfield. Though it is professionally advantageous for her to look motherly, it is quickly clear that this political organizer is no matriarch. Louisa May Alcott's Plumfield was less an institution than an extended family for Mother Bhaer to cherish and create: its pupils were the unofficially adopted siblings of her own and her sisters' children, whose characters and games soon blended with those of the March family, and over whose destinies "the mother" fretted incessantly. But this solicitude that was so important a part of nineteenth-century womanhood—in Gaskell's biographical defense of the woman beneath the artist, she remarks of Branwell's portrait of his sisters, "Emily's countenance struck me as full of power; Charlotte's of solicitude" (p. 155)—is Madame Beck's mask for her impersonal system of surveillance: "All being thus done decently and in order, my property was returned to its place, my clothes were carefully refolded. Of what nature were the conclusions deduced from this scrutiny? Were they favourable or otherwise? Vain question. Madame's face of stone (for of stone in its present night aspect it looked: It had been human, and, as I said before, motherly, in the salon) betrayed no response" (pp. 64-65).

The phrase "decently and in order" is a significant echo of the Roman Catholic "system" as perceived by *Jane Eyre's* Eliza Reed, whom Jane defines as an anti-human personification of "judgment without feeling": "I shall devote myself for a time to the examination of the Roman Catholic dogmas, and to a careful study of the workings of their system; if I find it to be, as I half suspect it is, the one best calculated to ensure the doing of all things decently and in order, I shall embrace the tenets of Rome and take the veil." And so she does, becoming in time "superior of the convent where she passed the period of her novitiate"; but Jane witholds from her the title, *Mother* Superior.[36]

By the time *Villette* was written, this woman who is a superior without the softening addendum, "Mother," is no longer a one-dimensional monster. She is merely thoroughly professional as she assimilates her three daughters into her system of administrative deceit. "Madame must have possessed high administrative powers: she ruled all these, together with four teachers, eight masters, six servants, and three children, managing at the same time to perfection the pupils' parents and friends; and that without apparent effort; without bustle, fatigue, fever, or any symptom of undue excitement: occupied she was—busy, rarely" (p. 67). Unlike Mother Bhaer, Madame Beck does not align her children with her pupils—in fact, we scarcely see her with the pupils at all—but raises them to the dignity of her employees. Her familial is transformed into her professional life, which she "rules" rather than nurtures.

In *Tom Brown's Schooldays,* the Doctor's public position is irrelevant to our boys'-eye view, which enshrines him wisely administering justice and rewards; we are told of the *History* he has written only to provide more food for our reverence. The great act of the feverishly adored Head in *Stalky & Co.* is an act of kinship: at the risk of his own life, he sucks diptheria mucus out of the throat of a dying pupil. But Madame Beck barely touches the domestic life of her school, as she is seen through the eyes of a shrewd adult who fully approves only what is fully adult. If she spies on Lucy, so does Lucy spy on her, with a quiet camaraderie in distant surveillance that we feel will stand Lucy in good stead when she too is mistress of a pensionnat: "She did not behave weakly [when disappointed in her bid for Dr. John], or make herself in any shape ridiculous. It is true she had neither strong feelings to overcome, nor tender feelings by which to be miserably pained. It is true likewise that she had an important avocation, a real business to fill her time, divert her thoughts, and divide her interest. It is especially true that she possessed a genuine good sense which is not given to all women nor to all men; and by dint of these combined advantages she behaved wisely—she behaved well. Brava! once more, Madame Beck" (p. 99). This tribute to the dignity of an unwomanly life, in which the training of children is neither an emotional outlet nor a familial surrogate, but "a real business," carrying one from emotion's humiliations to the male "art of ruling," defines a silent alliance between Lucy and Madame Beck which continues to the end of the novel.

Monstrous as this portrait of the administrative woman may seem to some, it presents a less cloying alternative to the fragile hothouse enclosure of John Bretton and his doting mother: "The two were now standing opposite to each other, one on each side the fireplace; their words were not very fond, but their mutual looks atoned for verbal deficiencies. At least the best treasure of Mrs. Bretton's life was certainly casketed in her son's bosom; her dearest pulse throbbed in his heart. As to him, of course another love shared his feelings with filial love; and, no doubt, as the new passion was the latest born, so he assigned it in his emotions Benjamin's portion" (p. 180). Mrs Bretton's heart is exclusive, locked in a son who makes continual affectionate digs about the day he will supersede her reign with his wife's; though when Dr. John does fall in love with pretty Polly, her father has a long scene in which he expounds on his incestuous woe at the loss of his little girl, while Mrs. Bretton's possibly deeper loss goes undramatized. More truly cloistered than the pensionnat, the two families we see in the novel are repositories of such embarrassingly arch eroticism between parent and child—both Polly and John have lost the parent of their own sex—and the engagement itself is so problematic,[37] that the movement of the novel seems at one with Lucy's recoil away from this exclusive intimacy: "I shall share no man's or woman's life in this world, as you understand sharing" (p. 414).

In *Villette*, the family is a tiny circle of questionable emotion, not a sphere of "household management" reaching toward the larger world. In his argument for women's participation in politics, John Stuart Mill logically extends the managing, administrative wife we have seen in the previous chapter by predicting the political success of "widows or wives of forty or fifty, by whom the knowledge of life and faculty of government which they have acquired in their families, could by the aid of appropriate studies be made available on a less contracted scale."[38] But Charlotte Brontë's experiences as governess and teacher may have made her doubt the likelihood of combining the maternal with the administrative perspective: she presents the jealous identification of the one and the cool surveillance of the other as mutually exclusive. Mrs. Pryor in *Shirley* goes so far as to abandon her daughter out of the mistaken fear that she may have inherited her father's character instead of being all her own. Her morbid privacy is set in contrast to the executive skill of Miss Ainley, the solitary spinster: "She was far better informed, better read, a deeper thinker than Miss Ainley, but of administrative energy, of executive activity, she had none. She would subscribe her own modest mite to a charitable object willingly,—a secret almsgiving suited her; but in public

plans, on a large scale, she could take no part: as to originating them, that was out of the question."[39]

If *Villette* is uncompromising in its divorce between the family and the state, it is also a welcome departure from the Victorian cant that justified woman's work only by making it a
natural outgrowth of familial duties.[40] In its denial that motherhood and government are the same thing, as in its heroine's
ability to love two men at the same time, *Villette* forces on the
reader facets of women not covered by the traditional definition of daughter, mother, wife. By virtue of its very detachment from household management, the pensionnat becomes a
little state, the government of which is government itself. But
Lucy's shrewd recognition of power is stripped of Tom Brown's
boyish idealization: "I say again, Madame was a very great
and a very capable woman. That school offered her for her
powers too limited a sphere; she ought to have swayed a nation: she should have been a leader of a turbulent legislative
assembly. Nobody could have browbeaten her, none irritated
her nerves, exhausted her patience, or over-reached her
astuteness. In her own single person, she could have com-
prised the duties of a first minister and a superintendent of
police. Wise, firm, faithless; secret, crafty, passionless;
watchful and inscrutable; acute and insensate—withal perfectly decorous—what more could be desired?" (p. 69).

In fact, this Machiavellian entity is already less an institution of learning than a veiled political arena, having subtly
appropriated the characteristics usually reserved for boys'
schools. It gains its power less from the income or ability than
from the rank of its pupils, some of whom are in the Queen's
train; so with Lucy's own school at the end: "Pupils came—
burghers at first—a higher class ere long" (p. 478). Moreover,
the various ceremonies and spectacles around which the school
chapters are organized progress stealthily from the demure
ceremonial fete of Madame Beck to the final phantasmagoric
fete in the park, in which history and legend, deception and
revelation, convent and empire, come together "[i]n a land of
enchantment, a garden most gorgeous, a plain sprinkled with
coloured meteors, a forest with sparks of purple and ruby and

golden fire gemming the foliage; a region, not of trees and shadow, but of strangest architectural wealth—of altar and temple, of pyramid, obelisk, and sphinx; incredible to say, the wonders and the symbols of Egypt teemed throughout the park of Villette" (p. 440). The double meaning of the French word *fête*, which travels from the total privacy and uniqueness of a birthday to the corporate festival of an empire's history, contains both the intimate and the political character of the school. Lucy's, and our, final discovery is that, through the machinations of the "secret junta," school, city, and nation are in league and at one.

Though the institution of cricket leads naturally into the art of government in literature about boys at school, a female academy can make such a leap only in "a land of enchantment." Charlotte Brontë's picture of such an academy, whose educational is at one with its political identity, may owe something to Tennyson's *The Princess*, whose opulent Amazonian College lies in another "garden most gorgeous," at the center of the poem's action. Like Madame Beck's pensionnat, Princess Ida's College is suffused with the lure of intensity and unreality that links it to his Palace of Art and his Camelot, "a city built to music," therefore eternal and impossible. Like Madame Beck in her consistent avoidance of the children in whom she trades, Ida sees the integrity of her College as the denial of the child within and without. As her perplexed father puts it: "knowledge, so my daughter held, Was all in all: they had but been, she thought, As children; they must lose the child, assume The women" (I, ll. 134-137). Ida is right: when she embraces a child, she begins to lose her empire. The greater consistency of Charlotte Brontë's women may be a response to the defection of Tennyson's Amazons: the poem was first published in 1847, and in 1848 Charlotte bought a copy for Emily. In 1851, the year *Villette* was begun, a new edition appeared containing vivid descriptions of the Prince's "weird seizures," in which the boundaries between the real and the visionary melt down as they do in Lucy Snowe's opium-suffused vision of the last great fete.

The "weird seizures" of Tennyson's Prince, which make all

around him seem "a hollow show," tend to engulf him when he confronts organized female power. His first attack of unreality springs from his meeting with Ida in full panoply of loyal maidens and tame leopards (III, ll. 167-180); his second from his banishment by the furious Princess and her "monstrous woman-guard" (IV, ll. 538-553); and his last from his encounter with Ida's army, fulfilling the prophecy that he will fight with shadows and fall (V, ll. 466-531). An air of similar unreality takes over *Villette* when we learn the extent of Madame Beck's organized power. Lucy's desperate confession to Père Silas, which seems to take place in the antipodes of solitude, eerily finds its way back to her employer through the intercession of Madame Walravens, whom Lucy dubs "Malevola," a preternatural female ruler to whom even Madame Beck bows down. This magical being seems a truer ruler of the feminine Villette than its gloomy little king, who is himself the prey of a ravaging female force—the vividly hallucinated goddess Hypochondria. The church Père Silas serves, whose interests serve those of the pensionnat, is all crooning maternality—it speaks in a pamphlet with "the mild effluence of a mother's love towards her tenderest and her youngest" (p. 402)—but it is also entwined with the greatest public power history boasts: "I had been made to witness a huge mingled procession of the church and the army—priests with relics, and soldiers with weapons" (p. 409). To these high powers Madame Beck adds her own. Both her academy and Ida's partake of the central sources of governmental power, for which they pay the price of an increasing unreality.[41]

For, finally, they are compelling incarnations of lies. Because *The Princess* is a comedy and Ida must recant, her error can be viewed with romantic indulgence: "My princess, O my princess! true she errs, But in her own grand way: being herself Three times more noble than three score of men, She sees herself in every woman else, And so she wears her error like a crown To blind the truth and me" (III, ll. 91-96). Lucy Snowe, who is not living a comedy and who knows she will not win, is a less forgiving anatomist than the Prince: "Not a soul in Madame Beck's house, from the scullion to the directress herself, but was above being ashamed of a lie; they thought nothing of it: to invent might not be precisely a virtue, but it was the most venial of faults" (p. 76). In this nocturnal setting of pervasive shadows, labyrinthine walks, and hidden enclosures, duplicity knits together all classes and types. Lucy's fierce Protestant quest for truth (which eventually becomes TRUTH as it recedes from her) is repeatedly defeated by the women who sidle and whisper about her, finally drugging her with opiate so that the lies of Madame Beck's community pierce her perceptions, forcing her integrity to dissolve into the hallucinatory intensity of her phantasmagoric nightwalk through the illuminated city. The power of the stern headmistress is at one with the noble error of the Amazonian Princess: both are able to "blind the truth" with fantasy and mystery until all avenues of apprehension are obscured.

Ida embraces the child and is flooded with maternality, renouncing empire for solicitude as she nurses her wounded lover back to health. At this point, the "hollow shows" of female power give way to female truth: "and all Her falser self slipt from her like a robe, And left her woman" (VII, ll. 145-147). But though Tennyson's empire of women fades like the "land of enchantment" it is, the plotting coven of *Villette* never stoops to nursing its antagonist rather than killing him. Lucy's thwarted love affair with M. Paul may be in part an Amazonian revision of the false final "truth" of *The Princess*: in Charlotte Brontë's academy there is no essential reality of solicitous "woman" to dissipate the specter of organized female power. M. Paul Emanuel, who is called a "Christian knight" in chapter 35 and who casts himself as the opponent of all Amazons, cuts a sadly futile figure in the role of visionary Prince, his fiery protestations suggesting a burlesque of the mighty life force Tennyson's hero represents.

The intensity of debate surrounding this dubious love story [42] obscures the fact that it springs into prominence only in the third volume of the novel, and only in the last chapters does Paul move from being Lucy's colleague to being her need. Though he is the supposed arbiter of her destiny when, desolate and lost, she first applies to the school, Madame Beck's chivalrous consultation of her talented cousin would never, one is sure, override her own decision: as always, the power of management is hers. Though Paul bursts into the novel as a self-proclaimed Napoleon, and we soon see that he does have some political base of his own, the impact of his public address more nearly resembles the personal influence of Mother Bhaer than it does the wide-ranging intrigues of the headmistress: "I do not think his audience were generally susceptible of sharing his flame in its purity; but some of the college youth caught fire as he eloquently told them what should be their path and endeavor in their country's and in Europe's future. They gave him a long, loud, ringing cheer, as he concluded; with all his fierceness, he was their favourite professor" (p. 303). There is something patronizing in his students' ability to see through his facade of tyranny to his underlying softness. They see him as Lucy does, less as oppressor than as tyrant manqué. Though he is a more vividly attractive character than any of the others, Paul's trajectory in the novel resembles those of Rochester and of the men in *Cranford*, who storm into the women's little world, set the dovecote fluttering, then suddenly and inexplicably collapse. With mingled disappointment and relief, Gaskell and Brontë reveal in all these novels that the Grand Turk is a man of straw.

As the late-blooming love story intensifies, Paul loses his solitary empire over the pensionnat, coming increasingly to resemble such a character as Hardy's Jude, whose life is in the power of women. Madame Beck commands him and ghoulish little Madame Walravens drains him of the income that is his independence; his soul and his actions are in the power of the maternal church, while his love pours forth in his ambiguous prayer to "Marie Reine du Ciel" (p. 408). The incessant pity of the Virgin Mother merges with that of his lost inamorata, the nun Justine-Marie, in a blended coalition of the feminine powers that control Paul's supposed autocracy. "[H]er business is as much with you as with me" (p. 356), Paul says to Lucy of the spectral nun; but the symbolic figure who is Lucy's alter ego and Nemesis is the love of Paul's vulnerable life.

Though we ultimately learn that the nun is "merely" prankish little de Hamal, she belongs in the setting she haunts, suggesting among other things contemporary wishes and fears that were grouped around the image of conventual power. The potency of her mournful solitude also brings her influence in league with that of the female "halcyon moon," which both is Lucy's life and controls it: "She and those stars seemed to me at once the types and witnesses of truth all regnant. The night-sky lit her reign: like its slow-wheeling progress, advanced her victory—that onward movement which had been, and is, and will be from eternity to eternity" (p. 455).[43] This Empress, whose pageant of victory appropriates the sky, will also appropriate the tides and storms under which her acolyte Paul Emanuel is drowned.

Through such images, the governing female coalition in the state seems to spread into the universe. The regnant feminine moon might embody the oddly assorted female Powers who people the novel's cosmos, several of whom are created by Lucy herself. The inflammatory power of the divine-demonic Vashti seems art's symbol of political and cosmic life, as Madame Beck, with her motherly facade and her soundless step, reveals her collusion with Madame Walravens, a barely human genius of the Rue des Mages. This presiding witchlike Malevola silently motivates the Mother Church. Hovering beyond the Church are such feminine personifications as the Reason and Imagination who battle for Lucy's perceptions; the Hypochondria who eats the King; and the "red, random beldame" Human Justice whom Lucy thrusts at the whiskers of the "pious mentors" she is supposed to want to impress. The idiosyncratic, faintly pagan "powers" who govern this world are female and communal; when Lucy receives the nun's habit as a mocking gift and destiny, she is initiated into a world as well as denied one.

For one story of *Villette* is Lucy's education, not only into her own emotions, but into "the art of ruling." In her ascension to government, at least, Madame Beck is her ally from first to last. It is she who snatches Lucy out of the "nursery obscurity" of a woman's sphere and makes her look in the face of power: "At that instant she did not wear a woman's aspect, but rather a man's. Power of a particular kind strongly limned itself in all her traits, and that power was not *my* kind of power: neither sympathy, nor congeniality, nor submission, were the emotions it awakened. I stood—not soothed, nor won, nor overwhelmed. It seemed as if a challenge of strength between opposing gifts was given, and I suddenly felt all the dishonour of my diffidence—all the pusillanimity of my slackness to aspire" (p. 72).

Despite her momentary hesitation between the "opposing gifts" of power and influence, government and sympathy, once she is in the classroom Lucy obeys her employer's challenge as wholeheartedly as Tom Brown did those of his mentors at Rugby: she exercises her own power with great relish, just as she will do in the theatricals when the assumption of male attire inspires her to compete with John Bretton rather than grovel before him. Her teaching performance consists of tearing up one student's composition and locking up another student with unsympathetic enjoyment and aplomb; never do we see her drop her autocratic guard to win her pupils with the personal influence women were supposed to cherish and exude. Lucy's skill in exerting power and her disregard of female influence become clearer when we realize that her teaching debut almost exactly duplicates that of the gruff, masculine Crimsworth in *The Professor*, though even he never goes so far as to incarcerate a student. Lucy has learned a good deal from her disapproving scrutiny of Madame Beck. "C'est bien," says her spying sponsor—and she is right.

At the end of the novel Lucy is given an even more abrupt and disturbing cue, to which she responds with equal aplomb: "Ladies, instead of the usual lesson with M. Emanuel, you will, this morning, read English with Mademoiselle Lucy." "I kept them at it the whole morning. I remember feeling a sentiment of impatience towards the pupils who sobbed. . . A rather weak-minded, low-spirited pupil kept it up when the others had done; relentless necessity obliged and assisted me so to accost her, that she dared not carry on the demonstration, that she was forced to conquer the convulsion" (p. 427). The unprecedented kiss she gives the girl afterward is similar in kind to the candy Paul had handed out to pupils he harangued.

Her ensuing agony notwithstanding, at Madame Beck's command she has taken on Paul's authority with dispatch, her power never weakening into the "obscure nursery" world of personal influence.

Having learned to rule, she too receives her little nation. Though it is surely wrong to say, as Millett does, that Lucy slyly coaxes Paul into giving her her "true home," the school that is not family but commonwealth, we need not trust Lucy's own hyperbole when she dubs him her king and the arbiter of her destiny; only Madame Beck's insistent example enables her to govern there successfully. In fact, as seen through Lucy's eyes, the end of the novel can be regarded as a triumph of decent and orderly deviousness. Having found her one honest man, this Diogenes collaborates with the forces, personal, institutional, and cosmic, that destroy him. The death of Paul seems the death of her own and her world's integrity: "There was no sham and no cheat, and no hollow unreal in him . . . He was born honest, and not false—artless, and not cunning—a freeman, and not a slave" (p. 479). But is Lucy herself honest in the final chapter, with its swerving back and forth between ambition and deference, death and rebirth, triumph and wretchedness? Her ambiguous feelings for Paul take shape in the strange remark: "I thought I loved him when he went away; I love him now in another degree; he is more my own" (p. 480). Like Mesdames Beck and Walravens, Lucy is now "in possession" of Paul Emanuel, aligned implicitly with the "secret junta" that governs school, city, and cosmos, the winds and the storms. She need never fall with Princess Ida from teacher and ruler to nurse.

Brontë's statement about Lucy, "From the beginning I never meant to appoint her lines in pleasant places,"[44] seems as much about success as it is about loss of love. Lucy's position at the end of the novel shares something with Miss Matty's; weakened and trembling at the mention of her mysteriously dead lover, she presides through every tremor over her Amazonian state. She announces proudly that with the help of Miss Marchmont's legacy, her externat (day school) has become a pensionnat (boarding school); the female community which was an emblem of her isolation is transfigured into a seal of her triumph. The dead Paul comes to function as an emblem of her own dead honesty as she assumes "power of a particular kind" and enters the camp of the prosperous: the thriving Mesdames Beck and Walravens and their henchman Père Silas, who obligingly bends the Church to their plots. Harmless and small as its name makes it sound, Villette, like Cranford, is in possession of the Amazons. The triumph of both is epistemological and political: they are invaders of perceptions, erecting self-defined male honesty into the Grand Turk until it seems to spontaneously crumble. The efficiency of Madame Beck and the sweetness of Miss Matty are the organizing centers of communities that triumph over outside standards of truth to create female worlds "all regnant." At the end of *Villette* Lucy lives in such a world; she is a stranger no longer.

Beyond the Self:
The Spectacle of History
and a New Religion

John Singer Sargent. *The Wyndham Sisters*
The Metropolitan Museum of Art, Catharine Lorillard Wolfe Collection,
Purchase, 1927, Catharine Lorillard Wolfe Fund

"Women—so said the books—are adepts at dissimulation." [1] With such shreds of mid-Victorian wisdom, George Gissing's Edmund Widdowson warms himself after his wife's desertion in favor of the new gospel of equality and independence brought her by the odd women. But before she dies, even drifting, weak-willed Monica is able to assert her truth as the truth: "I love the truth better than falsehood. . . In keeping away from him I am acting honestly" (p. 309). The "new truths" women bring to Henry James's The Bostonians (1884-85) and George Gissing's The Odd Women (1893) take on sudden authority in the face of society's deterioration.

In the 1850s Miss Matty's Cranford and Madame Beck's pensionnat were indeed "adepts at dissimulation"; these mid-Victorian communities were private visions of imagination and deceit that slyly obliterated public, masculine truth. But at the end of the century, history's majesty seemed to many men a waning thing, reduced to the "babble, babble" Tennyson's aged patriarch curses in "Locksley Hall Sixty Years After" (1886):

> Poor old Heraldry, poor old History, poor
> old Poetry, passing hence,
> In the common deluge drowning old political
> common sense! (11.249-250)

In the face of this pervasive exhaustion, institutionalized feminism held the promise of historical youth; fighting disenchantment, male authors turned for the first time to the vision of the female community as a new, if equivocal, source of power. For their own reasons, Henry James and George Gissing are the first authors examined in this book who have bestowed the laurel of reality and the crown of history on the feminist communities that overwhelm a fading aristocratic sensibility. [2]

Women today want to be the first and the only generation to

seize the time. Our contemporary Elizabeth Janeway exults: "Suddenly, and really for the first time, it is women who are in the forefront of change. . . For reality is on our side. We are working with history and not against it."[3] But this triumphant alliance has been forged and broken before. The Bostonians and The Odd Women are charged with the excitement of this new possession of reality by women: yet we who were supposed to solidify it have only recently managed to rediscover it. As our own century came into view, James and Gissing allowed their feminists to converge with history by invoking a reality that seemed as irrevocably present then as it does today; at the same time, their feminist visions were their compromise with historical change.

Both writers recoiled from the mass commercial ugliness of a democratic revolution. As James saw the lower classes, "their yearning toward the superior world makes up their very substance. Unlike the Flaubert of Un Coeur Simple, . . . he could see nothing but pathos and unreality in states of penury and servitude. . . The appurtenances of poverty were 'the merciless signs of mere mean stale feelings.' Poverty was the total failure of the human."[4] Gissing, too, found all poverty but the aesthetic and literary a repellent blight which it was impossible to eradicate by the varnish of mass education or improved income. "He shows no interest in the tribulations of the unaesthetic London poor, their resilience, courage, and laughter; he has no concern with social reform or political protest."[5]

Some of Gissing's early novels do suggest an implicit engagement with social reform, just as James struggles in The Princess Casamassima to incorporate the revolutionary underground into his art. Both men sensed a coming "common deluge" that threatened to drown the private and fastidious perceptions of art; thus, the woman's revolution may have brought about an uneasy marriage between their social guilt and their aesthetic instincts. Shrill-voiced or hardhearted as the new woman may have been, her ascension seemed preferable to the garbage of mass lower-class culture that surged below her. Unnatural as her coming reign might be, it would at least maintain good taste.

In the claims of the feminist movement, history provided the two with a subject that met their ambivalent needs. Though suffrage is only glancingly mentioned in *The Bostonians* and is ignored in *The Odd Women*, the crusade for it in the United States and Great Britain was an unprecedented symptom of women's reach into the public world: "By demanding a permanent, public role for all women, suffragists began to demolish the absolute, sexually defined barrier marking the public world of men off from the private world of women."[6] Recent revisionist historians have shown that, for all their obscurity, women have never been truly hidden from history, even if for centuries women's history has constituted an autonomous counterforce to male public events, "a separate woman's culture" like that of Cranford or the March cottage, with rules and a life of its own.[7] But whether woman's sphere remains a secret pocket of history or moves into convergence with great events, the varying realities of a female community remain its single constant force: "If any long-range trend is apparent from this work [in women's history], it is the central importance of supportive female networks in raising women's aspirations and encouraging their creativity."[8] Hidden or overt, the historical reality of women is the force of their communities, communities which in the American and English novels that follow signify the death of a known century and the promise of the unimaginable new. The sisterhood that existed as a countertruth, an enclave of deceit and quiet subversion, moves at the close of the nineteenth century into possession of its time.

The Bostonians

It isn't Boston—it's humanity![9]

To many *The Bostonians* seems a stillborn anomaly in the Jamesian canon. James regretfully found no place for it in the definitive New York edition of his work, which was his own gesture toward public definition; and his later critics have floundered in finding a language in which to discuss it, or even a tone on which they can agree. To one it is "a long, cold, and distinctly unpopular novel"; to another it is "admirably open, wonderfully funny, and humanly attractive."[10] No doubt one's critical perspective depends on one's human judgment of the central passion of the novel: Olive Chancellor, an inhibited Boston Brahmin who seeks sisterhood and salvation in the woman's movement, is stricken with an obsession to possess beautiful, pliant Verena Tarrant. Daughter and subject of a sleazy mesmerist with whom she is performing when we first meet her, Verena is endowed with the gift of compelling talk. Gripped with excitement, Olive buys the girl from her parents, thus initiating a bond which through Verena's mellifluous, magnetic speeches promises to make the fortunes of the feminist movement and to purchase Olive's happiness forever. The women's only antagonist is Olive's cousin Basil Ransom, a displaced Southerner adrift with medieval ideas in progressive New England, who falls in love with Verena and vows to restore her to her "normal" sphere of ornamental privacy.

Whether the emotion between Olive and Verena is human or inhuman, it is not as solitary a thing as it seems. In making the novel's psychic pivot "one of those friendships between women which are so common in New England," James captured a moment in which New England women were not only yearning to find Platonic elevation in each other, but were exhorted by men to do so. In 1885, the year in which *The Bostonians* was completed, a book appeared in Boston which held such friendships up to women as the crown of life: "If one-tenth of the efforts which women now make to fill their time with amusements, or to gratify outward ambition, were devoted to personal improvement, and to the cultivation of high-toned friendships with each other, it would do more than anything to enrich and embellish their lives, and to crown them with contentment."[11]

In its crowning claims for sisterhood *The Bostonians* could be an alternative sequel to *Little Women*, happily undomesticated if somewhat overwhelming in its emancipation. Alcott and James knew each other. Their philosophic fathers both orbited dreamily around the beaming Emerson, and in 1865,

when he was twenty-two, James wrote a respectful, if quali-
fied, review of Alcott's *Moods* for *The North American* and
lectured her sententiously in private, "as if he had been eighty
and I a girl."[12] Jo March's plaintive allegorizing of her noble
sister—"Beth is my conscience, and I *can't* give her up. I can't!
I can't!"[13]—is echoed in Verena's drier tribute to Olive: "You
do keep me up. . . . You are my conscience" (p. 159). The "marriage" Olive envisions between them has the same corporate
self-completeness as the mutually balancing circle of the
March sisters:

> To Olive it appeared that just this partnership of their two
> minds—each of them, by itself, lacking an important
> group of facets—made an organic whole which, for the
> work in hand, could not fail to be brilliantly effective . . .
> Olive perceived how fatally, without Verena's tender
> notes, her crusade would lack sweetness, what the Catho-
> lics call unction; and, on the other hand, how weak Ver-
> ena would be on the statistical and logical side if she her-
> self should not bring up the rear. Together, in short, they
> would be complete, they would have everything, and to-
> gether they would triumph. (p. 160)

Olive is echoing Alcott's faith that a solitary woman is a fragment of a greater female whole, an irresistible mystical body
with the power to cleanse history.

There is a more distinct echo of Alcott in *The Tragic Muse*
(1889-90), in the humiliating fiasco of aspiring tragedienne
Miriam Rooth's first audition before the great Madame Carré,
which she later recoups through indefatigable work and overweening confidence. In *Jo's Boys* (1886), Meg's hoydenish
daughter Josie gives an equally embarrassing performance before the great actress Miss Cameron, whose beloved protégée
she later becomes. For Alcott and James, histrionic ability
takes almost interchangeable theatrical and political forms;
these young women auditioning before the queens of their sex
represent the grooming of political as well as artistic power.

If James adapted Alcott's voice and vision in his "very American tale," he was intimately aware of another female community in his adopted England: Elizabeth Gaskell's *Cranford*,

with its self-depreciating power. *Cranford* was a beloved artifact in Cambridge, Massachusetts, where James lived as a young man. Writing to Gaskell in 1855, Charles Eliot Norton, James's mentor and first editor, endows it with the status of holy writ as it prepares his sacred father for a better world: "During the summer of 1853 as my Father's life was gradually drawing to its peaceful close, there was little left for those who loved him to do but endeavour to amuse the listless and languid hours of decline. It was then that your *Cranford*, which had been read aloud (and much of it more than once) in our family circle when it first appeared in 'Household Words,' was again read to him and gave him more entertainment and pleasure than any other book. It was indeed, I think, the last book that he cared to hear. You may imagine what sacred associations it now possesses for us,—and how glad I am, and I speak for my Mother & sisters as well as for myself, to have the opportunity to express our gratitude to you for it."[14] Reviewing Gaskell's career for *The Nation* in 1866, James placed *Cranford* as a work "manifestly destined in its modest way to become a classic."[15] This witty phrase captures precisely the book's blend of the overweening and the shrinking, the imperial and the demure, and casts it in the American idiom that was James's. *The Bostonians*, one strange fruit of this idiom, is part of a distinct tradition and carries its antecedents, from both England and New England, before it. Moreover, in James's total vision of his country, the world of women that is his Boston spreads out over the land he sees as his personal past and the historic future.[16] The focus of the novel sharpens in the context of James's total geography, where the might of collective American womanhood steps forth as history's irony and its promise.

If The American Girl did not exist, James would have had to invent her as a personification of the United States more appealing and appalling than Uncle Sam. While New England women tended to see themselves as a glorious America within America—Julia Ward Howe's *Reminiscences* equates the discovery of her own sex with "the addition of a new continent to the map of the world"[17]—to James women were simply, and ambiguously, America itself, a land whose men had disappeared either into soldiers' graves or into something mysterious and inconsequential called "business." His writings abound in obsessive references to the domination of America by women, references of an oddly insistent but uncertain tone, as if this female world is too important and unprecedented to be captured by familiar definitions.

James's personal and national ambivalence crystallizes around the death of his mother and his simultaneous (to him) abandonment by his mother country, out of which *The Bostonians* was born: "The disappearance of the home in Quincy Street, the now permanent absence of a Cambridge hearth, is probably the single deepest emotion out of which *The Bostonians* sprang . . . *The Bostonians* was the novel in which James wrote out the hidden emotional anguish of the collapse of his old American ties, and he coupled this with a kind of vibrating anger that Boston should be so unfriendly as to let him go." [18] His capacity for dependence and disgust seemed rooted in his mother, and he reacts to her death in visions where mother and country seem perceived interchangeably, as centers of transcendent comfort or cosmic vertigo. He greets her loss first with an Emersonian eulogy: "Her death has given me a passionate belief in certain transcendent things—the immanence of being as nobly created as hers—the immortality of such a virtue as that—the reunion of spirits in better conditions than these. She is no more of an angel today than she had always been; but I can't believe that by the accident of her death all her unspeakable tenderness is lost to the beings she so dearly loved. She is with us, she is of us—the eternal stillness is but a form of her love." Twenty years later, he confronts the family graves in Mount Auburn Cemetery on a bleak Cambridge evening in which "the highest deepest note of the whole thing" is a note of loss and numbness: "But why do I write of the all unutterable and the all abysmal? Why does my pen not drop from my hand on approaching the infinite pity and tragedy of all the past? It does, poor helpless pen, with what it meets of the ineffable, what it meets of the cold Medusa -face of life, of all the life *lived*, on every side. *Basta, basta!*" [19]

The land of swaddling angels is now haunted by Gorgons, women who are equally transcendent, but devouring.

But angel and Gorgon cannot be reduced to Mrs. James alone. This vacillation between renewal and decay, birth and blight, beginnings and endings, reflects the historical tone of feminized, turn-of-the-century New England as well as the psychic idiosyncracies of James's reaction to it. In "The Relation of College Women to Social Need," Vida Scudder wrote of educated women as a new, saving race, their unprecedented numbers revealing "the harmony of dramatic purpose that runs through the evolution of history. . . The time passionately demands new life-force, new mind-force, consecrated to the study of social evil and the lessening of social distress. The college woman, prepared by combination of nature and training to react on life from a new point of view, appears for the first time."[20] But for Van Wyck Brooks, looking backward, this New England that seemed to Scudder restored and renewed was a valley of the dry bones, its possession by women a sign of the death rather than the evolution of history: "The bony fingers of aging spinsters dominated the village scene, where one might have supposed the end of the world was at hand."[21]

With the ascendancy of woman to apocalyptic force, the anchor of home is supplanted by the pervasive communality of the hotel. In *The American Scene* (1904-5) James stands before the "gorgeous golden blur" of the Waldorf-Astoria, contemplating the sumptuous fruit of the death of home: "The moral in question, the high interest of the tale, is that you are in presence of a revelation of the possibilities of the hotel—for which the American spirit has found so unprecedented a use and a value; leading it on to express so a social, indeed positively an aesthetic ideal, and making it so, at this supreme pitch, a synonym for civilization, for the capture of conceived manners themselves, that one is verily tempted to ask if the hotel-spirit may not just be the American spirit most seeking and most finding itself." "Here was a social order in positively stable equilibrium. Here was a world whose relation to its form and medium was practically imperturbable; here was a conception of publicity *as* the vital medium organized with the authority with which the American genius for organization, put on its mettle, alone could organize it."[22] This replacement of home by hotel as a point of "positively stable equilibrium" in a society made up of dizzying changes is at one with the spread of women over the social life of the land. Louisa May Alcott's dream of national sisterhood has come true, with the result that no homely little cottage remains to lure the lone male from dreams of glory. The community of women has gorgeously communized American life.

Ironically, this appropriation of social life by women, which James regards with such fascinated horror, was originally (and perhaps disingenuously) intended as a holding action against the public push of feminism. In 1850 a pious woman exhorted her gentle readers to leave the inexorable power of government to men and to remain content with the nobler sphere of society: "May not we, the women of America, mould our social life by our intelligent convictions into a form which shall make it the fit handmaid of our political life in its grand simplicity and lofty aims?"[23] This decorous resignation will become for James an overwhelming national monument:

> The phenomenon may easily become, for a spectator, the sentence written largest in the American sky: when he is in search of the characteristic, what else so plays the part? The woman is two-thirds of the apparent life — which means that she is absolutely all of the social. . . The woman produced by a women-made society alone has obviously quite a new story—to which it is not for a moment to be gainsaid that the world at large has, for the last thirty years in particular, found itself lending an attentive, at times even a charmed ear. The extent and variety of this attention have been the specious measure of the personal success of the type in question, and are always referred to when its value happens to be challenged. "The American woman?—why, she has beguiled, she has conquered the globe: look at her fortune everywhere and fail to accept her if you can." (pp. 346-347)

The imperial conquest by the American female, product of a kind of social parthenogenesis whereby the male is bred out of the race, is the United States—and thus the future—itself.

Though *The American Scene* finds with relief that Washington is still a male bastion in a female nation, James is uneasy with such reassuring divisions as Maria McIntosh's between lofty little social life and its ruthless political counterpart. In "Pandora" (1884), a story written the year *The Bostonians* was begun, social and political life converge disturbingly in the person of Pandora Day, "the latest, freshest fruit of our great American evolution. She is the self-made girl!"[24] In the course of her story, Pandora effortlessly conquers Washington society until she bullies America's affable, silly President into appointing her fiancé Minister of Holland. There are some nervous jokes along the way about Pandora herself being made a foreign minister, and when we observe her fiancé's obliging facelessness at the end, we realize she has effectively become one. As a "woman produced by a women-made society," this "self-made girl" could never have been made by a man, though by the end she is able to make one. Containing in her name both a threat and a promise, the mythic Pandora Day is an amalgam of "certain transcendent things" James associated with his mother country. *The American Scene* describes women "in peerless possession" of his powerful homeland. *The Bostonians* lives through such a spreading possession, with its capacity for transcendence and the "cold Medusa-face" of its power.

With the partial exception of the hypnotically intense relation between Olive and Verena, the larger community of women in *The Bostonians* has none of the lovingly personal solicitude of its antecedents in *Little Women* and *Cranford*. Despite its mystically imagined power, it is as impalpable a unit as the invisible, economically powerless Bennet family in *Pride and Prejudice*. With the exception of the first scene in the dim parlor of Miss Birdseye, the fuzzily selfless abolitionist, figurehead of the movement, whose guests straggle suspiciously around while their benevolent hostess wonders who these people are she has invited, we are scarcely permitted to see the collective entity of womanhood we are told will sweep over the world. The female community is an abstraction. For its guiding spirit, Olive Chancellor, feminism's main drawback is the intrusion of other women: "Miss Chancellor would have been much happier if the movements she was interested in could have been carried on only by the people she liked, and if revolutions, somehow, didn't always have to begin with one's self—with internal convulsions, sacrifices, executions. A common end, unfortunately, however fine as regards a special result, does not make community impersonal" (pp. 113-114). On the face of it a contradiction in terms, this goal of impersonal community is the heart of Olive's mission. She dreams not of sisterhood, but "that a woman *could* live on persistently, clinging to a great, vivifying, redemptory idea, without the help of a man" (p. 393)—and ideally, one presumes, without the intercession of another woman. The impersonality of her private Utopia carries Olive beyond womanhood as her century defined it, endowing her with the monumental constriction of an institutional body: "a smile of exceeding faintness played about her lips—it was just perceptible enough to light up the native gravity of her face. It might have been likened to a thin ray of moonlight resting upon the wall of a prison" (p. 8).

It is easy enough to give this image a Freudian tinge and to visualize poor crazy Olive as the prisoner of her own unnatural desires and twisted aspirations; but if Olive is inmate, she is given the status of prison as well. The image which introduces her reminds us that in the last third of the nineteenth century, a fervent New England cause was separate "matriarchal" prisons, such as the one at Sherburne which Louisa May Alcott described with excitement in 1879: "Went with Dr. W. to the Woman's Prison, at Sherburne. A lovely drive, and very remarkable day and night. Read a story to the four hundred women, and heard many interesting tales. A much better place than Concord Prison, with its armed wardens, and 'knock down and drag out' methods. Only women here, and they work wonders by patience, love, common-sense, and the belief in salvation for all." The bleak smile with which Olive greets her antagonist is an emblem of this corporate female self-sustainment which will preside over the world of the future and uplift it. [25]

The institutional weight with which Olive is endowed on her first entrance is reinforced by the book's title, which suggests that with all their qualifications and conflicts, Olive and the rest are at one with their time and place. In *Villette*, despite their palpable inadequacies, the conventionally feminine Mrs. Bretton of Bretton and spaniel-like Polly Home had a similar harmony bestowed on them by their names, while Lucy Snowe was thrust by hers into some cosmic arctic Beyond. This oneness of Olive with her time defines the accuracy of her catty sister's first characterization: "She is very honest, is Olive Chancellor; she is full of rectitude. Nobody tells fibs in Boston; I don't know what to make of them all" (p. 3).

Olive's relentless honesty is a part of her undivided fusion with her life: "There are women who are unmarried by accident, and others who are unmarried by option; but Olive Chancellor was unmarried by every implication of her being. She was a spinster as Shelley was a lyric poet, or as the month of August is sultry" (p. 18). Like her dream of an impersonal community, Olive's asexuality is an allegiance that moves beyond humanity: "I have said that it was Miss Chancellor's plan of life not to lie, but such a plan was compatible with a kind of consideration for the truth which led her to shrink from producing it on poor occasions" (p. 288). Her "consideration for the truth" as a thing beyond the contingencies of the moment removes her from the secretly subversive enclaves of our mid-century women. Divorced from herself like the vaporously impersonal Miss Birdseye, Olive acts as a yardstick of honesty in all its grotesqueness, bestowing for a time the apparently omniscient perspective of which Miss Birdseye's name is a witty emblem: "Olive had taken [Verena] up, in the literal sense of the phrase, like a bird of the air, had spread an extraordinary pair of wings, and carried her through the dizzying void of space. Verena liked it, for the most part; liked to shoot upward without an effort of her own and look down upon all creation, upon all history, from such a height" (p. 79). The very ludicrousness of this image of Olive as American eagle carries a certain authenticity. "A woman without laughter,"

Olive may be funny as she takes to herself a God's-eye view, but nothing in the book says she is false.

From his opening drawl, "I pretend not to prevaricate" (p. 4), Basil Ransom "as a representative of his sex" (p. 5) is associated with a dissimulation that is traditionally feminine. [26] Far from expressing his gallant love of "the sex," the florid chivalry with which he smothers every woman he meets (and, in the case of Mrs. Luna, becomes smothered himself) is the honey of a universal rage: "Chivalry had to do with one's relations with people one hated, not with those one loved" (p. 403). This belated admission corroborates Olive's most paranoid and seemingly unbalanced observations: "Olive disliked [men] most when they were least unpleasant" (p. 294). "He didn't love [Verena], he hated her, he only wanted to smother her, to crush her, to kill her—as she would infallibly see that he would if she listened to him. It was because he knew that her voice had magic in it, and from the moment he caught its first note he had determined to destroy it" (p. 390). Without doubt Olive's speech is hysterical, but it is nevertheless an honest echo of Basil's involuntary response to Verena's voice in the night: "Murder, what a lovely voice!" (p. 366). What seems deranged in Olive is her conscious formulation of the duplicitous Basil's buried life.

Basil is not only a liar, but a carrier of lies. Like the relic-obsessed narrator of *The Aspern Papers* (1888), he contaminates the shabby but genuine integrity of a community of women with the seductive lie of love. At a key moment in the novel he confronts the incorruptibly honest Miss Birdseye with the advantages of deceit: " 'Do you wish me to conceal—?' murmured Miss Birdseye, panting a little . . . 'Well, I never did anything of that kind' " (pp. 225-226). Backed to the wall, she submits only in the name of that "truth" of which she is a disheveled exemplar: "Well, I believe in the victory of the truth. I won't say anything" (p. 226). Though the truth seems sadly un-victorious in this novel, at least as it is usually read, Olive's dismissal of men as "poor creatures" is quietly sanctioned by the reality James creates, since Basil is the most attractive man we see; while his ornate fantasy about women as decorative objects for private consumption is given the lie by every woman in the novel, of whom none but Verena is decorative and none but Olive's carnivorous sister, Mrs. Luna, lives a private life.

Serpentine landscapes seem to follow Basil. When he takes Verena for an idyllic walk in Central Park in order to initiate her into the "contempt and brutality" that make up his conservative doctrine, the two "[thread] the devious ways of the Ramble, [and lose] themselves in the Maze" (p. 335). Her conversion to his alternate truth is introduced by another image of random, floundering falsity: as she sees him "waiting for her at a bend of the road which lost itself, after a winding, straggling mile or two, in the indented, insulated 'point,' *where the wandering bee droned through the hot hours with a vague, misguided flight,* she felt that his tall, watching figure, with the low horizon behind, represented well the importance, the towering eminence he had in her mind" (p. 397; my italics). The droning directionless bee Verena is becoming takes poignancy from the certainty with which Olive scans history from Miss Birdseye's perspective in her plan to appropriate it "like a bird of the air." The bare view of the Charles River with which Olive is associated carries by contrast with Basil's lost and devious associations the authority of its honest ugliness.

Basil's role as the source of lies is associated with his isolation in time and place. No South is left to validate his identity; his plantation and his homeland have been destroyed in a war he thinks was incited by female Abolitionists from New England.[27] And he is locked into an ideology that is "about three hundred years behind the age." His lie is less personal than historical, for in this novel, truth is the partner not of morality, nature and sanity, but of history as James perceives it. Too many critics have dismissed Olive's perceptions because they see her as neurotic:[28] in the face of this pervasive historicity, her "new truths" are vindicated by the bushels of letters she receives on Cape Cod, while Basil sits alone in his law office in New York, waiting for someone to need him.

The truth upheld by the female community in the person of

its representative Olive is the truth of an age whose religion is publicity and its concurrent theatricality. The age is defined by Olive's uncharacteristically witty response to Boston theatergoing: "It was not so religious as going to evening-service at King's Chapel; but it was the next thing to it" (p. 119). The spiritualistic miasma that clings to Boston's feminist communities aligns them with a "truth" that is public and transcendent. [29] As it is defined in the novel, truth is one's theatrical debut on the stage of history. [30]

This inseparability of history and the theater is not unique to James's America: in the England of *The Princess Casamassima* (1886) and *The Tragic Muse* (1889-90) the entanglement between politics and the stage simply is more glamorously dazzling than that of London's earnest and shabby American cousin. The three major novels of the 1880s grow out of a single vision and set of concerns, in which the old world and the new illuminate each other in the suspicious similarity of their national and histrionic performances. Donald David Stone's otherwise exhaustive account of James in the 1880s oversimplifies in its contentions that "History is a mirage, for James's main characters, which they escape by disavowing" and "Art is an illusion which lasts, while history is a reality which passes." [31] Neither James nor his protagonists can escape a narrowly defined "history" for a private Skinner box of "art." The overarching irony of all these novels is the extent to which the confinements of history and the freedom of art pervade and create each other, and the characters who try to separate them can only be damned by losing both.

In *The Princess Casamassima* the initiation of the artist is at one with that of the incendiary. "Mr. Vetch had on a great occasion, within the year, obtained for the pair an order for two seats at a pantomime, and to Hyacinth the impression of that ecstatic evening had consecrated him, placed him for ever in the golden glow of the footlights." [32] Young Hyacinth Robinson's vision of his destiny is as prescient as the young Wordsworth's in Book IV of *The Prelude*. His shift to the golden glow of political footlights does not even require a shift of vocabulary: "Hyacinth waited for the voice that should allot him the particular part he was to play. His ambition was to play it with brilliancy, to offer an example—an example that might survive him—of pure youthful, almost juvenile, consecration" (p. 233).

Hyacinth's formal consecration to the cause of revolution is the result of a flamboyantly theatrical speech, and his final suicide is an equally stagy/political gesture which deftly makes him a martyr to both parties. We learn of it in a wonderfully grandiose curtain line: "Mr. Robinson has shot himself through the heart. He must have done it while you were fetching the milk" (p. 511). In a novel soaked in the aura of footlights, the Princess herself is of course the primary diva, embodying the worlds of politics and the stage from the moment we first see her at the theater, a covert revolutionary outshining the actors. But though the Princess incarnates the complex performances of public life, her companion Madame Grandoni speaks with the same intimate authority as Olive's sister did: "Christina has many faults, but she hasn't that one [of lying]; that's why I can live with her. She'll speak the truth always" (p. 210). Immersing her private needs in "the golden glow of the footlights" of a political mission, she generates, grotesquely, honesty and truth. She is an illuminatingly inverted descendant of Tennyson's Princess Ida, who, in her equally gorgeous confluence of feminism, education, and art, was simply, compellingly, false. By the time we reach James's Olive Chancellor and Princess Casamassima, a woman's entrance in the historical theater introduces an undeniable new truth which no dashing intrusion of a prince can gainsay.[33]

The budding actress Miriam Rooth in *The Tragic Muse* is James's final confrontation of the public woman in this group of novels. Though Miriam is not a secret political organizer, she is subtly balanced against her analogue, the thoroughly political Julia Dallow, whose irritated fiancé asks wearily of her pageant of houseparties: "Must you *always* live in public, Julia?"[34] Similarly, Peter Sherringham, whose role is that of a more civilized Basil demanding that the public woman subside "naturally" into being private and possessed, defines the monstrosity of the perpetually performing Miriam: "It struck him abruptly that a woman whose only being was to 'make believe,' to make believe that she had any and every being that you liked, that would serve a purpose, produce a certain effect, and whose identity resided in the continuity of her personations, so that she had no moral privacy, as he phrased it to himself, but lived in a high wind of exhibition, of figuration— such a woman was a kind of monster, in whom of necessity there would be nothing to like, because there would be nothing to take hold of" (p. 150).

But when Peter confronts Miriam with his discovery that she is a monster, her answer is the calm: " 'Yes, perhaps,' the girl replied, with her head on one side, as if she were looking at the pattern. 'But I'm very honest' " (p. 167). As with Olive and the Princess, honesty is born, not submerged, in the public woman, an assertion made with greater assurance in each of the three novels. The most assured, ebullient, and untragic of the trilogy of the 1880s, *The Tragic Muse* rewrites and exposes the controversial ending of *The Bostonians*, in which Basil invades the New York theater where Verena is about to give a crucial speech, breaks her frail will, and steers her into marriage, leaving Olive to mollify the enraged audience as Verena secretly weeps into her hood.

In *The Tragic Muse* Miriam and Peter replay in a comic key the backstage confrontation between Verena and Basil. Here, however, the performing woman can assert the integrity of her existence: Miriam/Verena not only refuses to marry Peter/Basil, but meets his soothing platitudes with a series of elegantly stinging retorts that are unfortunately beyond the perpetually mesmerized Verena. Her final turn of the screw is her selection of the unsavory Basil Dashwood as her husband-manager. Like Matthias Pardon in *The Bostonians*, Dashwood embodies the shrewd professional acumen of the untalented; it may be James's final comment on the romance of the old South and the public supremacy of the male sex to bestow Basil's name on a petty operator who gets the girl and gives up his career to manage hers. The lucidity and grace of the later novel lend shape to some of the convolutions of the earlier one.

The Tragic Muse opens with the portentous announcement that "All art is one" (p. 16), and the art of politics is included in this statement of theme. As one essay puts it: "Actor and politician have this in common, that they can only function in relation to an audience; that to catch this audience both speak and feign 'parts' that have been written and devised for them by others—they must be what they are not." In its sense of this alliance between two public arts that tell a perverse but immutable "truth," *The Bostonians* is indeed "a backstage drama—will the show go on?"[35]

Seen in this context of performance and triumphant theatricality, the relation between Olive and Verena is less purely a matter of submerged eroticism than it may seem. Its "unnatural" intensity is a consequence not simply of its implicit alliance with "the love that dare not speak its name," but of the magically unnatural generation of creativity and art, the love between impresario and star. The eighties and nineties abounded in impassioned, unnatural unions such as those between Henry Irving and Ellen Terry, Henry Higgins and Eliza Doolittle, and Svengali and Trilby, whose agents literally invade each others' personalities to produce the "new truth" that is not a child. In depicting such a relation between two women, James made the process of mutual identification more subtle and complex, for when Olive flings herself onstage after Verena's defection, her desperate appearance suggests that of the archetypal mousy understudy who becomes a star.

James has carefully prepared us for a surprising triumph on Olive's part. Shortly after the widely quoted passage on her masochistic hunger for martyrdom, he adds quietly: "Olive had a fear of everything, but her greatest fear was of being afraid. She wished immensely to be generous, and how could one be generous unless one ran a risk? She had erected it into a sort of rule of conduct that whenever she saw a risk she was to take it; and she had frequent humiliations at finding herself safe after all" (p. 14). In a sense, Olive's greatest martyrdom would be personal acclaim by the audience she despises; but her fastidiousness hides the yearning of the secret ham. At the gathering at Miss Birdseye's, she gibbers nervously to Mrs. Farrinder: "I want to enter the lives of women who are lonely, who are piteous. I want to be near to them—to help them. I want to do something—oh, I should like so to speak!" (p. 36)

And later on, the thorough trooper Verena evaluates one of Olive's self-forgetting harangues: "Why, Olive, you are quite a speaker yourself! . . . You would far surpass me if you would let yourself go" (pp. 139-140). For Olive, letting herself go and letting Verena go may be equally therapeutic means of realizing her vision of woman standing alone and "clinging to a great, vivifying, redemptory idea"—which she spreads over her age.

If the impresario Olive is a secret star, pliant Verena is closer to Trilby than to Victoria Woodhull. She enters the novel performing under her father's mesmeric influence, and in her subsequent conversions to Olive's new truth and Basil's old one, she vacantly replaces the compulsion of Selah Tarrant's initial Svengali. When she falls under Basil's counterspell at the end of the novel, she explains her abdication in the Trilby-like phrase, "I was paralyzed" (p. 460). Basil sees her not as the medium of an ideology, but as a complete performer; he drinks her voice in with no sense of the words it utters. In their futile debate toward the end of the novel, both dismiss the mighty "cause" as if it were mere program music: " 'I confess I should like to know what is to become of all that [talented] part of me, if I retire into private life, and live, as you say, simply to be charming for you. I shall be like a singer with a beautiful voice (you have told me yourself my voice is beautiful), who has accepted some decree of never raising a note. Isn't that a great waste, a great violation of nature?' . . . 'Believe me, Miss Tarrant, these things will take care of themselves. You won't sing in the Music Hall, but you will sing to me; you will sing to every one who knows you and approaches you' " (pp. 401-402).

This recurrent impression of Verena as a singer in her passive, compulsive response to the influence of others may not be purely coincidental. James became friendly with George Du Maurier in 1884, the year *The Bostonians* was begun; ten years later the stunning success of *Trilby* as novel and play was a bitter pill: " 'See what it is to take the measure of the foot—as we say—of the gross Anglo-Saxon public,' he remarked to Daudet. 'The rare Meredith is not that kind of shoemaker—nor,' added Henry, 'the poor James.' "[36]

James's rare ungraciousness presumably stems from the

fact that years before, he himself had been offered the idea for *Trilby*—and rejected it. In 1889 he wrote in his notebook: "Last evening before dinner I took a walk with G. Du Maurier, in the mild March twilight (there was a blessed sense of spring in the air), through the empty streets near Porchester Terrace, and he told me over an idea of his which he thought very good—and I do too—for a short story—he had already mentioned [it] to me—a year or two ago, in a walk at Hampstead, but it had passed from my mind. Last night it struck me as curious picturesque, and distinctly usable: though the want of musical knowledge would hinder *me* somewhat in handling it."[37] But it is just possible that the success of *Trilby* stung him so much not because he had refused the idea of a beautiful mesmerized girl who is a mere "subject" for the "sacred fire" of others, but because he had already taken and transplanted it from music to politics in a novel of his country that no one had liked.

Verena's kinship with Trilby further undermines the authenticity of Basil's chivalry and his love: conventional marriage offers only escape from the truth of the performing self. Moreover, males lack the power to endow a woman with fulfillment, for in a world where the public faces of art and politics are so nearly interchangeable, the men must struggle for billing in an increasingly feminized history, as we see the journalist Matthias Pardon doing throughout: "Besides, it was a woman's question; what they wanted was for women, and it should be by women. It had happened to the young Matthias more than once to be shown the way to the door, but the path of retreat had never yet seemed to him so unpleasant. He was naturally amiable, but it had not hitherto befallen him to be made to feel that he was not—and could not be—a factor in contemporary history; here was a rapacious woman who proposed to keep that favorable setting for herself" (p. 147). Olive's banishment of Pardon has the historical audacity of Elizabeth Cady Stanton's "woman herself must do this work," and under this stern injunction the men equate surviving at all with getting one's name in the paper. If the struggle for existence is the struggle to break into print, "it is to the world of Matthias Pardon, and Selah Tarrant, we have to look for the most consistent portrait of the age."[38] Tarrant's hope of heaven embodies the pathos of these peripheral men: "The wish of his soul was that he might be interviewed; that made him hover at the editorial elbow" (p. 106).

In his awareness that a self-promoting society requires him to publish or perish, Basil Ransom is no different from the grubbier Tarrant and Pardon. If his obsessive dogmatizing links him to Olive, his feeling that the acceptance of a single essay by an obscure periodical makes "an era in my life" sufficient to justify his existence forges a stronger link with the other men in the novel, who in their pathetic print-bound obscurity anticipate the tenants on Gissing's *New Grub Street*. Indeed, Verena's first involuntary tenderness for Basil comes when he exposes to her his humiliatingly unpublished state: he reminds her of her unpublished father, whom she is accustomed to pity and obey. It is no wonder that in the final abdication of her flight with him, her mother springs out of her habitual torpor and hurls herself upon Verena in a "furious onset" of rage, prayers, and tears: she knows better than Olive the hopelessness of such a marriage. Rather than marrying the "normal" antagonist and double of twisted unnatural Olive, Verena retreats to the home cycle by eloping with a more romantically colored version of her shady father.

It is as debatable as the nature of history itself whether "the age" in *The Bostonians* belongs to its scrambling men, who maintain a tenuous identity as long as they have the hope of seeing their names on a page, or to the visionary gleam of its women. For Basil, "it's a feminine, a nervous, hysterical, chattering, canting age . . . which, if we don't soon look out, will usher in the reign of mediocrity, of the feeblest and flattest and the most pretentious that has ever been" (p. 343). Allowing Basil his own hysterical and canting tone, "the age" we see does seem implacably possessed by its variegated women. [39] But insofar as Olive embodies it, its "chattering, canting" rhetoric disappears into the silence that is associated with her throughout. The mutuality of her "dumb embrace" with Verena (p. 310) is held against Basil's surely more "hysterical" concept of marriage: "if he should become her husband he should know a way to strike her dumb" (p. 329). At Marmion, Dr. Prance describes the women's nervousness as stillness: "you can hear the silence vibrate" (p. 416). Shortly thereafter, we do: "Verena leaned her head back and closed her eyes, and for an hour, as nightfall settled in the room, neither of the young women spoke. Distinctly, it was a kind of shame" (p. 425). The silence defines the shame, of their intensity and of Verena's betrayal. But most portentous is the "quick, complete, tremendous silence" which greets Olive's appearance onstage at the end, where the book leaves her.

This silence that confronts Olive is a majestic question mark. It is so common to assume that her first performance is her lifelong humiliation[40] that critics of James seem to have succumbed to the intensity of her own self-hate: "I am going to be hissed and hooted and insulted!" (p. 463). But perhaps, after all, the waves part for Olive. The dramatic hush she creates looks forward to that moment in *The Turn of the Screw* (1898) when the governess first sees an apparition: "It was as if, while I took in, what I did take in, all the rest of the scene had been stricken with death. I can hear again, as I write, the intense hush in which the sounds of evening dropped. The rooks stopped cawing in the golden sky and the friendly hour lost for the unspeakable minute all its voice."[41] Such a silence marks an unnatural change in the universe. The ghost in the garden, Olive on the stage, reveal an invasion of commonality by an equivocal power that must change the present and the future and throw the past in new perspective. Whatever the value of such an invasion, it is an irrevocable emergence.

The very end of the novel juxtaposes Olive's "rush to the front" with Verena's hidden tears. This important moment seems to repeat itself in a majestic passage written in 1905 for the New York edition of *The Princess Casamassima*, in which the Princess repudiates Hyacinth's adoration: "And she turned from him as with a beat of great white wings that raised her straight out of the bad air of the personal. It took her up too high, it put an end to their talk; expressing an indifference to what it might interest him to think of her to-day, and even a contempt for it, which brought tears to his eyes" (p. 495). This quasi-mystical ascent away from nature and regret crystallizes the tone of Olive's debut. "Like the heroine that she was" (p. 462), she seems to balloon into the purity of history, while "the bad air of the personal," with concurrent lies and tears, mourns its loss.

James's historical prophecy about women sweeping over and embodying his virgin land has been muddled by the subsequent diminution of feminism after the vote was finally gained. It was easy for later writers to assume that feminism was as morbid an eruption to James as it seemed to them, but a remark he made about the British suffrage movement in 1908 might stand as his own diagnosis of his Bostonians: "All the signs of the beginning of a great movement, in spite of the ease of ridiculing them for desiring martyrdom on such cheap terms, 'for the terms *are* cheap.' "[42] The martyrdom, not the movement, is legitimately ridiculous; this female thirst for self-destruction has recently been given the soberer, more secular label, "fear of success." James's freedom from defensive derision is underlined by the fact that, in 1908, passionate support began in Boston for the militant suffragists in England; a torpid New England party was revivified by its adoption of British tactics and its adulatory response to the Pankhursts.[43] Though by that time the novel was a far-off failure to him, James may have remained a Bostonian despite himself. His respect for the new militancy of the crusade suggests the sadly anachronistic and ahistorical nature of some later assumptions about his attitudes: "[T]he doctrinaire demand for the equality of the sexes may well seem to promise but a wry and constricted story, a tale of mere eccentricity . . . It would seem to be susceptible only of comic treatment, and the comedy it seems to propose is not of an attractive kind[.]"[44] But to James, women's demands were less funny than inexorable. The bitter comedy lay in the movement's self-subversion of its own strength.

When Olive furiously mounts the stage, readers may assume, consciously or unconsciously, that James wrote out a terrible prevision of his own devastating debut ten years later, when, as the author of *Guy Domville,* he was so "hissed and hooted and insulted" that he never recovered from the exposure. In Leon Edel's magnificent description of this event, the theater and politics converge irrevocably in the crisis of James's adult life:

> He brought James on, leading him by the hand. The novelist, having heard applause, came forward shyly, hesitantly; and at that moment the gallery exploded. Jeers, hisses, catcalls were followed by great waves of applause from that part of the audience which esteemed James and had recognized the better qualities of the play. *The two audiences had declared war.* The intellectual and artistic elite answered the howls of derision; the howls grew strong in defiance. This was an unusual kind of passion in an English theatre, where feelings were so seldom expressed. "All the forces of civilization in the house," Henry later wrote to his brother, "waged a battle of the most gallant, prolonged and sustained applause with the hoots and jeers and catcalls of the roughs, whose roars (like those of a cage of beasts at some infernal zoo) were only exacerbated by the conflict."[45]

For Edel, the trauma of James's life was an incident in the British class struggle, as the "two audiences," the elite and the roughs, battled for possession of the innocent artist. His excruciating debut was a symptom of the class war in his adopted country; but Olive's equally vulnerable entrance in the city she personifies is a touchstone of American feminism, particularly in its Bostonian incarnation. In a manner that Alcott's *Work* exemplifies perfectly when Christie's triumph as a speaker brings ladies and workingwomen into communion, Boston feminism saw American womanhood as the transcendent triumphant fact that swept over differences of class, age, and race: "True empathy based on experiences common to sex rather than on those particular to class, ethnic origin or religion was the ultimate goal."[46] This one far-off divine event in Olive's life seems less a private sexual captivation of Verena than a breaking out of Brahminism into this mystical solvent of "true womanhood." Its consummation is left poised at the end of the novel, but this "great, vivifying, redemptory idea" of sex as a common purging wave over the social war differentiates James's "very *American* tale" from its British counterpart.

The Odd Women

Did you ever see such a pack of women; there seems to be nothing else; it wouldn't be a bad joke if half of them took the wrong turning and drove into the river instead of going to the Castle—and for all they'll get there![47]

George Moore, *A Drama in Muslin* (1886)

I wish girls fell down and died of hunger in the streets, instead of creeping to their garrets and the hospitals. I should like to see their dead bodies collected together in some open place for the crowd to stare at.[48]

George Gissing, *The Odd Women* (1893)

The surge of women in *The Bostonians* carries some of the mythic ferocity of a potential master race; but the superfluous masses in *The Odd Women* are defined as the body count of an oppressed class. "Virtually alone among his generation, [Gissing] seems to have perceived that the emancipation of women and the liberation of the working classes were in practice linked."[49] Both are social, not metaphysical, creations. While Olive saw men as "the other, the brutal, bloodstained, ravening *race*" (p. 37; my italics), her militant counterpart Rhoda Nunn deplores a "feeble, purposeless, hopeless woman; type of a whole *class*; living only to deteriorate" (p. 291; my italics).

Gissing's community of women is defined by its relative power in the economic market. The focus of its existence is not a historically resonant city such as Boston, but the salutary practicality of Mary Barfoot's vocational school, designed to save England's masses of unmarried women from eking out desperate lives in impoverished gentility by providing them with the skills for office work. Mary Barfoot and Rhoda Nunn, its heads, respectively embody the philanthropic and the protestant attitudes toward professional training for women without men: for Mary the school is an endowment for the socially unfortunate; for Rhoda it is a radical blow against marriage, the family, and a social system whose demands are the degradation of women. For both, as a cushion or a weapon, the school will alleviate such humiliations as those of the Madden sisters, whose chivalrous father, trusting to the appearance of equally chivalrous husbands, made no provision for them; trained only to wait for men, they now wait only for destitution and merciful death. Society's flattery has led to starvation and the dumb inability even to dream of purpose and power.

That society rather than sex is the primary fact in Gissing's novel is made clear by a diligent pupil, of whom we are clearly supposed to approve: " 'I really don't think, aunt, that there can be any solidarity of ladies with servant girls,' responded Miss Haven, encouraged by a look from Rhoda" (p. 53). Louisa May Alcott, a conscious Brahmin who wrote vigorously in *Work* about her stint as a servant girl, would not have understood this sort of feminism; but the vocational school that is Gissing's community of women is more closely knit to the cause of work than is Alcott's novel whose title celebrates it. Gissing's community is a means toward employment and inclusion, while Alcott's great reality of work breaks down at the end in favor of her crowning vision of mystical sisterhood. British communities have tended to emulate rather than escape from the larger masculine society which encloses them. It is no accident that Barbara Bodichon's *Women and Work* (1859) and Olive Schreiner's *Woman and Labour* (1911) were two of England's most influential feminist texts.

Rhoda's attempts to take the older Madden sisters in hand may at best enable them to cling to reality for a few more years and "restore their self-respect. After all, they might have a mission, a task in the world" (p. 64). In *The Bostonians*, despite some perfunctory mention of suffrage and legal reform, "a mission" was nothing so socially concrete as "a task"; it was a strange new confluence of art, religion, and reform, whose spirit was most clearly heard in its silence. But the odd women are to find their salvation by joining the world rather than saving it. Their particular Great Good Place is not the public platform of the Music Hall, but the quiet dignity of the office.

"Offices" meant perdition in Jane Austen's *Emma*. To the elegant and gifted Jane Fairfax, their sale not just of human flesh, but of human intellect, was a far more degrading transaction than marriage to the unreliable Frank Churchill. But by the time of *The Odd Women*, even the squeamish and conventional Madden sisters feel their beloved Monica, youngest of the family and its treasure, "would be better off 'in business' than in a more strictly genteel position" (p. 11). Rhoda's mission shows that the wheel has come full circle. Her work for Mary Barfoot offers not only the opportunity of "combining benevolence with business," but a great escape: "When my mother left me that little sum of money I took a bold step. I went to Bristol to learn everything I could that would help me out of school life" (p. 22). In her determined aim at "offices," the moment has come when the mission of work is cut off from its confusion with maternity.

Rhoda's escape from school takes us back to *Villette*, whose school was an escape from enclosure in the family, "the obscure nursery world" of governess or companion. Madame Beck, a sinister evolution out of the managing, administrative mother of Victorian convention, made of her school a little state which in imagination at least swelled into empire; but Gissing's administrative Mary Barfoot lacks Madame Beck's deceptive facade of bustling maternity. "She could have managed a large and complicated business, could have filled a place on a board of directors, have taken an active part in municipal government—nay, perchance in national" (p. 54). No token alliance is suggested between Mary's potential power and that of the "womanly" life or professions: the hierarchy of achievement begins with offices. The governing woman has always existed in the nineteenth-century British novel, but Gissing allows her to graduate out of the sphere and appurtenances of womanhood into the sweep of impersonal adulthood.

The sexless world of the office, the new woman's mission, is being abandoned by the men as the women exuberantly aspire to it. During their equivocal courtship the aimless and neurotic Widdowson tells Monica bitterly: "I have always hated office work, and business of every kind; yet I could never see an opening in any other direction. I have been all my life a clerk—like so many thousands of other men . . . A clerk's life—a life of the office without any hope of rising—that is a hideous fate!" (p. 43). His world-weariness is a dreary comment on the efforts of Mary and Rhoda, whose greatest triumphs come when one of their girls achieves a clerkship. Similarly Mary's enlightened cousin Everard Barfoot, who claims total sympathy for the odd women, has wearily abandoned the working world in favor of "the spectacle of existence." When Miss Haven delights her teachers by finding a place on a paper, he asks blandly: "Why doesn't she aim at some better position?" (p. 141). The hope of work that is meat and drink to the women has become dust and ashes to the men. The novel's most dampening line is Everard's "I think there is a vast amount of unnecessary labour" (p. 82). This sad distinction between the sexes is embodied in the inheritances Edmund Widdowson, Everard Barfoot, and Mary Barfoot all receive at the age of around forty. While the men can now replace a life of hated work with one of somewhat shoddy drifting, Mary is redeemed because she can begin her work at last. As the Carlylean struggle fades into the Paterian spectacle, Gissing hints that his women are preparing themselves to take over the means of production; while those of James were possessing themselves of society's mind and soul, leaving the still masculine but tangential enclave of business to the corners of history. But in both, men have relinquished command while women reach for spiritual and social control. Thus, in both, the love stories are a deflection from, rather than a fulfillment of, woman's mission. Edmund Widdowson's marriage to Monica Madden and Everard Barfoot's romance with Rhoda Nunn offer only aimlessness and angst to lives that hold at least the possibilities of meaning.

As woman's sphere of government moves from home to

school to office, the family virtually dissolves in Gissing's world, and with it the anchor of home. The dying and sadly ineffective patriarch in *In The Year of Jubilee* (1894) fulminates against one type of new woman who is semi-fallen and semi-odd: "Town and country, it's all the same. They're educated; oh yes, they're educated! What sort of wives do they make, with their education? What sort of mothers are they? Before long, there'll be no such thing as a home. They don't know what the word means. They'd like to live in hotels, and trollop about the streets day and night."[50] As the Waldorf-Astoria glittered ironically for James as the one stable community in the devouring mutability of womanized American life, so "home" in Gissing's world searches nervously for new locations beyond the family. In the same novel, Lionel Tarrant, who loves his wife, and Arthur Peachey, who hates his, find home only by escaping it: "Ah, if [Peachey] were but unmarried, what a life he might make for himself now that the day's labour brought its ample reward! He would have rooms in London, and a still, clean lodging somewhere among the lanes and fields. His ideals expressed the homeliness of the man" (p. 243).

Here and throughout Gissing's novels, home is the world beyond the hearth. For Edwin Reardon in *New Grub Street* (1891) it is not wife and baby, but the journey to Greece he and Biffen never take. In *The Odd Women* Everard entices Rhoda with the vision not of a home but of travel: " 'By the Orient Express?' . . . Rhoda [said] colouring, for the words that had escaped her meant too much for mere jest" (p. 260). Gillian Tindall sums up this drift out of seclusion and private space: "the boarding-house, that antithesis of the settled family home and classic refuge of the pretentious yet precarious, might be described as the archetypal Gissing setting: it provides such scope for social disorientation, guilty secrets, misleading appearances, unsuitable matches, affected conversations, emotion in a vacuum, and other staples of Gissing's repertoire."[51]

In *The Odd Women* the point of order and truth that home conventionally provided is Mary Barfoot's vocational school. When Rhoda holds "a slice of good beef" out to starving Virginia Madden, she transmutes the sustenance the hearth had offered to Dickens' hungry army of waifs and strays. Her community of skill and purpose staves off the desperation of the family of women. Home and the family replace Dickens' fractured city as the source of waste and devastation from which there is no redemption, but only escape. In the saga of the shabby-genteel Maddens, Cranford's "elegant economy"— and the various forms of "hunger, rebellion, and rage" that flourished in all the communities of women we have looked at—hits bottom in starvation and drunkenness, cloaked only by Virginia's pretense of vegetarianism, while the unladylike pimples on Alice's forehead proclaim the truth. The family of sisters in *Pride and Prejudice* existed to disappear; but lacking the machinery of the marriage market to absorb it into the world—even pretty Monica can meet her future husband only in an unsavory fashion that smells of disaster—such a family exists in *The Odd Women* to be destroyed. The selfless, sparkling sisterhood Mrs. Ellis seems to have envisioned in her "little community of young women" has declined into a colony of victims.[52] The death of a sister is no longer an occasion for protracted mourning and the salutary penance of not having been good enough for the departed, as it was in *Little Women*. Having lost its inner life as a unit, the family has been reduced to a Malthusian community of numbers:

> Isabel was soon worked into illness. Brain trouble came on, resulting in melancholia. A charitable institution ultimately received her, and there, at two-and-twenty, the poor hard-featured girl drowned herself in a bath.
> Their numbers had thus been reduced by half. Up to now, the income of their eight hundred pounds had served, impartially, the ends now of this, now of that one, doing a little good to all, saving them from many an hour of bitterness which must else have been added to their lot. By a new arrangement, the capital was at length made over to Alice and Virginia jointly, the youngest sister having a claim on them to the extent of an annual nine pounds. A trifle, but it would buy her clothing—and then Monica was sure to marry! Thank Heaven, she was sure to marry! (p. 12)

On the face of it, the irony of *Pride and Prejudice* condemned Mrs. Bennet's obsession with numbers, but now the only identity left to the family of women is statistical. When Widdowson tries to retain his wife by moving the three remaining sisters back to their childhood home at Clevedon, his bounty falls grimly flat, for, as far as we see, the family has no unified past to remember. But when Monica dies, and this last hope of a conventional home dies with her, the two remaining sisters are faintly restored. Feeding on the hope of Monica's baby daughter and their recurrent dream of a school, the tattered colony of women survives as a saving remnant to meet the future.

They manage to do so only with the help of Rhoda, whose school flourishes "like the green bay-tree" at the end of the novel. In the world of this novel, sisterhood can survive and nourish only if it is impersonal—a rule which may echo Olive Chancellor's implicit lesson at the end of *The Bostonians,* when she takes center stage alone. Rhoda's visit to the Maddens in Gissing's final scene carries a faint suggestion that the dilapidated familial past and the skilled new future will coalesce in the frail baby growing up in a world of women. For, like Olive, Rhoda brings honesty into a world of timid deceit. "Why should mother say what she doesn't mean?" (p. 5), she asks as a child, with ingenuous incomprehension of a self-effacing lie. Like Olive's, her honesty carries her away from nature and spontaneity into history. When she refuses to readmit a pupil who had eloped with a married man, Mary pleads for the girl on behalf of a nature opposed to Rhoda's "truth":

> "That hardness of heart is not natural to you. You have encouraged yourself in it, and you are warping a very noble character."
> "I wish only to be honest . . . [the girl] was happily *not* my sister, and I remained free to speak the simple truth about her case. It isn't personal feeling that directs a great movement in civilization." (p. 133)

In her rejection of Everard, womanhood, and love, her honesty flourishes in firm opposition to the personal and natural: "Was not her honesty, her dignity, struggling against the impulses of her heart?" (p. 325). As a standard of truth in the novel, Rhoda's honesty goes beyond the self to align her with her age, in a manner pinpointed by the newly (and equivocally) emancipated Amy Reardon in *New Grub Street:* "She was becoming a typical woman of the new time, the woman who has developed concurrently with journalistic enterprise."[53] The new woman is inseparable from the new history, which, as in *The Bostonians,* is born in the incontrovertible reality of the newspapers.

As new women, the disillusioned Amy and the crusading Rhoda assert the honesty of the headlines against the lie of books: "Best or worst, novels are all the same. Nothing but love, love, love; what silly nonsense it is! Why don't people write about the really important things of life? . . . What downright lies are accepted as indisputable! That about love being a woman's whole life; who believes it really? Love is the most insignificant thing in women's lives. It occupies a few months, possibly a year or two, and even then I doubt if it is often the first consideration" (NGS, p. 297). Rhoda erects Amy's complaint into doctrine: "If every novelist could be strangled and thrown into the sea we should have some chance of reforming women. The girl's nature was corrupted with sentimentality, like that of all but every woman who is intelligent enough to read what is called the best fiction, but not intelligent enough to understand its vice. Love—love—love; a sickening sameness of vulgarity. What is more vulgar than the ideal of novelists? They won't represent the actual world; it would be too dull for their readers. In real life, how many men and women *fall in love?* Not one in every ten thousand, I am convinced" (p. 58). This clarion call for an honesty that means honor rather than wish and need is the new religion motivating woman's emergence from the private fantasy of a novel to the shared dailiness of journalistic truth. The nexus of women's community is no longer the privacy of love and dreams but the clarity of historical reality.

As in *The Bostonians,* it is the men who carry into this community the disease of love, nature, and lies. Widdowson calls Monica from a dreary laboring life to traditional patriarchal marriage, a name that means bereavement, and an aimless, random, excluded life devoid of the roots only Mary and Rhoda could give. She agrees to marry him in a chapter caustically titled "At Nature's Bidding," from which "The Joys of Home" and "The First Lie" follow inexorably. The commentary tells us that, if Monica transmits the lies, Widdowson is their source: "She despised herself, and hated him for the degradation which resulted from his lordship over her" (p. 210).

The assumptions of patriarchal marriage are made to seem at this moment of history both insane and estranged, but Everard's magniloquent proposal of a "free union" has scarcely more integrity. Like Monica's, Rhoda's temptation into love is the beginning of lies and concealment, as she tries in humiliatingly indirect fashion to worm information out of openhearted Millie Vesper. The lovers' final rupture rests on Everard's misleading equivocation about his harmless relation with Monica, with whom Rhoda thinks he is in love; but even without this mutual incomprehension, the free union is a chimera, founded on deceit: "Legally married; the proposal of free union was to be a test only. Loving her as he had never thought to love, there still remained with him so much of the temper in which he first wooed her that he could be satisfied with nothing short of unconditional surrender. Delighting in her independence of mind, he still desired to see her in complete subjugation to him, to inspire her with unreflecting passion" (p. 261). This apparent alternative to Monica's degradation crumbles into a more exotic variant of it; the freedom of the Orient Express becomes a lure for "unconditional surrender." Finally, the association of men with dissimulation dissolves entirely into Bevis' interminable babble of protestations to Monica. When she begs him to rescue her from her marriage, he spews out romantic exaltations designed only to get rid of her. Widdowson's tormented "Hypocrite! Liar!" (p. 244), which seems to be the marriage motif in this novel, could apply equally well to marriage's apparent alternatives. Only among the shabby unenlightened, such as the childlike, belated union of Mr. and Mrs. Mickelwaite, is romance still reality.

The central characters are left only with the female community's messianic promise: "It's better to be a woman, in our day. With us all the joy of advance, the glory of conquering. Men have only material progress to think about. But we—we are winning souls, propagating a new religion, purifying the earth!" (p. 87). Mary is too polite to add to this Olive Chancellor-ish cry that the women are appropriating "material progress" as a primary goal as well. Later on, Everard will humbly accept his cousin's identification with the age, asking with the futility of James's Matthias Pardon that she put him, too, in league with history: "You make me feel that I am in touch with the great movements of our time. It's delightful to know you. But come now, isn't there any way in which I could help?" (pp. 141-142). Both Mary and Rhoda can love Everard as passionately as the earnest David Copperfield once loved a Dora who was incompetent to sharpen a pen for his strenuously exacting work, but he cannot be absorbed into the new religion. He is finally "not quite serious" (p. 326); like the other men in the novel, his lack of authenticity forbids him to embrace this inexorable new phase of evolution. As Gissing perceives it, human advance still depends on the importance of being earnest.

This new religion which spurns nature in favor of honesty and work is pervaded with a subtle theatricality. Unlike James, Gissing felt nothing of the glamour of the stage; he seemed to link it instead to encroaching democracy: "One of the consequences of this prejudice was a pronounced dislike of theaters and plays, which he associated with crowds."[54] Accordingly, his *Charles Dickens* (1898) depicts the great man's theatricality as a murderous blot on the scutcheon: "The garish lights had done their work upon him, but he did not recognize it; he imagined that he had but to sit down in his house at Gadshill, and resume the true, the honourable occupation of his life."[55] But "the honourable occupation" of Rhoda's life is the religion which is at one with theater. In her first and final interviews with Everard, she greets him as actress and nun: "He wondered how she would present herself, in what costume. Her garb proved to be a plain dress of blue serge, certainly not calculated for effect [of course this drab unconcern is itself an effect]; but his eye at once distinguished the fact that she had arranged her hair as she wore it when he first knew her, a fashion subsequently abandoned for one that he thought more becoming" (p. 323).

Everything about Rhoda is a public statement, rather than the private secret which to her is at one with a lie. She defines her life according to the truth it will illustrate rather than the experience it might contain: "She herself was no longer one of the 'odd women'; fortune had—or seemed to have—been kind to her; none the less her sense of a mission remained. No longer an example of perfect female independence, and unable therefore to use the same language as before, she might illustrate woman's claim of equality in marriage.—If her experience proved no obstacle" (p. 270). As in Miriam Rooth's formation into an actress, experience exists only to feed one's power of illustration. The personal and felt becomes obsolete in the face of the impersonal community that is both church and theater.

This community of women exists only as a motivating dream. Never do we see Mary Barfoot's vocational school functioning, and it is difficult to imagine how actual classes in typing could bear all this ecstacy and hope. Yet though the community is more phantom Grail than actual Camelot, relations between women take on a quiet primacy that makes of them a more fundamental motivating force than "natural" love between the sexes. Monica marries in large part to escape the ubiquity of a world of women, since her life has passed from the starved isolation of her sisters to the vulgar intrusions of the dormitory to Mary and Rhoda's "old maid factory." Yet her hysterical passion for Bevis springs from the loss of this very female anchor: "Perhaps the reason was that she felt herself more hopelessly an outcast from the world of honourable women, and therefore longed in her desolation for the support of a man's love" (p. 245). Even conventional Monica needs women more than she does men. When she dies, it is a matter of course that her child will go to her sisters, ill and unreliable as she knows them to be, rather than to its rich and well-intentioned father.

For Rhoda, too, the course of her one love in life is determined by her awareness of other women. She exults when it is offered because it will put her in truer relation with her own sex, rather than intimacy with the other: "Secretly she deemed it a hard thing never to have known that common triumph of her sex. And, moreover, it took away from the merit of her position as a leader and encourager of women living independently. There might be some who said, or thought, that she made a virtue of necessity . . . Offer what he might, she would not accept it; but the secret chagrin that was upon her would be removed. Love would no longer be the privilege of other women. To reject a lover in so many respects desirable, whom so many women might envy her, would fortify her self-esteem, and enable her to go forward in the chosen path with firmer tread" (pp. 147-148). Ultimately she adheres to this program, insisting on marriage when it seems best for her image, and acquiescing to a free union, which she knows Everard no longer wants, because she knows Mary and Mrs. Cosgrove would support her. Bonds with her own sex determine her feelings for the other.

This primacy of women is at one with the fact that in their great movements and their petty destitutions, only they are seen as movers and victims of history. Alice and Virginia's dinner of mashed potatoes and milk is not an isolated humiliation; Alice makes it an analogue of the greatest famine and the greatest revolt her century had known: " 'The Irish peasantry live almost entirely on that,' croaked Alice, 'and they are physically a fine race' " (p. 20). This wretched consolation throws the sisters in league with a diminished but dangerous land struggling for self-rule, and with another novel about superfluous women in history that Gissing may have known: George Moore's *A Drama in Muslin: A Realistic Novel* (1886).

The 'muslin martyrs" in Moore's Irish novel, desperate girls struggling to survive in an increasingly impoverished marriage market, have no "mission" to remove them from the humiliating facelessness of superfluity: "There is no hope in life for them but the vague hope of a husband" (p. 267). Their degradation goes beyond the Madden sisters' in that they have become the "good beef" Virginia merely longs for. Preparing for the Spinsters' Ball, which quickly turns into a rout, one of them sings feverishly:

Five-and-forty spinsters baked in a pie!
When the pie was opened the maids began to sing.
Wasn't that a dainty dish to set before the king?   (p. 85)

Unlike that of *Pride and Prejudice*, the hopeless waiting of the girls is presented explicitly as a historical rather than a moral condition. As the turbulent peasants who constitute the Land League fight to take over the soil they have worked for centuries, the gentry is stripped of its sustenance and the class into which the girls must marry disappears. Alice Barton, the novel's "plain" heroine, sees her encroaching spinsterhood looking at her in the death of the Irish landscape: "Cold and weary, she sat watching the night falling over the waste of immaculate snow . . . But through her gazing eyes the plain of virginal snow, flecked with the cold blue shadows of the trees, sank into her soul, bleaching it of every hope of joy; and, gathering suggestions from the surroundings, she saw a white path extending before her—a sterile way that she would have to tread—a desolate way, with no songs in its sullen air, but only sad sighs, and only stainless tears, falling, falling, ever falling—falling silently" (pp. 97-98). The snow is general all over Ireland, as the hidden desolation that is Moore's image of spinsterhood spreads out into a national emblem as pervasive as the shroud of snow which is national lovelessness in Joyce's "The Dead."[56]

Moore continually juxtaposes these hopeless young women in white, whom nothing unites but wistful memories of their girlhood unity in a convent and the receding hope of husbands, with the threat of the peasant uprising: "The history of a nation as often lies hidden in social wrongs and domestic griefs as in the story of revolution, and if it be for the historian to narrate the one, it is for the novelist to dissect and explain the other; and who would say which is of the most vital importance —the thunder of the people against the oppression of the Castle, or the unnatural sterility, the cruel idleness of mind and body of the muslin martyrs who cover with their white skirts the shames of Cork Hill?" (pp. 203-204).

But potentially at least, the women are not as passive as they seem in this tableau. The hunchback Lady Cecilia Cullen, a life-hating, man-hating religious mystic whose lesbianism becomes her fervent creed, is luridly presented, not as a freakish outgrowth of this unnatural world, but as its representative product. With Alice, who seems, like Olive Chancellor, to be a spinster to the marrow of her bones, the manless Cecilia has the mantle of the zeitgeist bestowed on her:

> but beneath the great feminine tide there is an under-current of hatred and revolt. This is particularly observable in the leaders of the movement; women who in the tumult of their aspirations . . . forget the immutability of the laws of life, and with virulent virtue and protest condemn love —that is to say love in the sense of sexual intercourse— and proclaim a higher mission for woman than to be the mother of men: . . . But as the corporeal and incorporeal hereditaments of Alice Barton and Lady Cecilia Cullen were examined fully in the beginning of this chapter, it is only necessary to here indicate the order of ideas—the moral atmosphere of the time—to understand the efflorescence of the two minds, and to realise how curiously representative they are of this last quarter of the nineteenth century.   (pp. 195-196)

The shrill war between endorsement and condemnation of these unnatural but typical women produces the cul-de-sac of the end of the novel: the revolt of the peasants fizzles out, and so does that of the muslin martyrs. Cecilia, who by this time is virtually frothing at the mouth, retreats to the convent which was presented as a quasi-idyllic but unreal sisterhood in the opening scene; and Alice is married off in a particularly unsavory way by capturing the doctor of her pretty sister, a belle who has always outshone her but who is now hideously ill as a result of her own and her mother's follies. The "bloody tenacious mucus" over her sister's "once almost jewel-like teeth" propels Alice to the safety of a smug and arty Kensington suburb, and with dignified noblesse oblige, she takes the wasted old maid in at the end, able to be a sister now that the marriage war is over.

In escaping the celibate, embattled community at home, Alice retreats from her country and time. Her marriage is a denial of her age, rather than a renewal of it: "Of humanity we must not think too much; for the present we can best serve it by learning to love each other" (p. 324). Though surrounded now by sardonic qualifications, this Dickensian solution must serve against the waste of women who are not waiting for history to redeem them, as they were in *Pride and Prejudice*, but who have become barren history itself.

Gissing's vision of the odd woman as an expression of her age's ideals rather than an isolate within them is at one with Moore's. As James's Bostonians appropriated the mind of America, so the muslin martyrs and the odd women are dignified by becoming national and epochal emblems. But the "new religion" of Mary and Rhoda, like that of Olive Chancellor, carries the possibility that the community of odd women may create history as well as express it, that instead of praying for redemption as Moore's women do, they can become redeemers themselves. In the novels examined in this chapter, sisterhood is no longer an island of personal sanctity in a world of war; it is an impersonal community that hones one to impersonal ends.

This shift of direction is most apparent in a scene near the end of *The Odd Women* in which Monica confronts Rhoda with Everard's fidelity and her own despair. The scene probably owes something to the similar confrontation between Dorothea Casaubon and Rosamond Lydgate in *Middlemarch*, in which the desperate Rosamond puts self aside to bring Will and Dorothea together. In *Middlemarch* the meeting creates an oasis of fellowship in a dim and tangled world; when the women clutch each other "as if they had been in a shipwreck," the novel's snarled relations briefly cohere in their embrace.

Monica's confession results in no such sobbing intensity of communion, nor does it alter the characters' relation; instead, it fuels Rhoda's vocation "to live alone and work steadily for a definite object" (p. 37). When told that the man she loves loves her, she incorporates this triumph into her self-sufficiency: "Scornful austerity had given place to a smile, stern indeed, but exultant" (p. 313). And her inspiriting advice to the wretched girl moves her to the solitary glory of vocation, not communion: "Herself strongly moved, Rhoda had never spoken so impressively, had never given counsel of such earnest significance. She felt her power in quite a new way, without touch of vanity, without posing or any trivial self-consciousness. When she least expected it an opportunity had come for exerting the moral influence on which she prided herself, and which she hoped to make the ennobling element of her life. All the better that the case was one calling for courage, for contempt of vulgar reticences; the combative soul in her became stronger when faced by such conditions" (pp. 315-316). Rhoda is so fixed in her vision of power that it scarcely matters that her "moral influence" on Monica is nonexistent: her bracing prescription of health and nature is irrelevant to the girl's pitiful, inevitable death in childbirth. Sisterhood no longer belongs to the personal and solicitous, but to the visionary and the cosmic sphere. If the present is enfeebled, the future is founded upon a rock.

Despite its intensity of purpose, the relation between Mary and Rhoda is equally impersonal. When Mary hesitantly asks Rhoda whether she has ever been in love, a long-standing reticence is obviously being pierced; and even here the women need the excuse of their prodigal pupil to venture into what James called "the bad air of the personal." Monica reminds Everard that "A woman may be as much a mystery to another woman as she is to a man" (p. 195), and this reserve is important in discussing possibilities of lesbianism in The Odd Women.[57] Mary and Rhoda are bound by a militant vision of a life beyond desire, and in such a cause sexuality, even personality, is allowed only oblique appearance. Diagnoses of lesbianism bring a misleading emphasis to our understanding of this group of novels. Despite the silent possibility of "a kind of shame" between Olive and Verena, or the fiercely erotic mysticism in which Cecilia encircles Alice in A Drama in Muslin, sexuality is one ingredient of a vision which aspires to the lonely self-transcendence of the religious spirit. Crusading or defeated, these communities of women are knit together by a visionary allegiance whose sphere is less the bedroom than the battlefield, and they are fed by the honesty that is not intimacy, but solitude and honor.

There is an unbridgeable temperamental gap between James, whose sly laughter seems at times to expose the funniness of human sexuality itself, and Gissing, in his grim display of society's oddities and victims. But alone in our canon they endow communities of women with the impersonal virtues of men, allowing them to stand as incarnations of honesty in a world of lies and shifting appearances. For all their antihumanity, only these male-conceived communities become "an image of this mighty world" rather than an excrescence on it. Whatever homosexuality they convey is a far more muted and tacit presence than the consecrated "marriage" between Ishmael and Queequeg which is death and life in Moby-Dick; but like that of Melville's Pequod, the final images of James's Bostonians and Gissing's odd women are collective and representative, rather than private and fulfilled.

In our tradition, only these two male writers endow their women with the burden of historical reality communities of men assume as a matter of course. This anomaly accounts in part for their odd tone, somewhere between laughter and lament, vision and nightmare, as a coming reign of women seems about to embody humanity evolving beyond itself, lifting the race beyond egoism and need to the pinnacle of transcendence or the void of extinction. This paradoxical promise of elevation or death by a world of women gives its tone to Gissing's unpublished essay "Hope of Pessimism" (October 1882), which ends like The Odd Women with an equivocal prophecy: "a childless race will dedicate its breath to the eternal silence, and Mercy will have redeemed the world."[58] Endowed like Gissing's personified Pessimism with the power of truth, these communities of women make up "a childless race" that is the last breath of the future in a weary century and an aging world.

A World at War:
One Big Miss Brodie

Pablo Picasso. *Les Demoiselles D'Avignon*
The Museum of Modern Art, New York; acquired through
the Lillie P. Bliss Bequest

O Lysistrata, Peace sworn on a buckler!

Union among women, perceived by every generation that experiences it as unprecedented in history, is one of the unacknowledged fruits of war. The Civil War fratricide generated the charmed domestic sorority of *Little Women* as well as a postwar America peerlessly possessed by Henry James's "woman produced by a women-made society alone." Yet feminists and nonfeminists alike claimed that the purity and harmony of her nature, together with her isolation from the greed of history, endowed woman with the unique mission of ending forever the wars that deprived and relieved her of men: the task of the newly banded community was to root out the human evil that was one source of its power. Caught in such a contradiction, as she proselytizes a millennium of peace in recurrent martial imagery, Olive Chancellor can only remain dumb in the face of Basil's taunt that "in spite of your expressions of horror you delight in the shock of battle" (p. 92). It is from such shocks that her purified community is born.

This paradox of war and peace reaches back to Aristophanes' dark comedy. Though one editor of his *Lysistrata* describes the pity "of the plight of women, whose lives war leaves sunless and empty," once the army of wives has captured the Acropolis they revel in their new militarism: "ah, ha, you thought it was a herd of slaves You had to tackle, and you didn't guess The thirst for glory ardent in our blood."[1] As the organization of women moved in the nineteenth century from comic conceit to troubling reality, women's gratitude toward "the shock of battle" they claimed to deplore became more intense and more confused.

Mary A. Livermore's millennial article "Coöperative Womanhood in the State" (1891) is a prophetic blueprint for the divided nature of the female communities two world wars would produce. In her exuberant hope for woman's emergence into public, political life, Mrs. Livermore looks thankfully back to the Civil War which brought women in league for the first time with each other and with their government: "The barriers of sect, caste, and conventionalism, which had heretofore separated them, were burned away in the fervid heat of their loyalty." Now that war has taught women "to draw more closely together, to keep in touch with each other in thought and purpose, to unite in an organization 'superior to any existing society,' " she dreams of an organization within the national government of "a republic of women, duly organized and officered, . . . [which] would train women for the next great step in the evolution of humanity, when women shall sit side by side in government, and the nations shall learn war no more."[2] In proposing to abolish war, this nobly presiding republic of women is turning against the violent cause of its own birth.

Counterpointing the pacifist organizations that presented a frail, largely female bulwark against World War I was a note of exaltation at the Amazonian countries created by the war, whose military elation spread from the suffrage battle to the nation at large: "Throughout my stay in England I searched for, but could not find, the self-effacing spinster of former days. In her place was a capable woman, bright-eyed, happy. She was occupied and bustled at her work. She jumped on and off moving vehicles with the alertness if not the unconsciousness of the expert male. . . England was a world of women— women in uniforms."[3] The force that destroys men brings power and vigor to the community of women, and the dream of its postwar inheritance.

These images of war and peace come together in Charlotte Perkins Gilman's Utopian fantasies, "Herland" (1915) and "With Her in Ourland" (1916). Herland is a placid Shangri-la "in a state of perfect cultivation," "an enormous garden" of wise women whose men destroyed each other in a war at the beginning of the Christian era.[4] Blessed by a mysteriously sympathetic power with the gift of parthenogenesis, this land of universal mothers generates a consecrated civilization without families, kings, and priests: "All the surrounding devotion our women have put into their private families, these women put into their country and race. All the loyalty and service men expect of wives, they gave, not singly to men, but collectively to one another."[5] Such a world seems identical with Livermore's "next great step in the evolution of humanity," a republic of women, progressive yet lovingly embracing its traditions, generated by the last great battle of the species. In the sequel, these "great-minded over-mothers" are envisioned bringing a war-torn patriarchy to its knees: "And what a glorious time they will have—cleaning up the world!"[6]

Gilman's pacifism is strangely joined with gratitude toward a war that allows a country of women to inherit the earth at last. Her parables of succession are supported by the more straightforward exhortations she wrote for her periodical The Forerunner in the early years of the war: the holocaust that seems the death of civilization is for women "A World Beginning,"[7] their kingdom of heaven on earth:

> Women, united, to serve and teach,
>   Peace, wealth and power shall find;
> In every work that hands can reach,
>   Great heart and seeing mind,
> In loving labor for all and each—
>   Mothers to all mankind.[8]

"The great-minded over-mothers" of Herland are the staunch progenitors of such contemporary female Utopias as Joanna Russ's evanescent Whileaway.[9] But while Herlands presided, Whileaway, originally called "For-A-While," exists in perpetual transience; "the Might-be of our dreams," which is always a lost world, is first discovered in the act of disappearing under invasion. The greater vulnerability of this lyrically imagined planet of women in the face of insane and patriarchal Earth suggests, not a shrinking back into fragile "femininity," but the lack of a great war to provide the stimulus of a worthy antagonist and the necessity of a second birth.

One image of the twentieth century has been a community of

women healing a world whose violent adventures allow it to thrive: Florence Nightingale's mid-Victorian regiment of women has returned from far-off Scutari to transfigure and possess its homeland. But in England, characteristically, this ambiguously cleansing vision is rarely the Utopian awakening of an undiscovered country: American expansion is in England a domestic exchange. Instead of exploring and creating new frontiers, women quietly inherit the old ones.

E. M. Forster's Howards End (1910) is a prophecy of war forestalled by the intervention of a healing sisterhood. Transplanted heirs of the best romantic spirit of the German enemy, Margaret and Helen Schlegel are abetted by that "great-minded over-mother" Mrs. Wilcox in their triumph over England's ruling spirit of business, empire, and form. In their acquisition of the estate which is continuity, connection, and home, the only real battle is a brief skirmish of the sexes: "A new feeling came over [Margaret]; she was fighting for women against men. She did not care about rights, but if men came into Howards End, it should be over her body." Though Leonard Bast is sacrificed to this victory of Amazonian idealism, all is well at the end, as Helen's solicitous motherhood broods over the ritual year and Margaret nurses her husband, Mr. Wilcox, symbol of a broken, "pitiably tired" patriarchy.

Margaret and Helen's triumph, over which the dead Mrs. Wilcox presides mysteriously like a female God, is a triumph of privacy in England. Culture and the heart supplant the outer national life of "telegrams and anger"; theirs is the succession of the interior, far from the public forum of Gissing's odd women. Though their cultivation makes them feminists as a matter of course, their healing function secludes them from the historical theater: "Not out of them are the shows of history erected: the world would be a grey, bloodless place were it entirely composed of Miss Schlegels. But the world being what it is, perhaps they shine out in it like stars."[10] Such a sisterhood exists to soothe history, not to usurp it; rather than being odd women, who dream of appropriating the sources of power, the Schlegels are part-women, who tend them, Helen as exclusive mother and Margaret as exclusive wife, in a vital house somewhere between country and town in which they can monitor both but belong to neither.

Women did not soothe World War I out of existence, but the image of this community persisted. Dorothy Sayers' *Gaudy Night* (1935) opens with a resplendent picture of the stately towers of Shrewsbury, a women's college at Oxford. As the irascible outside world plunges toward World War II, Shrewsbury's devotion to the perfection of its own work makes of it an oasis of detachment, governed by wise and faithful women. But unlike the staunch mothers of Herlands, the scholars of Shrewsbury are increasingly tainted with the possibility of madness and rage as the mystery unfolds. Though Lord Peter Wimsey's elegant detection finally exonerates them of all but emotional shortsightedness, the purity of their spiritual fervor has been contaminated by the surrounding violence, and these strong women recede rather shamefacedly out of the action to be replaced, in *Busman's Honeymoon* (1937), by the self-congratulatory, cloying idyll of Lord Peter's marriage to Harriet Vane. As so often happens in cultural history, the war that seems to infuse women's solidarity with vigor and purpose leads in the end to renewed, more stringent confinement within home and its attendant mythology. Caught between the dominions of love and war, the vision of self-governing Shrewsbury fades away.[11]

Virginia Woolf's *Three Guineas* (1938) returns to this dilemma of the integrity and good faith of a community of women squeezed between national and domestic tyrannies. Turning over the question of how women can prevent war, she imagines a paradox, a "Society of Outsiders," living on a fine line that weaves between servility and power: "Simply . . . that we, daughters of educated men, are between the devil and the deep sea. Behind us lies the patriarchal system; the private house, with its nullity, its immorality, its hypocrisy, its servility. Before us lies the public world, the professional system, with its possessiveness, its jealousy, its pugnacity, its greed. The one shuts us up like slaves in a harem; the other forces us to circle, like caterpillars head to tail, round and round the mulberry tree, the sacred tree, of property."[12] To save civilization, Woolf's perpetually paradoxical Society of Outsiders must be endowed with a free world all its own.

"Let us then draw rapidly in outline the kind of society which the daughters of educated men found and join outside your society but in co-operation with its ends" (p. 106). For a moment Virginia Woolf sounds like Sarah Stickney Ellis, envisioning her experimental community of unselfish little girls and wondering how it would function. But Woolf's visionary daughters of England are to be endowed with a College "built on lines of its own," and they will have the power not merely to join but to reshape the professions to their own humane, co-operative dimensions. Like Herland, Howards End, and Sayers' early, majestic Shrewsbury, Woolf's Outsiders' Society presides untouched from its own center of gravity. Taking being and shape from the exigencies of war—"when before has an educated man asked a woman how in her opinion war can be prevented?" (p. 3)—such a Society, fresh, unenvious, unscarred, alone has the power of abolition and renewal. The guineas that will give it life are the same coin that can defeat death.

The Outsiders' Society must be secluded from the pageantry of power, academic as well as military, as the Schlegel sisters drew back from the official reality of telegrams and anger. In gathering their inheritance, in coin or house and land, these communities of women must preserve a delicate balance between purity and power, seclusion and control. But Woolf suggests in an icy sentence the difficulty of such a preservation, for "the public and the private worlds are inseparably connected; . . . the tyrannies and servilities of the one are the tyrannies and servilities of the other" (p. 142). In such a hopeless cohesion, her no-man's-land can find no air to breathe. After the Second World War, Muriel Spark returned to Woolf's vision of an Outsiders' Society of women, "built on lines of its own," with a sharp awareness of the irony inherent in its supposed inviolability between two poles of tyranny. To define the integrity of their seclusion, Spark's contemporary communities of women absorb the rapacity of history to give themselves the resonance of myth.

The Prime of Miss Jean Brodie

It is absurd in modern times that the nuns should have to get up twice in the middle of the night to sing the Matins and the Lauds. But modern times come into a historical context, and as far as I'm concerned history doesn't work. Here, in the Abbey of Crewe, we have discarded history. We have entered the sphere, dear Sisters, of mythology . . . Here, within the ambience of mythology, we have consummate satisfaction, we have peace.[13]

The Abbess of Crewe (1974)

The triumphal seizure of history by the female communities of James and Gissing culminates in Muriel Spark's Abbess' soaring rejection of the new sphere. But Spark's women are so fiercely and so firmly aware of their historical resonance that this apparent rejection is more truly a recreation of history to accord with the primacy of their own gigantic self-images. Our communities of women have passed from being the self-renouncing attendants to the covert antagonists of a history that has consistently taken the shape of literal or economic warfare. At the turn of the century they rose to being its appropriators, then, in a brief vision of hope in a calamitous time, they took the role of its redeemers. Finally, Muriel Spark's women incorporate the blackness of this history as an element in their own self-created divinity: "We are leaving the sphere of history and are about to enter that of mythology. Mythology is nothing more than history garbled; likewise history is mythology garbled and it is nothing more in all the history of man" (Ab. Crewe, p. 92). Taken together, Spark's novels shape conventional female duplicity into a new theology that assimilates the myth of history.

The Bachelors (1960), Spark's single delineation of a community of men, exists abstractly in a timeless lost city of London. Ronald's final judgment that his London is "all demonology" seems an echo of eternity, placing these fractured souls forever on a spiritual spectrum. But Spark's most fully realized community of women, the Marcia Blaine School for Girls in *The Prime of Miss Jean Brodie* (1961), attains immortality from its inextricable connection to history and time: "It is time now to speak of the long walk through the old parts of Edinburgh where Miss Brodie took her set, dressed in their deep violet coats and black velour hats with the green and white crest, one Friday in March when the school's central heating system had broken down and everyone else had been muffled up and sent home."[14] The Brodie set lives at the other pole from the bachelors' self-justifying limbo. Their collective identity springs from their alliance with particular moments and places of which they become an indelible emblem.

Jean Brodie's "prime" itself exemplifies the holiness of time: as well as designating the best and richest part of a whole, the *Oxford English Dictionary* reminds us that "prime" also means "beginning," both of the world (as in "primeval") and of the ecclesiastical holy day. Historically and spiritually, it announces a birth and a creation, not just of an individual, but of a human and divine epoch. The Marcia Blaine School seems at first even more diminutive and remote than Jane Austen's bits of ivory, as do Spark's later colonies of women, the May of Teck Club in *The Girls of Slender Means* and the Abbey of Crewe; but like the divided Jerusalem in *The Mandelbaum Gate* (1965), this apparent enclave is revealed as one of creation's vital spots. The centrality hidden within its apparent eccentric obscurity makes of it a lighter and less seemingly distressing variant of the Maud Long Ward in *Memento Mori* (1959). Beyond the dailiness of time, nature, and gender, this female geriatric ward in which the women squabble with each other as they wait to die becomes the only reality the novel's title allows. The inhabitants of the Maud Long Ward appear as stinted and remote as Hesiod's eyeless, colorless Graie, but their community possesses the overwhelming power of the first of the four last things: "Remember you must die."

Jean Brodie's girls at the beginning of life possess a similar import, though according to our previous definitions, the Brodie set is not a community at all. Composed of turbulent adolescents and a monomaniacal teacher, it may seem at first to demonstrate the impossibility of its own existence: "Buried in this largely comic novel there is a severe and uncompromising dogmatic message: that all groups, communions and institutions are false and more or less corrupting except the one that is founded on the truths of Christian orthodoxy—and even that one is not particularly attractive or virtuous."[15] But Spark's dishonest, disloyal communities may reflect what Frederick Karl sees as the passage of history: "We can no longer speak of 'community' in any nineteenth-century sense."[16] Rife with egoism and backbiting, Spark's communities may be the only saving remnants the twentieth century can accommodate.

In the Brodie set everybody is famous for something; all "heroines in the making," the girls are held together only by their lack of team spirit and their collective fantasy of Miss Brodie. There is none of the cooperative communion of the March sisterhood or of Cranford, both of them reproaches to a torn world; nor is there the abstract integrity of James's Bostonians and Gissing's odd women. Instead, vagaries of individual temperament make of the Brodie set a Blakean Giant Form: "Sandy looked back at her companions, and understood them as a body with Miss Brodie for the head. She perceived herself, the absent Jenny, the ever-blamed Mary, Rose, Eunice and Monica, all in a frightening little moment, in unified compliance to the destiny of Miss Brodie, as if God had willed them to birth for that purpose" (p. 38). The unity of the Brodie set is organic and preordained rather than loving and willed. Its indelible bond is stronger than selfhood, not so much resembling the power of Mussolini's Rome as becoming it: "It occurred to Sandy, there at the end of the Middle Meadow Walk, that the Brodie set was Miss Brodie's fascisti, not to the naked eye, marching along, but all knit together for her need and in another way, marching along" (p. 40). The invisible bond is holy as well as historic; this "body" that partakes of unseen power is also, for David Lodge, Spark's travesty of the mystical body of the Christian church.[17] State and church are reformed in a band of straggly little girls holding their heads "up, up"; under the aegis of Jean Brodie, a female community is a mystical body that partakes of all things.

Jean Brodie herself is a collective creation. The dazzle that is her identity is the conjunction of her own fantasies with those of her set, making her very being a gorgeous garble of nature and art, document and epic, history and myth: "When we go indoors we shall look on the map at Flanders, and the spot where my lover was laid before you were born" (p. 16). Unwinding her tragic romance in the garden each autumn before an audience of weeping little girls, Miss Brodie is by the book's definition within the bounds of truth when she reassures the prosaic headmistress: "We are having a history lesson" (p. 17). For throughout Spark's work, the self is inseparable from history and from the imaginative dance both evoke. In her early biography of Emily Brontë, the first passionately religious Spark heroine who can find nothing worthy of obeisance but herself, the subject of the work becomes inseparable from the dreams she generates: "All great genius attracts legend to itself. Legend is the common means of expressing the manifestation of genius in certain people, who cannot be described in ordinary terms. For this reason the legendary data which adhere to people of genius, should be respected. . . Such legend is the repository of a vital aspect of truth; and ought not to be swept aside simply because it is not ascertainable; neither, of course, should it be taken as literal truth."[18] It is in this sense that we must accept the "mendacious truth"[19] of Jean Brodie's history lessons in the garden: as that "true history" which is myth and parable, snare and transfiguration in one voice.

As a legend and a maker of "dedicated women," Jean Brodie is the divine-demonic creation of a world at war. Her new fascisti parade past lines of men who are broken and hopeless: "Sandy felt that she was not staring across the road at the endless queue of brothers, but that it was pulling her eyes toward it. She felt once more very frightened. Some of the men looked over at the girls, but without seeing them. The girls had reached the tram stop. The men were talking and spitting a great deal. Some were laughing with hacking laughs merging into coughs and ending up with spits" (p. 49). But simultaneously war's female casualties plunge into wonderful new regions: "There were legions of her kind during the nineteen-thirties, women from the age of thirty and upward, who

crowded their war-bereaved spinsterhood with voyages of discovery into new ideas and energetic practices in art or social
welfare, education or religion" (p. 52). This juxtaposition of
diseased and destitute men with elated visionary women com-
pletes the process begun in *The Bostonians* and *The Odd Women*. The ravages of history create new pioneers. The limbo of
the dole line and of these voyages of discovery are the two
faces of an age defined only as a space between wars.

A creation of past and coming wars, Jean Brodie is also the
personification of her city. "She was an Edinburgh Festival all
on her own" (p. 34); the blood of William Brodie, respectable
cabinetmaker and gallant criminal, comes alive in her "exotic
suicidal enchantment"; only she can transfigure the obscene
streets of Old Town into history; and only she shines as the city
does: "It was then that Miss Brodie looked beautiful and
fragile, just as dark heavy Edinburgh itself could suddenly be
changed into a floating city when the light was a special pearly
white and fell upon one of the gracefully fashioned streets" (p.
136).

Because she is the head of a mystical body, she can be both
Edinburgh and the cosmopolitan world beyond it, as was her
idol, Mary Queen of Scots, the national legend who had no
country: "We of Edinburgh owe a lot to the French. We are
Europeans" (p. 41). At various times in the book, she is described as Julius Caesar, Joan of Arc, the Mona Lisa, a Roman
gladiator, a Roman matron, noble Brittania, and God. The
sexual eclecticism of her epic identities reminds us again that
she is all things; and her cosmopolitanism links her to the
simultaneous dispossession and discovery of *Three Guineas:*
"[A]s a woman, I have no country. As a woman I want no
country. As a woman my country is the whole world" (p. 109).
As a woman, as the head of a mystical body, Jean Brodie personifies at once her city, her countryside, and the exotic range
of the world beyond: "Miss Brodie looked admirable in her
heather-blue tweed with the brown of a recent holiday in Egypt
still warming her skin. Miss Brodie was gazing out over Edinburgh as she spoke" (p. 130). As her life is history, so her body
is geography.

When the adult Sandy, now visited as nun and seer, is told about history in a boys' world—"We boys were very keen on Auden and that group of course. We wanted to go and fight in the Spanish Civil War. On the Republican side, of course" (p. 43)—she can only stammer confusedly, "it was all different for us." For no girl can experience the effortless transition whereby the holy wars of school become those of adult reality, as they do in Tom Brown's tribute to his friend East as he moves from cricket captain to officer: "no fellow could handle boys better, and I suppose soldiers are very like boys."[20] Similarly, Rudyard Kipling's Stalky is able to become a legendary leader in mysterious India, "the great man of his Century," by the shrewd application of schoolboy tricks to the greater school of the battlefield. But in Spark's novel, "we boys" in their idealistic assurance seem thin and facile as Miss Brodie desperately shoves Joyce Emily on a doomed train heading for Franco's Loyalists. The mad disjunction of this act reminds us that, in a girl's world, the passage from academic to political arena can take place only in "a land of enchantment" like that of *Villette* or in a mystical leap both ridiculous and dangerous.

On the face of it, politics are as hazy to the Brodie set as the Civil War was to Alcott's little women: "The Spanish Civil War was something going on outside in the newspapers and only once a month in the school debating society" (p. 144). Nevertheless, Sandy is mistaken in telling the headmistress that Miss Brodie is not attracted by politics "except as a side interest." Her conception of politics as a convenient mechanism with which she can betray the teacher whose powers are ominously appropriating God's is a more radical error, for it exposes Sandy's ignorance of the Sparkian process whereby history and myth interweave to become theology and the self. In the compulsive autobiography that is her history lesson, Jean Brodie *is* politics, just as Spark's Emily Brontë "became her own Absolute" and died of it. Sandy's disclaimer to Miss Mackay, "I'm not really interested in world affairs, . . . only in putting a stop to Miss Brodie" (p. 152), is a desperately false distinction, for the woman whose reality is inseparable from her legend is one with the "world affairs" Sandy tries to repudiate. Though she fulfills her last assignment for the teacher she betrayed and becomes famous for promulgating Miss Brodie's "Transfiguration of the Commonplace," Sandy fails to apply the doctrine of Transubstantiation on which the creed of her chosen church rests: she forgets that the head of the mystical body incarnates all the power of all the affairs of the world. Just as the world she tried to escape came pouring into her convent, so her anti-God Miss Brodie cannot be separated from the myth that is history and the history that is myth.

Spark's parable about a community of women as a fascist state is not an isolated conceit. In 1936, just as Miss Brodie is beginning to put her best energy into politics, a book appeared in the United States which equated the fascist threat with women's new tendency to organize: "We men who have reason for gratitude to some one woman, have reason also to be on our guard against women in the group, women organized, women on the march, even when the menacing confederation includes Her. . . The influence which women exercise in mass is funny when not distressing, distressing when not pernicious. To realize her true talent for inspiration, woman should be isolated." The author goes on to define a "menacing confederation" close to that of Jean Brodie's Edinburgh: "Women in the mass are now reducing men to slaves. . . Heaven defend us from the one evil yet untasted, a feminist dictator!"[21] This diatribe is a caricature of Jean Brodie's Edinburgh, in which men are reduced to a function and even the postwar world is envisioned as a community of women: the "lawful glamour" of Miss Lockhart's science room, symbol of the senior school and adulthood, whose competent leader, like the Cold War world, "could . . . blow up the school with her jar of gunpowder and would never dream of doing so" (p. 139).

All somehow defective, the men in the novel exist only to feed the women's perpetually spun myth; even the exhibitionist whose exposure was supposed to traumatize pretty Jenny shrinks into an excuse for the girls' running saga of the romantic policewoman who asked questions about him. Jean Brodie's Hugh takes life only from his lyrical death; like Lucy Snowe's

Paul Emanuel, he is "more my own" and thus more loved when lost, obligingly playing multiple roles in her evolving history lesson. One-armed Mr. Lloyd and short-legged Mr. Lowther look suspiciously alike; as the men in *Doctors of Philosophy*, Spark's play about female professors, are all variants of "Charlie," to be desired and repudiated in a vacuum by her histrionic women, so Miss Brodie's lovers are conveniently interchangeable: Jean Brodie extracts art and music from them to enhance the pageant of her emotions as Sandy extracts Catholicism from Teddy Lloyd's discarded "husk." The maimed artist Teddy expresses a historical as well as a personal truth when he paints the world as an incessant portrait of "one big Miss Brodie," for the world we see in the novel *is* Jean Brodie's Giant Form, in the face of which the abstract idealism of "Auden and that group" is irrelevant. The novel is her "prime" in its meaning of "primary; from which others are derived and on which they depend": with the exception of Rose, who being granted by Miss Brodie/God instinct but not insight is permitted to shake off her education, her set finds its source of being in her alone. Jenny is mistaken in attributing to a man the power to resurrect "an erotic wonder in life" that is pure mystic Brodie:

> It happened she was standing with a man whom she did not know very well outside a famous building in Rome, waiting for the rain to stop. She was surprised by a re-awakening of that same buoyant and airy discovery of sex, a total sensation which it was impossible to say was physical or mental, only that it contained the lost and guileless delight of her eleventh year. She supposed herself to have fallen in love with the man, who might, she thought, have been moved towards her in his own way out of a world of his own, the associations of which were largely unknown to her. There was nothing whatever to be done about it, for Jenny had been contentedly married for sixteen years past; but the concise happening filled her with astonishment whenever it came to mind in later days, and with a sense of the hidden possibilities in all things.   (pp. 99-100)

Even clumsy Mary Macgregor locates her only happy memories in Miss Brodie's "stories and opinions" before she dies im-

prisoned by a hotel fire; and for Sandy, transfigured or disguised as Sister Helen, all influences, "literary or political or
personal," take the shape of "a Miss Jean Brodie in her prime"
(p. 156). Although "prime" has an occasional meaning of "sexual excitement," Jean Brodie's pervasive creation is worlds
away from Charlotte Perkins Gilman's "Mothers to all mankind": mothers have withered out of this female world entirely.
In Spark's myth of perpetual self-generation, biology is an excrescence; the family has no part in her visionary community
of chosen vibrant souls.

"She thinks she is Providence, thought Sandy, she thinks she
is the God of Calvin, she sees the beginning and the end" (p.
147). Sandy's jealousy cannot alter the fact that Jean Brodie is
the only God the book permits us to see. The Church in which
Sandy finds tenuous refuge from herself and her times is no
more than a dramatic postulate; by the laws of this woman-
possessed novel, only Jean Brodie has sufficient potency to
create a world Miss Lockhart's science room alone can destroy.

Moreover, Sandy's betrayal is transmuted into an act of
faith in a leader who, like Mary Queen of Scots and Mussolini,
can find consummation of her image only in martyrdom. Out of
the ridiculous individual, Sandy extracts mythic and immutable truth: "The whine in her voice—' . . . betrayed me, betrayed me'—bored and afflicted Sandy. It is seven years,
thought Sandy, since I betrayed this tiresome woman. What
does she mean by 'betray'? She was looking at the hills as if to
see there the first and unbetrayable Miss Brodie, indifferent to
criticism as a crag" (p. 75). It is this first and unbetrayable
Miss Brodie whom Sandy preserves by denouncing the neurotic
schoolteacher who is her perishable shadow. It is she whose
magnetic "prime" is the beginning and the end of the book,
swallowing and transfiguring the larger reality into which it is
supposed to conduct its pupils and finally emerging as the only
reality there is. A lodestone of historical and spiritual power,
the prime of Miss Jean Brodie exposes the thinness of humanitarianism and culture: like the callow boys running after
"Auden and that group," women who "belong to the Fabian
Society and are pacifists" shrink into "gross materialists" (p.

131). Virginia Woolf's restorative Outsiders' Society, tenuously poised at the margins of power, becomes impossible to sustain. The female community has been invaded by the power of history and religion, achieving insistent, if insistently savage, transcendence.

Spark's later novels about women frequently cast *The Prime of Miss Jean Brodie* into even balder, more reduced and parabolic form. *The Girls of Slender Means* (1963) replaces the golden idyll of schooldays with the pastoral symbol of the May of Teck Club, a springlike oasis in the bomb-ripped London of World War II, existing "for the Pecuniary Convenience and Social Protection of Ladies of Slender Means below the age of Thirty Years."[22] But we soon learn that an undetonated bomb is buried in the Club's peaceful garden. Its explosion provides the book's sole catastrophe and leads to the conversion and ultimate martyrdom of Nick, the idealistic hero who, like most of the book's men, persists in forming images of paradise out of this community of girls: "In fact, it was not an unjust notion, that it was a miniature expression of a free society, that it was a community held together by the graceful attributes of a common poverty. He observed that at no point did poverty arrest the vitality of its members but rather nourished it. Poverty differs vastly from want, he thought" (p. 103). For Nick, the Club is like the March sisterhood or Cranford, a self-denying enclave in a world at war. But the spuriousness of such a female idyll is exposed by the book's grim and quiet comedy.

The bomb ticking silently in the garden contains all the original power and sin of this Edenic enterprise. In its potency it is a neat abstraction of the Jean Brodie of the earlier book, sitting in the equally lovely garden of the Marcia Blaine School, intoning her compelling history lesson; but to the power of her art has been added that of the science teacher's stored-up gunpowder, which she would never dream of using. The bomb in the garden is an emblem of all Spark's myths of the female community in history, on whom she bestows the primitive adaptiveness behind the pastoral dream: "As they realised themselves in varying degrees, few people alive at the time were more delightful, more ingenious, more movingly lovely, and, as it might happen, more savage, than the girls of slender means" (p. 6). Even Joanna Childe, the Club's elocutionist and ultimate martyr, who loftily recites "The Wreck of the Deutschland" on any occasion, finds poetry an equally savage sublimation of her "strong obscure emotions": "Joanna Childe had been drawn to this profession by her good voice and love of poetry which she loved rather as it might be assumed a cat loves birds; poetry, especially the declamatory sort, excited and possessed her; she would pounce on the stuff, play with it quivering in her mind, and when she had got it by heart, she spoke it forth with devouring relish" (p. 8). The bomb is planted more deeply in Spark's garden than was the primitivism in William Golding's *Lord of the Flies* (1955); unlike the boys on Golding's microcosmic island, the girls of slender means find in their resident martyr only the artistic quintessence of their own lovely savagery.

The very seclusion of Spark's communities of women assures us that they are not pastoral alternatives to a world at war but symbols of it. The slenderness of the May of Teck girls is their strength: the foodless, impalpable family of *Pride and Prejudice*, the fasting of *Little Women*, the "elegant economy" of *Cranford*, the "hunger, rebellion and rage" of *Villette*, the starvation of *The Odd Women*, become the compulsive dieting of our last hungry community which allows the most elegantly thin girls to slither out the bathroom window, first for secret sex on the rooftops, then to escape the burning Club in which they are trapped when the bomb explodes. The slenderness that allows the girls to worm in and out of the little window is the strength of an Outsiders' Society that prevents their being confined in any one life; for windows "had accumulated much meaning, having been the main danger-zone between domestic life and the war going on outside" (p. 5). This "danger-zone" is the true heroic setting of the girls of slender means, allowing them to straddle Virginia Woolf's private house and her history which is war, no longer for the higher purpose of saving the world from itself, but simply to live in it wherever need allows.

In his peculiar idealism, Nick insists that the ravishing

Selina, in whom he chooses to embody the community he is in love with, perceive how beautiful a thing her deprivation is: "It was incredible to him that she should not share with him an understanding of the lovely attributes of dispossession and poverty, her body was so austere and economically furnished" (p. 113). But to the girls themselves, their dispossession is less beautiful than their shared aspirations. Though Selina's return to the burning Club to rescue the Schiaparelli dress the girls have lovingly passed back and forth between them is the vision of evil that drives Nick to conversion, her apparent betrayal is also an act of salvation: in stealing the dress and leaving the girls to burn, Selina has rescued the symbol of their community, a truer memento of the Club than any individual member would have been. As Sandy's betrayal of Jean Brodie preserved her unbetrayable and immortal image, so that the myth of her prime could enshrine the unity of her temperamental, disparate "set," so the shared elegant dress is the unity of vision to which the Club aspires. The community was never "held together by the graceful attributes of a common poverty," but by the dress that was their common dream of transcending it. In choosing to rescue the soul of the community rather than its perishable, discrete bodies, Selina, like the Brodie set, triumphantly denies facile male humanitarianism in favor of the emblem, myth, and vision of a female world.

This world's salvation is survival. From time to time the novel flashes forward to bits of telephone conversations between the girls, showing them firmly entrenched in the postwar "pandemonium" of telephones and power as they discuss Nick's death as a martyr and a nuisance. "Nowhere's safe," he had moaned in his Utopian longings, but this community has safely negotiated the "danger-zone" between domesticity and war, according to the tenuous credo of Selina's Poise Course: "Poise is perfect balance" (p. 57). Selina's reiterated slogan is the slick complement of Joanna's high-minded "The Wreck of the Deutschland." Underlying her vision of the noble nuns' destruction is the covert code of female survival, to whose anti-heroic but indestructible persistence all the novels we have looked at testify.

The anti-humanism of Spark's societies goes beyond the impersonality of James's and Gissing's, which transcended the self in behalf of the higher reality of a cause. For communities which in their obsessed grandeur retain a "perfect balance" between two spheres by incorporating and devouring them both, self and cause are one. With their "concealing, hiding, secreting, covering, screening, cloaking, veiling, shrouding, shading, muffling, masking, disguising, ensconcing, eclipsing, keeping in ignorance, blinding, hoodwinking, mystifying, posing, puzzling, perplexing, embarrassing, bewildering, reserving, suppressing, bamboozling, et cetera" (pp. 101-102), the nuns in *The Abbess Of Crewe* (1974) rise through their involuted duplicity to an epic, absolute status never approximated by Spark's masculine model of Nixon's community of men at the Watergate: "Gertrude, you know I have become an object of art, the end of which is to give pleasure" (p. 113). Surely not even the most ingenious dream could make Richard Nixon say that; but under the administration of the Abbess Alexandra, the Abbey of Crewe becomes a magic artifact according to Spark's definition: "The novelist, presumptuous, arbitrary, scheming, and faking, lying like the fiend, makes things like worlds, plots absurdly like God's."[23]

"Presumptuous, arbitrary, scheming, and faking," the Abbess of Crewe has gone beyond Jean Brodie's and Selina's aspirations toward myth: she has shed her humanity and lives entirely in that self-created sphere. When we last see her, exposed and enshrined, she eschews all kinship with natural forms and achieves the immortal status of a monumental thing: "She sails indeed on the fine day of her desire into waters exceptionally smooth, and stands on the upper deck, straight as a white ship's funnel, marvelling how the wide sea billows from shore to shore like that cornfield of sublimity which never should be reaped nor was ever sown, orient and immortal wheat" (p. 116). The language of human abstraction and of religious transcendence are one. Having lost its humanity to become an amalgam of abstract giant forms, the Abbey of Crewe resembles the Brodie set as a cubist painting: "Mildred and Walburga stand up as she enters, and she looks neither at one nor the other, but stands without moving, and they with her, like Stonehenge" (pp. 99-100). Perpetually plotting in their bugged convent, Spark's nuns would yawn at the self-conscious stateliness of those in Rumer Godden's *In This House of Brede* (1969), just as her Doctors of Philosophy never bothered with the rhetoric of dedication that resounds in *Gaudy Night*. But her language bestows on them a magnitude of anti-nobility and nonhumanity simply because they appropriate the reality her world makes available to us, casting off the cornfields that can be reaped and sown to exist on a plane of absolute created myth.

As the manless world of *The Abbess of Crewe* supersedes and makes gorgeous the masculine history it seems to emulate, so Lise in *The Driver's Seat* (1970), with her insistent costume of dissonant colors, plots to make her murder an immutable truth which will shed transfiguration on the functionaries who swarm about her: "[The waiter], too, will give his small piece of evidence to the police on the following day, as will also the toilet attendant, trembling at the event which has touched upon her life without the asking."[24] Since she has no inner life we are allowed to see, Lise's psychology has disappeared into her colors, as her life has disappeared into her apprehension of her destiny. In her world, too, men are invisible or materialized instruments of her dream. The deposed Sheik who crosses her path in the Hilton seems a fleeting ghost of the evaporated masculine power of Gaskell and Brontë's Grand Turk. Mrs. Fiedke, sweetly banal through most of the story, acts as choric explicator of the secret primacy of a woman's world: "They are demanding equal rights with us . . . That's why I never vote with the Liberals . . . There was a time they would stand up and open a door for you. They would take their hat off. But they want their equality today. All I say is that if God had intended them to be as good as us he wouldn't have made them different from us to the naked eye. They don't want to be all dressed alike any more. Which is only a move against us. You couldn't run an army like that, let alone the male sex . . . They won't be content with equal rights only. Next thing they'll want the upper hand, mark my words. Diamond earrings, I've read in the paper" (pp. 78-79).

On the surface a rather archly whimsical inversion, Mrs. Fiedke's speech defines a hidden Sparkian world in which women are in "the driver's seat" of a mysterious metaphysical collusion that underlies the social world we see. Within her contemporary settings Spark returns us to the myth with which we began—that of the female community of the Fates. Lise in the driver's seat following out the plot of her own murder, Lise as God arranging and shaping a dream of a world, distills all Spark's organizing women into a figure that transcendentalizes the managing, marrying mother of Victorian convention and the impersonal visionary of early feminism: a woman both possessed and in possession, who is no longer the antagonist of masculine "reality" and "truth," but its symbolic embodiment and eternal form, the driving force behind men's violent history.

"I was born on the first day of the second month of the last year of the First World War, a Friday."[25] One of Spark's most recent stories, a characteristic legend of the self as artist, traces back to their origin in consciousness her communities of women in history. In infancy, we learn, the author was omniscient and thus in psychic unity with the war: "Babies, in their waking hours, know everything that is going on everywhere in the world; they can tune in to any conversation they choose, switch on to any scene. We have all experienced this power" (p. 37). In fact, only Muriel Spark's chosen "set" are in communion with the powers she evokes, but her inclusion of the reader in the artist's prime experiences is as harmlessly polite a lie as was Wordsworth's "Heaven lies about us in our infancy." The difference is that for Spark, from the first, war lies within, corroborating Ellen Moers's suggestion that women remember with special nostalgia the noninnocent brutality of childhood.[26] The legend of "The First Year of my Life" shrinks the Brodie set, the May of Teck Club, and the rest to a mythic female baby who carries the slaughter, irony, and hope of her age within her and finally decides to smile at it.

This baby with magical knowledge and war in her heart assures us that the boundaries of separation have quietly broken down in Muriel Spark's parables of female communities. Apparently as slight and as remote from the main theater of action as were Jane Austen's Longbourn or Elizabeth Gaskell's Cranford, these communities incorporate a dimension traditionally denied to women—the violence of history and religion. Knowledge of war is discernible in their smiles; possession of this forbidden fruit makes their world no longer a remote Utopia or Gorgon-haunted dystopia, but one in league with its time and with our own. The autonomous and self-sustaining communities of nineteenth-century women, perforce cooperative because deprived of outside reality and power, lose focus and perfection with this acquisition of previously masculine territory. In moving through the window of "domestic life" to "the war going on outside," female communities take increasingly abstract and asymmetrical shapes.

The movement of this book has been one of aspiration and expansion, as for the most part women's history itself has been. In literature at least, expansion has involved less an extension than a repudiation of the family: not even the matriarchies of Austen and Alcott could retain their authority in face of the public world of men. Gaskell's Cranford and Brontë's Villette were far-off enclaves of "Amazons" whose nonfamilial organizations gave them a certain dreamlike power over masculine autocracy. But ironically, only the male authors James and Gissing have endowed their speechifying societies with "reality" and "truth," freeing them from self-enclosed, sirenlike deceit to invade the authenticity of public life. In these conquered worlds, the family has vanished utterly.

Though the Brodie set, the May of Teck Club, and the Abbey of Crewe restore to their members the self-protective duplicity which seems intrinsic to the literary woman's voice,[27] and though these communities might well house the anti-Christ rather than Spark's own Catholic "norm," the powers with which their novels endow them complete the destruction of the woman's world as a haven of separate, cherished values. Their geographical separatism is the irony of their identity, allowing them to embody with greater intensity the historical and spiritual violence that surrounds them. In denying her communities the virtues of separation, Spark is not the idiosyncratic maverick she has seemed to some. Her portraits of powerful eccentric women who withdraw from the male battle-field to embody it align her implicitly with her age.

If Simone de Beauvoir's gloomy classic, *The Second Sex* (published in the United States in 1953), inaugurates the second feminist revolt whose boundaries we are still expanding, that revolt begins with a prescient warning against the lure of separatism:

> Sometimes the "feminine world" is contrasted with the masculine universe, but we must insist again that women have never constituted a closed and independent society; they form an integral part of the group, which is governed by males and in which they have a subordinate place. They are united only in a mechanical solidarity from the mere fact of their similarity, but they lack that organic solidarity on which every unified community is based; they are always compelled—at the time of the mysteries of Eleusis as today in clubs, salons, social-service institutes —to band together in order to establish a counter-universe, but they always set it up within the frame of the masculine universe. Hence the paradox of their situation: they belong at one and the same time to the male world and to a sphere in which that world is challenged; shut up in their world, surrounded by the other, they can settle down nowhere in peace. Their docility must always be matched by a refusal, their refusal by an acceptance.[28]

This lugubrious analysis of the fantasy of a feminine "counter-universe" is the death knell of the nineteenth-century dream of a cyclonic female force purging and purifying its world, or alternately, infecting it with its own diseased identity. Whether beneficent or malign, in the world as it is the impact of such an enclave is a dream. The sources of power are irrefutably male, and to deny them is to deny the potential power of a woman's own existence.

Such an anatomy illuminates the ego-driven corruption of Muriel Spark's communities, whose pastoral veneer is their subtlest joke; and it exposes forever the sentimental self-glorification of Charlotte Perkins Gilman's "Herland" and the other Utopias with which this chapter began, in which a nurturing female world checks male militarism while remaining pure of its violence and hunger for power. In de Beauvoir's opinion, a true community of women is impossible precisely because of its isolation from power: it must cancel itself out by its own enforced "purity." Having shaken off the nineteenth-century "cult of true womanhood," communities of women today must emulate their antagonist in order to exist at all. Despairing of this possibility, de Beauvoir envisions women as perpetually trapped in their biological "immanence," hopelessly barred from male "transcendence." The static cycle of barren gestation is the curse of women; men alone can aspire to and achieve the quest beyond mortality.

Though de Beauvoir's analysis is an indelible part of our present understanding of communities of women, in imaginative literature at least her gloom is unfounded. If in life female separatism still has the aura of a self-glorifying game because of its ambivalent denial of the institutionalized reality of male power,[29] its fictional incarnations achieve indisputable transcendence. Spark's Nixonian nuns are not the only contemporary community to partake through "masculine" thievery of "orient and immortal wheat": imaginatively recast, female communities typically achieve transcendence through their appropriation of male tactics in the quest for power. In contemporary visions, "domestic life" and "the war going on outside" are triumphantly one.

Nightwood (1936), Djuna Barnes's novel about the hypnotic impact of a lesbian triangle on the surrounding society, is a forecast of this new vision. Far from being outcast, the obsessed, half-somnolent love ballet between Robin Vote, Nora Flood, and Jenny Petherbridge easily supplants the authority of dynastic tradition yearned for by Robin's husband, Baron Felix Volkbein. But as Nora reveals, its triumph springs not from the alternate nature of a nurturing female world, but from the lesbian's emulation of the male historical imagination: " 'Man,' she said, her eyelids quivering, 'conditioning himself to fear, made God; as the prehistoric, conditioning himself to hope, made man—the cooling of the earth, the receding of the sea. And I, who want power, chose a girl who resembles a boy.' "[30]

Having thus eroded Felix's patriarchy by incorporating its ambitions, the women exert an oddly mystical potency over the doctor, that traditional nineteenth-century embodiment of the humane values that combine the healing goals of religion and science. But in this book the doctor is a holy grotesque, his solemnly ritualized transvestism an admission of women's historical and supernatural primacy: "Ritual itself constitutes an instruction. So we come back to the place from which I set out; pray to the good God; she will keep you. Personally I call her 'she' because of the way she made me; it somehow balances the mistake" (p. 150). The doctor's prostration before women is an admission of kinship rather than defeat. The power granted to these women of the "third sex" is as much historical and mystical as it is erotic: like Spark's "female god," Jean Brodie, whose primacy is dangerous precisely because it is immortal, Barnes's trinity assimilates rather than opposes the masculine values it supersedes. As in contemporary feminist literature, lesbianism is not the private aberration Freudians sniff out, but a public endowment, a token of women's new power to abandon the impotent pseudo-sanctity of their "counter-universe" for political and psychic centrality.

But the transcendence of *Nightwood* is permeated by shadows and secrecy. It finds its equivocal emblem in front of "a contrived altar, before a Madonna," as Robin and a dog merge into a grotesque Pietà: "He ran this way and that, low down in his throat crying, and she grinning and crying with him; crying in shorter and shorter spaces, moving head to head, until she gave up, lying out, her hands beside her, her face turned and weeping; and the dog too gave up then, and lay down, his eyes bloodshot, his head flat along her knees" (p. 170). Female divinity abases itself in a ritual self-celebration with Sparkian overtones of travesty and Black Mass. But despite the impact of its magic, transcendence seems possible only as part of the surreal metamorphoses of night and the unconscious, when, according to Nora, "the night does something to a person's identity, even when asleep" (p. 81). It has remained for a more recent novel to bring corporate female transcendence into the daylight, allowing it to take possession of the sun.

Monique Wittig's *Les Guérillères* (1969) is the incantatory account of the training and triumph of a female army. Here, the buried warfare of Spark's communities explodes in a new Amazonianism, but one that is sensuous and fulfilled, with none of the stigma of mutilation carried by the Greek name. Though Wittig's warriors are defined almost entirely by their bodies, her ecstatic vision recasts collective feminity from apparent "lacunae" into vessels of triumph: "Somewhere there is a siren. Her green body is covered with scales. Her face is bare. The undersides of her arms are a rosy colour. Sometimes she begins to sing. The women say that of her song nothing is to be heard but a continuous O. That is why this song evokes for them, like everything that recalls the O, the zero or the circle, the vulval ring."[31]

The apparent zero of the vulva, token of traditional and Freudian visions of female incompleteness, is transmuted by female art into the circle of eternity. The song of the siren is no longer the lure of deceit but the hymn of a new reality, as pathos is transmuted into the power of "the circle, the circumference, the ring, the O, the zero, the sphere" which is the emblem of the book. With the reimagination of the vulva comes the appropriation of masculine heroic mythology to the rhythms of a female world: "They say it is impossible to mistake the symbolism of the Round Table that dominated their meetings. They say that, at the period when the texts were compiled, the quests for the Grail were singular unique attempts to describe the zero the circle the ring the spherical cup containing the blood" (p. 45). Though female anatomy is still destiny, it is reconceived as an instrument of transcendence through the release of war and worship.

For the warriors' vulvae are not merely vessels of eternity, but containers of Amaterasu, "the sun goddess, the greatest of the goddesses," whose exemplary rage is the army's motivation: "The women say that they expose their genitals so that the sun may be reflected therein as in a mirror. They say that they retain its brilliance. They say that the pubic hair is like a spider's web that captures the rays. They are seen running with great strides. They are all illuminated at their centre, starting from the pubes the hooded clitorides the folded double labia. The glare they shed when they stand still and turn to face one makes the eye turn elsewhere unable to stand the sight" (p. 19). Metamorphosis here is not part of the secrets of night, but of the triumphant pageant of the sun, as the vulva escapes the receptive stasis of Simone de Beauvoir's tragic female immanence to shoot rays of victory and transcendence. The male quest is joyfully rooted in the female body.

Moreover, unlike their Greek ancestors, Wittig's Amazons have no scarcity of breasts. Though their military and eternal device is the 0 of the vulva, their breasts too are translated from passive nourishing vessels to instruments of aggression: "Some laugh out loud and manifest their aggressiveness by thrusting their bare breasts forward brutally" (p. 100). This female army has so effectively captured traditionally male myth and militarism that its ultimate victory over men is an anticlimax: it has achieved its triumph in its transfigured nature, which no longer needs the grotesquely convoluted postulate of Barnes's "third sex." In appropriating war and religion while remaining militantly female, Wittig's army might be the body of which Spark's more seemingly respectable communities are the spirit. Both these organizations of women deny the segregation of a female world by taking to themselves the violent heart of surrounding masculinity.

In its central movement of aggression and attack, Wittig's novel leaves behind the static settings of Spark's to take on the very form of literature about communities of men: the rhythms of the quest. Traditionally, as my Introduction defined, a band of brothers in fiction engages in a quest for a state or goal beyond themselves, be it a Grail, a white whale, or a kingdom, while communities of women achieve instead the triumph of their own self-completeness. Despite radical changes in content, this formal distinction has been maintained until very recently. Perhaps because such searing exposures as de Beauvoir's of the inescapable contradiction of self-completeness without power have made the old form impossible, a female haven has lost its imaginative efficacy in recent fiction. In Doris Lessing's The Golden Notebook (1962), Molly's and Anna's attempt to construct, through friendship and a shared dream of themselves as "free women," a community of two that will outface the soils of men is notable only for its fragility and ultimate failure: the belief in a permanent female refuge superior to the madness of men and history cannot survive the depredations of both. When they are resignedly "integrated with British life" at the end of the novel, the women must part; such integration is incompatible with sisterhood. The vision of Spark's almost contemporaneous Brodie set (1961) survived in its novel, not because it withdrew from men and history, but because it assimilated them.

The last advance of this steadily encroaching genre apparently has been the appropriation of the odyssean form of male communities. Having incorporated war, God, and the quest, our tradition might have nowhere left to go. Ti-Grace Atkinson's collection of speeches and essays, Amazon Odyssey (1974), might be its final visionary leap. Although Atkinson's potpourri is not, strictly speaking, a novel, its saga of the heartbreaking schisms in the women's movement, together with the painstaking battle plans and "strategy charts" interspersed with passionate invocations to the (ideally) female audience, make up a fervent and purely imaginative vision of a female community in a radical feminist future.

The title Amazon Odyssey defines Atkinson's alliance with Wittig's vision of war and the quest as inherent components of today's female community. Throughout, Atkinson insists that her band of women has learned its lesson from men: "And I want to respond, here and now, to the complaint that I am trying to put women on a war footing. Any group being shot at is immediately confronted with a 'dilemma.' It can die. Or it can confront and, possibly, at the very least, take some of the opposition with it. People who turn their backs on aggression tend to lose wars."[32] Atkinson spells out the implicit assumption of militant female communities as they are envisioned today: the power of the supposed "counter-universe" stems from its self-realization as part of the larger society that denies it. She makes explicit the battlefield code inherent in so many alliances between women: "For the moment, until I've laid out my general political analysis relevant to feminism and lesbianism, consider this proposition: I'm enormously less interested in whom you sleep with than I am in with whom you're prepared to die" (p. 138). Sisterhood is now a military discipline in this curt farewell to Austen's and Alcott's bands of women waiting together for the war to end.

Since her vision of community is pervaded by her quest, Atkinson dedicates her book "to those who fought and got away—but never went home." There can be no terminus of "home" for the radical female quest, only the beginning of hope for change: "Obviously, 'change' can never occur *in situ*. But at least some fundamental, solid, and reasoned direction should be in hand. And some methodology for reaching the charted destination should be consciously in process. These two minimal—and somewhat modest—basics are what I consider, at present, the end of my Odyssey" (p. xxiii). The new female code denies the permanence and completeness of setting the old one indefatigably constructed.

Following the subterranean patterns of Barnes's and Spark's novels, Atkinson insists on the centrality of women who are only apparently hidden from history. Though women embody history's primal oppression, oppression is, in her definition, history's vital essence. Women's victimization thus contains the radical promise of all human transformation: "Part of the feminist theory that I projected very early (and that was rejected as blasphemous for so long) was that 'women' were the beginning of the political notion of class, and, as such, were the foundation and contained the conceptual essence of oppression as a phenomenon in its totality" (p. ccxxix). Finding themselves at the heart of history, women's mission is to destroy the corruptions of religion—as Atkinson attempts to do when she lectures at Catholic University and breaks into a jeremiad against the Catholic Church—and to restore a purely female worship of, presumably, the "female god" of Barnes, Spark, and Wittig: "*Radical Feminism* was conceptualized and begun in 1968 . . . (I nicknamed it 'Genesis.') *Juniata II* was produced in 1969 and presented in early 1970 . . . (I nicknamed these four subsets the '*Apostles*,' because the pieces represented initial thrusts of evangelical missions.) On '*Violence* . . . ,' which has two parts, was written in late 1971 . . . It was a period of devastation and wrath. (I called it—'*Revelations*.')" (p. ccxlvii). The religion of men is destroyed only to be restored in an Amazonian sphere, as part of its newly appropriated odyssey.

Atkinson's angry, visionary book formulates many of the premises according to which communities of women have been created in the twentieth century. Most crucially, it destroys the possibility of a female world as a sheltered shared enclave whose values are private and unique. Her categories and her assumptions preclude a female counteruniverse: "The Institution of Sexual Intercourse" (p. 13); "no other activity in the world [but pregnancy], short of war, with that high a mortality rate would be legalized" (p. 15); "Radical Feminism and Love" (p. 41); a woman in love "is disarming herself to go into the enemy camp" (p. 45); "Lesbianism and Feminism" (p. 83); "Almost no feminist work has been done on 'mental health' . . . I believe this is yet another fruitful area for feminist (i.e., political) investigation" (p. 115). Love, pregnancy, sex, and madness, those dear constituents of the private female world, are forcibly yoked to public, political life, leaving us stranded in the reality of our century, free from any womanliness into which to retreat.

Violence, God, history, and the quest: their incorporation into a woman's world might suggest that by quietly broadening its base, the tradition I have defined will no longer survive in the novel, having evaporated by taking everything to itself. In this century at least, it has been strikingly free of humanity. Barnes's triad is perpetually somnambulistic, intoning cosmic things without seeming to develop consciousness or emotion. Spark's communities evolve into progressively visionary abstractions, her nuns finally disappearing into sheer monumentality "like Stonehenge." Wittig's warriors become the equally abstract and indistinguishable pattern of their vulvae, which themselves disappear into the stark black circle of the book's device. The women's names that are ritualistically chanted seem a human joke, since they are attached to no characters we come to know:

> DEMONA EPONINA GABRIELA
> FULVIA ALEXANDRA JUSTINE (p. 43),

and so on. Though these names take on their own incantatory life, the empty resonance of their sound is also the death of the real people we used to read novels to meet. Atkinson's community of women goes so far as to be totally invisible, as an audience is to an absorbed speaker. Since her real feminist communities are nests of corruption and betrayal, her visionary community consists only of the invisible sisters that the fervor of her words will invoke. In a sense we have circled back to Jane Austen's impalpable Bennet family, waiting for the opening of the door to make its world concrete.

Oddly, in gaining the appurtenances and mythology of men, women in this fictional tradition are losing their life as characters. Perhaps once women have proved their strength to themselves, it will be possible to return to the individuality of Meg, Jo, Beth, and Amy, or to the humanly interdependent courtesy of Cranford. What these nineteenth-century enclaves will have lost is their besieged penury and self-denying anger. But the survival of our tradition in literature will gain from them a reminder that living communities of women require an embrace of the full reality of human society.

Notes

1. Introduction: The Communal Eye

1. Herodotus, *The Persian Wars*, trans. George Rawlinson (New York: Random House, 1942), p. 336. For a definitive study of the relation between the uncooked and the barbaric, see Claude Lévi-Strauss, *The Raw and the Cooked: Introduction to a Science of Mythology: I*, trans. John and Doreen Weightman (1964; New York and Evanston: Harper & Row, 1969).

2. Sarah B. Pomeroy, *Goddesses, Whores, Wives, and Slaves: Women in Classical Antiquity* (New York: Schocken Books, 1975), p. 25.

3. "Oubli ou Silence, voilà la puissance de mort qui se dresse en face de la puissance de vie, Mémoire, mère des Muses. Derrière l'Eloge et le Blâme, le couple fondamental des puissances antithétiques est formé par Mnémosyné et Léthé. La vie du guerrier se joue entre ces deux pôles." Marcel Detienne, *Les Maitres de Vérité dans la Grèce Archaique*, 2nd ed. (1967; Paris: François Maspero, 1973), p. 22; the translation is my own.

4. Charlotte Wolff, *Love between Women* (New York: Harper & Row, 1971), p. 211.

5. Rudyard Kipling, *The Man Who Would Be King* (New York: Doubleday & McClure Co., 1909), p. 1. Future references to this edition will appear in the text.

6. Sarah Orne Jewett, *The Country of the Pointed Firs and Other Stories* (New York: Doubleday, & Co., 1956), p. 233. Future references to this edition will appear in the text.

7. See especially Françoise Basch, *Relative Creatures: Victorian Women in Society and the Novel*, trans. Anthony Rudolf (New York: Schocken Books, 1974), p. xiii: "Most females in English fiction of the first part of the Victorian era are caricatured or idealized figures; at any rate they are simplified, and seem to conform to a few stereotypes inspired by a tyrannical and narrow ideal of the woman in the home." Perhaps this sweeping statement is true, but there is a sense in which Basch's title has already created the truncated woman her book claims to discover. Joanna Russ, in "Why Women Can't Write," in *Images of Women in Fiction: Feminist Perspectives*, ed. Susan Koppelman Cornillon, rev. (Bowling Green, Ohio: Bowling Green University Popular Press, 1973), p. 5, lashes at our entire tradition in the name of its stricken heroines: "Our literature is not about

women. It is not about men and women equally. It is . . . [about] not women but images of women [who] exist only in relation to the protagonist (who is male)."

8. Dinah Mulock Craik, *A Woman's Thoughts about Women,* American ed. (New York: Rudd and Carleton, 1858), p. 30. Future references to this edition will appear in the text.

9. Elizabeth Janeway, *Man's World, Woman's Place: A Study in Social Mythology* (New York: William Morrow & Co., 1971), p. 111.

10. Elizabeth Janeway, *Between Myth and Morning: Women Awakening* (New York: William Morrow & Co., 1975), p. 7; Patricia Meyer Spacks, *The Female Imagination* (New York: Alfred A. Knopf, 1975); Ellen Moers, *Literary Women* (New York: Doubleday & Co., 1976); Carroll Smith-Rosenberg, "The Female World of Love and Ritual: Relations between Women in Nineteenth Century America," *Signs: Journal of Women in Culture and Society,* 1 (Autumn 1975), 1-29; Yolanda and Robert Murphy, *Women of the Forest* (New York: Columbia University Press, 1975).

11. "True Colleges for Women," from the *Imperial Review,* 1867, 8; quoted in Duncan Crow, *The Victorian Woman* (New York: Stein and Day, 1972), p. 199.

12. Mary Wollstonecraft, *A Vindication of the Rights of Woman,* ed. Charles W. Hagelman, Jr. (New York: W. W. Norton & Co., 1967), pp. 194-195.

13. In *Woman's Work and Woman's Culture,* ed. Josephine Butler (London: Macmillan & Co., 1869), pp. 290-330.

14. Elizabeth Gaskell, *The Life of Charlotte Brontë,* ed. Alan Shelston (Middlesex: Penguin Books, 1975), p. 132.

15. Sarah Stickney Ellis, *The Women of England: Their Social Duties and Domestic Habits,* American ed. (New York: J. & H. G. Langley, 1843), p. 28. Future references to this edition will appear in the text.

16. From 2,765,000 in 1851 to 2,956,000 in 1861 and 3,228,700 in 1871—an increase of 16.8 percent. The figures are given in J. A. and Olive Banks, *Feminism and Family Planning in Victorian England* (Liverpool: Liverpool University Press, 1964), p. 27.

17. Dora Greenwell, "Our Single Women," *North British Review,* 36 (February 1862), 63, 78-79.

18. Eliza Lynn Linton, "The Shrieking Sisterhood," *The Saturday Review,* 29 (March 12, 1870), 341.

19. July 17, 1887. Quoted in Elaine Showalter, "Dinah Mulock Craik and the Tactics of Sentiment: A Case Study of Victorian Female Authorship," *Feminist Studies* 2 (1975), 20. Showalter's article is an excellent study of the paradoxes and confusions of a woman who tried to go her own way in a society without standing against that society.

20. Dinah Mulock Craik, "On Sisterhood," in *About Money and Other Things*, American ed. (New York: Harper & Brothers, 1887), pp. 147-148.

21. The half-wistful dream of a restoration of convents is offered by two Victorian liberals, a man and a woman, in a manner that seems to crystallize the difference between a woman's life as it was perceived and as it was lived. First, the man: "But above all, [the convents] were at least an alternative to matrimony . . . I am far indeed from desiring the restoration of the conventual system, with its vows of perpetual celibacy and servitude; but it is right to re-member that with many evils it brought at least some compensations. To be unmarried was then to be the spouse of Christ, the revered "mother," the member of a Sisterhood surrounded with all the honour and sanctity of the Church—nowadays it is to live and die in the dreary lodgings, and under the half-contemptuous title of an old maid"; John Boyd-Kinnear, "The Social Position of the Present Age," in Josephine Butler, p. 352. Next, the woman: "I believe more than one half the women who go into the Catholic Church join her because she gives work to her children. Happier by far is a Sister of Charity or Mercy than a young lady at home without a work or a lover. We do not mean to say work will take the place of love in life; that is impos-sible; does it with men? But we ardently desire that women should not make *love their profession*"; Barbara Leigh Smith Bodichon, *Women and Work*, American ed. (New York: C. S. Francis & Co., 1859), p. 27; Bodichon's italics. For Boyd-Kinnear, a convent offers a restoration of the old relation of wife, mother, sister, a simulation of woman's relative role within the family. For Bodichon as for Dinah Mulock Craik, it offers the blessed work which promised many a release from love and family. The need the sisterhood would fill is vividly present, though quite different, to the sympathetic man and the aspiring woman.

22. Edith Simcox, "Eight Years of Co-operative Shirtmaking," *The Nineteenth Century*, 15 (June 1884), 1039, 1046.

23. Quoted in K. A. McKenzie, *Edith Simcox and George Eliot* (London: Oxford University Press, 1951), pp. 90-91.

24. See, for instance, her widely quoted letter to Mrs. Peter Alfred Taylor, February 1, 1853: " 'Enfranchisement of women' only makes creeping progress; and that is best, for woman does not yet deserve a much better lot than man gives her." Her chivalrous movement of man away from the position of oppressor toward that of moral arbiter seems doubly disingenuous in view of the letter's earlier dry, double-edged praise of Francis Newman: "Never men-tion me to him in the character of editress. I think—at least I am told—that he has no high esteem of woman's powers and functions. But let that pass. He is a very pure, noble being and it is good only to

look at such." *The George Eliot Letters,* ed. Gordon Haight, 7 vols. (New Haven: Yale University Press, 1954-55), II, 85.

25. See Susan R. Gorsky, "Old Maids and New Women: Alternatives to Marriage in Englishwoman's Novels, 1847-1915," *Journal of Popular Culture,* 7 (Summer 1973), 68-85, for a study of the effects of this particular Victorian doublethink on popular fiction.

26. George W. Burnap, *Lectures on the Sphere and Duties of Women and Other Subjects* (Baltimore: John Murphy, 1841), pp. 50-51, 124-126; italics mine. Burnap's brisk "corps de reserve" looks forward to the "glorious phalanx of old maids" celebrated by the Unitarian minister Theodore Parker.

27. Margaret Fuller, *Woman in the Nineteenth Century* (New York: W. W. Norton & Co., Inc., 1971), pp. 37, 62-63.

28. Quoted in Eleanor Flexner, *Century of Struggle: The Woman's Rights Movement in the United States,* rev. ed. (Cambridge, Mass.: Harvard University Press, 1975), p. 77. For an account of the Seneca Falls Convention, see ch. 5, pp. 71-77.

29. For an account of Emily Davies' campaign, see Josephine Kamm, *Hope Deferred: Girls' Education in English History* (London: Methuen & Co., 1965), pp. 250-270.

30. Jill Conway, "Women Reformers and American Culture, 1870-1930," *Journal of Social History,* 5 (Winter 1971-72), 173.

31. Sarah Edgarton to Mrs. Luella J. B. Chase, January 8, 1840; quoted in William B. Taylor and Christopher Lasch, "Two 'Kindred Spirits': Sorority and Family in New England, 1839-1846," *New England Quarterly,* 36 (March 1963), 32.

32. Quoted in William L. O'Neill, *Everyone Was Brave: A History of Feminism in America,* rev. ed. (1969; Chicago: Quadrangle Books, 1971), p. 85.

33. Quoted in Charles McCool Snyder, *Dr. Mary Walker: The Little Lady in Pants* (New York: Vantage Press, 1962), pp. 129-130.

34. Derek Stanford, *Muriel Spark* (Fontwell: Centaur Press, 1963), p. 27.

35. Rudyard Kipling, *Stalky & Co.* (New York: Doubleday & McClure Co., 1899), p. 110. For a discussion of the "priestly state" of boyhood in this novel, see Steven Marcus, *Representations: Essays on Literature and Society* (New York: Random House, 1975), pp. 61-75.

36. Thomas Hughes, *Tom Brown at Oxford* (1861; Philadelphia: Henry T. Coates & Co., n.d.), p. 400.

2. Waiting Together: Two Families

1. David Roberts, "The Paterfamilias of the Victorian Governing Classes," forthcoming in Anthony Wohl's collection of essays about the Victorian family; Mrs. Isabella Beeton, *The Book of House-*

hold *Management,* rev. ed. (1861; London: Warwick House, 1880), pp. 1, 17.

2. Patricia Meyer Spacks, *The Female Imagination* (New York: Alfred A. Knopf, 1975), p. 121.

3. Jane Austen, *Pride and Prejudice,* ed. R. W. Chapman (London: Oxford University Press, 1932), p. 341. Future references to this edition will appear in the text.

4. Jane Aiken Hodge, *Only A Novel: The Double Life of Jane Austen* (Greenwich, Conn.: Fawcett Publications, 1973), pp. 238-239.

5. Louisa May Alcott, *Little Women* (New York: Grosset & Dunlap, 1947), p. 539. Future references to this edition will appear in the text under the abbreviation *LW.*

6. See note to p. 351 of his edition of the novel: "Sir Maurice Hill has favoured me with a dissertation on Longbourn, in which he shows that *dining room* is impossible; they must have been in the *drawing room* upstairs. Professor R. A. Humphreys points out (1968) that *drawing room* is also impossible: in the first place, Mrs. Bennet tells Lady Catherine that they never sat there after dinner; secondly, on going down stairs (for the room was up stairs) Lady Catherine opened the doors 'into the dining-parlour and drawing-room' (p. 352). He suggests that the room must have been Mrs. Bennet's dressing-room" (p. 396). The actual inhabitants of Longbourn House never find it worth this sort of minute attention.

7. Dorothy Van Ghent, *The English Novel: Form and Function* (1953; rpt. New York: Harper & Row, 1961), p. 103. Ellen Moers's discussion of "female realism" in *Literary Women* (New York: Doubleday & Co., 1976), pp. 67-89, uses *Pride and Prejudice* and *Little Women* to construct a female tradition honoring the "Monday voices" of concrete and pragmatic workaday reality. But in the Bennet family at least, money and the job are most strongly felt by virtue of their thwarting absence.

8. As it almost invariably does in Patricia Beer's witty book, *Reader, I Married Him: A Study of the Women Characters of Jane Austen, Charlotte Brontë, Elizabeth Gaskell and George Eliot* (New York: Barnes & Noble, 1974), p. 76.

9. Jane Austen, *The Watsons,* in *Minor Works,* ed. R. W. Chapman (London: Oxford University Press, 1969), p. 321

10. For Austen's relation to the tradition of the familial Eden, see R. F. Brissenden, "*Mansfield Park:* Freedom and the Family," in *Jane Austen: Bicentenary Essays,* ed. John Halperin (Cambridge: Cambridge University Press, 1975), pp. 156-171.

11. Jane Austen, *Sense and Sensibility,* ed. R. W. Chapman (London: Oxford University Press, 1933), pp. 12, 72.

12. Jane Austen, *Emma,* ed. R. W. Chapman (London: Oxford University Press, 1933), p. 165.

13. See Chapter 1. For more detailed studies of the kinship between Austen and Wollstonecraft, see Nina Auerbach, "O Brave New World: Evolution and Revolution in *Persuasion*," *ELH*, 39 (March 1972), 112-128; and Lloyd W. Brown, "Jane Austen and the Feminist Tradition," *Nineteenth-Century Fiction*, 28 (December 1973), 321-338. For both writers the world is so constituted that a community of women can only multiply the deficiencies of exclusion from the sources of masculine strength.

14. July 26, 1809. *Jane Austen's Letters to her sister Cassandra and Others*, ed. R. W. Chapman (London: Oxford University Press, 1952), p. 68.

15. *Emma*, p. 249; Hodge, p. 207; Brigid Brophy, "Jane Austen and the Stuarts," in *Critical Essays on Jane Austen*, ed. B. C. Southam (New York: Barnes & Noble, 1969), p. 28.

16. See B. C. Southam, *Jane Austen's Literary Manuscripts* (Oxford: Clarendon Press, 1964), pp. 55-60.

17. James Edward Austen-Leigh, *Memoir of Jane Austen* (1870; rpt. Oxford: Clarendon Press, 1967), pp. 85-86.

18. Admiral Croft's wife in *Persuasion* is in some ways an exception, as she is to many things in Jane Austen's delineation of women: "But by coolly giving the reins a better direction herself, they happily passed the danger; and by once afterwards judiciously putting out her hand, they neither fell into a rut, nor ran foul of a dung-cart; and Anne, with some amusement at their style of driving, which she imagined no bad representation of the general guidance of their affairs, found herself safely deposited by them at the cottage." *Northanger Abbey* and *Persuasion*, ed. R. W. Chapman (London: Oxford University Press, 1933), p. 92. But Anne's imagining that her ride with them is symbolic is somewhat sanguine, since the Admiral commands the ships on which he allows his wife passage. Moreover, Mrs. Croft has no children and no household to run: originating in a man's world, her power is benign.

19. Julia Prewit Brown, "The Bonds of Irony: A Study of Jane Austen's Novels," Ph.D. diss., Columbia, 1975, p. 126.

20. Harriet Martineau, *Society in America*, 2 vols. (New York: Saunders & Otley, 1837), II, 276.

21. See Marvin Mudrick, *Jane Austen: Irony as Defense and Discovery* (Princeton: Princeton University Press, 1952), p. 103: "By her insulting condescension toward Elizabeth, [Lady Catherine] helps Darcy to balance off his distaste of Mrs. Bennet's not dissimilar shortcomings"; and Joseph Wiesenfarth, *The Errand of Form: An Assay of Jane Austen's Art* (New York: Fordham University Press, 1967), p. 63: "The wonderful interference of the egregious Lady Catherine de Bourgh in his affairs has yet to make Darcy realize that his

aunt's title is nothing more than a cover that keeps the skeleton in the family closet from rattling as loudly as the bumbling Mrs. Bennet."

22. May 24, 1813. *Jane Austen's Letters*, p. 312.

23. Jane Austen, *The History of England*, in *Minor Works*, p. 145.

24. May 31, 1811. *Jane Austen's Letters*, p. 73. Francis R. Hart, "The Spaces of Privacy: Jane Austen," *Nineteenth-Century Fiction*, 30 (December 1975), 305-333, is a wonderful discussion of the strength and complexity of Jane Austen's ideal of privacy.

25. See Kenneth L. Moler, *Jane Austen's Art of Allusion* (Lincoln: University of Nebraska Press, 1968), pp. 75-108, for a discussion of the managing, marrying Darcy in relation to his Godlike prototype, Sir Charles Grandison. It is part of Austen's feminization of Richardson's material that in *Pride and Prejudice* it is initially the mother's "business" to get her daughters married, and Darcy merely replaces her in the job.

26. Letter to Sam May, quoted in Madeleine B. Stern, *Louisa May Alcott* (Norman: University of Oklahoma Press, 1950), pp. 189-190.

27. Ralph Waldo Emerson's 1856 *Journal* lauds Bronson Alcott's ability to escape the very world of things to which Louisa adheres: "The comfort of Alcott's mind is, the connection in which he sees whatever he sees. He is never dazzled by a spot of colour, or a gleam of light, to value the thing by itself; but forever and ever is prepossessed by the individual one behind it and all." Quoted in *Bronson Alcott's Fruitlands*, compiled by Clara Endicott Sears (Boston: Houghton Mifflin Co., 1915), p. 5.

28. Patricia Meyer Spacks's students "resented the way Jo is finally disposed of" as clamorously as Alcott's first young readers did (Spacks, p. 100). For them, and for Spacks as well, being denied the conventional romantic marriage is Jo's punishment for her aggression. But Elizabeth Janeway gives her a sweeping cheer for avoiding it, thus becoming "the one young woman in nineteenth-century fiction who maintains her individual independence." "It is worth noting that the two other adored nineteenth-century heroines who say No to the hero's proposal give way in the end, when circumstances and the hero have changed: Elizabeth Bennet and Jane Eyre. But Jo [like Melville's stubbornly American Bartleby] says No and does not shift." Elizabeth Janeway, *Between Myth and Morning: Women Awakening* (New York: William Morrow & Co., 1975), pp. 235, 237. Janeway was the first to make plain the high-spirited sedition behind the pieties of *Little Women*; but both critics still define Jo by her response to a proposal, which is not for Alcott a crucial area of definition.

29. Quoted in *Louisa May Alcott: Her Life, Letters, and Jour-*

nals, ed. Ednah D. Cheyney (Boston: Roberts Brothers, 1890), p. 132.

30. In Spacks's grim view of the novel, "Discipline . . . is what women little and big require. They must be controlled or their passion for pickled limes and finery and freedom will precipitate chaos" (p. 101).

31. Mr. March's myopic detachment from female rituals and concerns recalls the more pernicious Dr. Blimber's intransigent erudition in the face of his boys' needs. "A warning from her mother checked any further remarks, and the whole family ate in heroic silence, till Mr. March mildly observed, 'Salad was one of the favorite dishes of the ancients, and Evelyn'—here a general explosion of laughter cut short the 'history of sallets,' to the great surprise of the learned gentleman" (*LW,* p. 194). Compare *Dombey and Son,* ch. 12, where Dr. Blimber intones over and over, "It is remarkable, Mr. Feeder, that the Romans"—while a boy is choking his throat out. At Amy's wedding party, at which Jo is finally falling in love, the good man discusses with ominous idiocy "the burial customs of the ancients" (p. 502).

32. In fact, as we see them in the first part, none of the girls thinks of being married; it seems to strike their aspirations unawares.

33. Journal entry, November 1, 1868. In Cheyney, p. 201.

34. *The New York Ledger,* 24 (April 11, 1868).

35. Cheyney, p. 187.

36. Louisa May Alcott, *An Old-Fashioned Girl* (Boston: Roberts Brothers, 1890), pp. 267-268, 378; hereafter cited as *OFG.*

37. Untitled manuscript, Alcott papers, 59M-309 (21), Houghton Library, Harvard University, Cambridge, Massachusetts. The manuscript is unpaginated after the first few pages.

38. The title is coined in Sarah Diamant's invaluable study, "Louisa May Alcott and the Woman Problem," Ph.D. diss., Cornell, 1974, pp. 181-196, the only serious full-length treatment of Alcott available. I think that Diamant makes too much of the lesbianism suggested by the heroines' promises of faith, without noticing that sisterhood here takes the form of passionate chastity, as in Persis' "On the continent I will mail myself like a vestal virgin and keep the vow I make my chosen goddess, Diana." The emotion here is the same as that of Jo's blunt wish that she could marry Meg to keep her in the family: allegiance is more important than sexuality.

39. Louisa May Alcott, *Work: A Story of Experience* (Boston: Roberts Brothers, 1885), p. 364. Future references to this edition will appear in the text.

40. The contrast between the selfless sharing of the female community and the "reality" of masculine laissez-faire economics suggests that Alcott may have been influenced by Elizabeth Gaskell's popular *Cranford,* which is explicitly linked to the cooperative artis-

tic jollity of *An Old-Fashioned Girl:* " 'How does the new book come on?' asked Polly, sucking her orange in public with a composure which would have scandalized the good ladies of 'Cranford' " (*OFG*, p. 268). Though she points to the superior strength and purpose of her own creation, Alcott nods in passing to another world of women and shows her awareness that she is writing in a tradition.

41. Journal entry, December 1862. Cheyney, p. 140.

42. Compare with this plenitude of names the distant formality of Elizabeth Bennet's return home to the unshared family crisis: "And my mother—How is she? How are you all?" "My mother is tolerably well, I trust; though her spirits are greatly shaken" (p. 286).

43. Janeway, p. 237, makes a similar point. Both M-G-M versions of the novel (George Cukor, 1933; Mervyn LeRoy, 1949), soften Bhaer's role from censor to critic of Jo's scribbling: the wise professor presents her with the old chestnut young writers in movies seem never to have heard before, "Write about what you know." Jo obediently writes about Beth and the book is a masterpiece. But the teacher-lover Alcott created is never so constructive.

44. Louisa May Alcott, *Little Men* (1871; rpt. New York: Grosset & Dunlap, 1947), pp. 42, 369. Future references to this edition will appear in the text under the abbreviation LM.

45. For a description of the Shaker community, see Charles Nordhoff, *The Communistic Societies of the United States,* with a Prefatory Essay by Franklin H. Littell (1875; rpt. New York: Schocken Books, 1965), pp. 117-255. For an account of Bronson Alcott's nervous collapse after Charles Lane deserted his community for that of the Shakers, see Sears, pp. 126-127, and Janeway, p. 236.

46. Louisa May Alcott, *Jo's Boys* (1886; rpt. New York: Grosset & Dunlap, 1949), p. 263. Future references to this edition will appear in the text under the abbreviation JB.

3. Beyond the Family: Idyll and Inferno

1. *The Ladies' Companion,* 9 (September 1838), 274.

2. Leonore Davidoff, *The Best Circles: Women and Society in Victorian England* (Totowa, N.J.: Rowan and Littlefield, 1973), pp. 14-15.

3. See Annette Hopkins, *Elizabeth Gaskell: Her Life and Work* (London: John Lehmann, 1952), pp. 119, 245.

4. Letter from Matthew Arnold to Mrs. Forster, April 14, 1853; in *Letters of Matthew Arnold,* collected and arranged by George W. E. Russell, 2 vols. (New York and London: Macmillan, 1895), I, 33-34.

5. Margaret Oliphant, "Modern Novelists—Great and Small," *Blackwood's Edinburgh Magazine,* 77 (May 1855), 558.

6. Elizabeth Gaskell, *Cranford* (1853; rpt. London: J. M. Dent &

Sons, 1969), p. 22. Future references to this edition will appear in the text.

7. "The independence of women seemed rather less unnatural to the Greeks than to other ancients, on account of the fabulous Amazons (whom they believed to be historical), and the partial example afforded by the Spartan women; who, though no less subordinate by law than in other Greek states, were more free in fact, and being trained to bodily exercises in the same manner with men, gave ample proof that they were not naturally disqualified for them"; John Stuart Mill, *The Subjection of Women* (1869; rpt. Cambridge, Mass.: M.I.T. Press, 1970), p. 14.

8. Quoted in Elizabeth Gaskell, *The Life of Charlotte Brontë* (1857; rpt. Middlesex: Penguin Books, 1975), p. 436. Future references to this edition will appear in the text.

9. See Aina Rubenius, *The Woman Question in Mrs. Gaskell's Life and Works* (Cambridge, Mass.: Harvard University Press, 1950), pp. 224-226.

10. *Cranford* has an odd critical history. It is usually dismissed as too charming for its own good. Edgar Wright, *Mrs. Gaskell: The Basis for Reassessment* (London: Oxford University Press, 1965), p. 8, discusses the damage this beloved book has done to its author's critical reputation. Rubenius loftily ignores it in her search for a feminist Elizabeth Gaskell; Susan R. Gorsky, "Old Maids and New Women: Alternatives to Marriage in Englishwomen's Novels, 1847-1915," *Journal of Popular Culture*, 7 (Summer 1973), 68-85, finds in its ladylike suffocation a world feminism helped the novel to outgrow. From a Freudian perspective, Martin Dodsworth's amazing "Women Without Men at Cranford," *Essays in Criticism*, 13 (April 1963), 132-145, Cranford is a pernicious hotbed of feminism and frustration, whose "horror" the uninitiated reader must be made to see. *Cranford* is *sui generis*, too sad for feminists and too strong for their antagonists. Patricia Wolfe, "Structure and Movement in *Cranford*," *Nineteenth-Century Fiction*, 23 (September 1968), 161-176, strikes a nice balance, forgetting Cranford's charm in favor of its hidden strengths.

11. Patricia Beer, *Reader, I Married Him: A Study of the Women Characters of Jane Austen, Charlotte Brontë, Elizabeth Gaskell and George Eliot* (New York: Barnes & Noble, 1974), p. 159.

12. Dodsworth, p. 135.

13. According to Dodsworth, p. 136, "The story of Martha and Jem provides a standard of sexual behaviour by which we may measure the adequacy of their betters' response to love and affection." Because the pair mate only at the call and convenience of these betters, this pseudo-Lawrentian judgment seems socially, psychologically, and artistically at variance with the novel Gaskell wrote.

14. In *Villette*, Charlotte Brontë will outdo her friend Elizabeth

Gaskell's Eastern silliness by dropping a turban on the sleeping head of the mock-god but true beefeater, Dr. John Bretton, who we are told earlier "was more than the Grand Turk in [Polly's] estimation." The teasing but recurrent erection of this personification of masculine autocracy seems to be the other pole of the transvestite image both writers find so amusing and appealing. The exotic costumes of Grand Turk and transvestite, and the abrupt passage of so many of their men from one to the other, suggest that both women found something inherently funny in Victorian ideals of manliness. The quiet laughter in their novels may be the deadliest component of the Amazonianism Margaret Oliphant found rampant in these two writers.

15. Emily to Catherine and Selina Winkworth, August 30, 1850; in *Memorials of Two Sisters: Susanna and Catherine Winkworth*, ed. Margaret J. Shaen (London: Longmans, Green and Co., 1908), p. 60.

16. On the strain of deceit that runs through Gaskell's narrative voice, see P. N. Furbank, "Mendacity in Mrs. Gaskell," *Encounter*, 40 (June 1973), 51-55. Furbank is right to isolate the note of duplicity that seems so important a part of the female voice in literature, but he seems somewhat overindignant at finding lies in works that are fictions to begin with.

17. Aristophanes, *Lysistrata*, trans. Jack Lindsay, in *The Complete Plays of Aristophanes*, ed. and with an introduction by Moses Hadas (New York: Bantam Books, 1962), p. 292.

18. According to Van Wyck Brooks, *Pride and Prejudice* and *Cranford* were Sarah Orne Jewett's favorite, appropriately Amazonian, novels. See *New England: Indian Summer, 1865-1915* (New York: E. P. Dutton & Co., 1940), p. 351.

19. Sarah Orne Jewett, *The Country of the Pointed Firs and Other Stories* (New York: Doubleday & Co., 1956), pp. 200, 206-207.

20. See her letter to Catherine Winkworth, August 25, 1850, which rushes on excitedly about the life she had just discovered, and which makes of Mr. Brontë an even more insanely savage Grand Turk than he appears in the biography. The letter is excerpted in the Penguin Library edition of the *Life*; the full text can be found in *The Letters of Mrs. Gaskell*, ed. J. A. V. Chapple and Arthur Pollard (Cambridge, Mass.: Harvard University Press, 1966), pp. 123-126.

21. *Cranford*, pp. 222-223, and Hopkins, p. 352.

22. *Cranford*, pp. 64-74, and *Life*, pp. 399-400.

23. Margaret Lane, *The Brontë Story: A Reconstruction of Mrs. Gaskell's Life of Charlotte Brontë* (London: William Heinemann, 1953), pp. 102-103, 159.

24. Winifred Gérin, *Charlotte Brontë: The Evolution of Genius* (Oxford: Oxford University Press, 1967), p. 294.

25. Gaskell, pp. 131-132. Gérin, p. 69, prints the letter in its entirety.

26. See, for example, Earl A. Knies's insistence in *The Art of Charlotte Brontë* (Athens: University of Ohio Press, 1969), p. 205, that "Charlotte's vision was primarily a private one" and she ventures beyond this sphere at her aesthetic peril.

27. Helene Moglen, *Charlotte Brontë: The Self Conceived* (New York: W. W. Norton & Co., 1976), p. 78.

28. "In Mr. Brontë's mind, then and later, the rooted belief that his daughter's feeble health would never be equal to the demands of marriage, was at the origin of his opposition to all her suitors"; Gérin, p. 440.

29. Richard Chase, "The Brontës: A Centennial Observance," *The Kenyon Review,* 9 (Autumn 1947); reprinted in *The Brontës: A Collection of Critical Essays,* ed. Ian Gregor (Englewood Cliffs, N.J.: Prentice-Hall, 1970), p. 20. Elizabeth Hardwick, *Seduction and Betrayal: Women and Literature* (New York: Random House, 1974), p. 10.

30. Quoted in Gaskell, pp. 189, 375; and in Margot Peters, *Unquiet Soul: A Biography of Charlotte Brontë* (New York: Doubleday & Co., 1975), p. 96. Peters' biography provides an astute and definitive discussion of the shifting relations between the sisters, replete with the misunderstandings and competitiveness that other biographers have glossed over.

31. This slashing attack on the "unsexed" Currer Bell coincided ironically with the death of Emily and the decline of Anne. See Elizabeth Rigby, "*Vanity Fair*—and *Jane Eyre,*" *Quarterly Review,* 84 (December 1848), 162-176.

32. Peters, p. 6

33. Charlotte Brontë, *Villette* (1853; rpt. New York: Harper Colophon Books, 1972), p. 224. Future references to this edition will appear in the text.

34. Charlotte Brontë, *The Professor,* Shakespeare Head Brontë (1857; rpt. Oxford; Shakespeare Head Press, 1931), pp. 66-67, 98-99.

35. Thomas Hughes, *Tom Brown's Schooldays,* Everyman's Library (1857; rpt. London & Toronto: J. M. Dent & Sons, 1924), pp. 259-260.

36. Charlotte Brontë, *Jane Eyre* (1847; rpt. New York: W. W. Norton & Co., 1971), p. 212. See, in contrast, Boyd-Kinnear's tenderhearted wish that women turn to sisterhoods for fulfillment of the familial roles life has denied them; Chapter 1, note 21.

37. For a fuller discussion of this sunny pair, see Nina Auerbach, "Charlotte Brontë: The Two Countries," *University of Toronto Quarterly,* 42 (Summer 1973), 339-341.

38. Mill, p. 99.

39. Charlotte Brontë, *Shirley* (1849; rpt, Middlesex: Penguin Books, 1974), p. 269.

40. Such justifications of unorthodox lives are still pervasive, infiltrating even sympathetic attempts to rehabilitate women in literature. Patricia Wolfe, for instance, defends Matty's childlessness against Freudian disapproval in the following terms: "She is a mother-figure to a larger and more important family—the Cranford community" (p. 173). If anything, the self-abasing Matty is Cranford's divine child; but like Madame Beck's pensionnat, Cranford is by definition not a family, and it seems needlessly apologetic to make it one.

41. Robert A. Colby discusses the pensionnat as a theater for the political and religious conflicts of the day, but he fails to draw the crucial distinction between Jane Eyre the governess and Lucy the teacher. In choosing to work in an institution rather than a household, Lucy is consciously entering the larger arena of government and power and leaving the home behind. See "*Villette:* Lucy Snowe and the Good Governess," in *Fiction With a Purpose: Major and Minor Nineteenth-Century Novels* (Bloomington: Indiana University Press, 1967), pp. 178-212.

42. Kate Millett's lively attack on Paul in *Sexual Politics* (New York: Avon Books, 1971), pp. 192-202, paradoxically throws him more into the foreground than Charlotte Brontë does. The book rarely makes us feel that he has the power to implement his patriarchal diatribes; Lucy laughs at them, and so should we. Some recent rebuttals of Millett's doctrinaire reading are M. A. Blom, "Charlotte Brontë, Feminist *Manquée,*" *Bucknell Review,* 21 (Spring 1973), 87-102; Carolyn V. Platt, "How Feminist is *Villette?*" *Women and Literature,* 3 (Spring 1975), 16-27; and Patricia Meyer Spacks, *The Female Imagination* (New York: Alfred A. Knopf, 1975), pp. 32-35.

43. On some connotations of the moon in Charlotte Brontë's novels, see Robert Heilman, "Charlotte Brontë, Reason, and the Moon," *Nineteenth-Century Fiction,* 14 (March 1960), 283-302. Also see Charles Burkhart, *Charlotte Brontë: A Psychosexual Study of her Novels* (London: Victor Gollancz, 1973), p. 108: "Lucy's paeans to the moon are those of its priestesses, odes to a female god."

44. To George Smith; quoted in Gaskell, p. 484.

4. Beyond the Self: The Spectacle of History and a New Religion

1. George Gissing, *The Odd Women* (1893; rpt. New York: W. W. Norton & Co., 1971), p. 237. Future references to this edition will appear in the text.

2. Nan Bauer Maglin, "Fictional Feminists in *The Bostonians* and *The Odd Women,*" in *Images of Women in Fiction: Feminist Perspectives,* ed. Susan Koppleman Cornillon (Bowling Green, Ohio:

Bowling Green University Popular Press, 1973), pp. 218-219. misleadingly divides the novelists into opposing camps, with Gissing as friend and James as foe of feminism. But both seem painfully ambivalent toward what they see as its historical inevitability in the new world to come.

3. Elizabeth Janeway, *Between Myth and Morning: Women Awakening* (New York: William Morrow and Co., 1975), pp. 138-139, 144.

4. F. W. Dupee, *Henry James* (1951; rpt. New York: William Morrow and Co., 1974), p. 122.

5. Jerome H. Buckley, "A World of Literature: Gissing's *New Grub Street*," in *The Worlds of Victorian Fiction*, ed. Jerome H. Buckley (Cambridge, Mass.: Harvard University Press, 1975), p. 223. For a detailed account of Gissing's often contradictory social attitudes, see Jacob Korg, *George Gissing: A Critical Biography* (Seattle: University of Washington Press, 1963).

6. Ellen DuBois, "The Radicalism of the Woman Suffrage Movement: Notes Toward the Reconstruction of Nineteenth-Century Feminism," *Feminist Studies*, 3 (Fall 1975), 65.

7. Gerda Lerner, "Placing Women in History: Definitions and Challenges," *Feminist Studies*, 3 (Fall 1975), 13

8. Barbara Sicherman, "Review Essay: American History," *Signs: Journal of Women in Culture and Society*, 1 (Winter 1975), 480.

9. Henry James, *The Bostonians* (1884; rpt. New York: The Modern Library, 1956), p. 21. Future references to this edition will appear in the text.

10. Leon Edel, *Henry James, The Untried Years: 1843-1870* (Philadelphia and New York: J. B. Lippincott Co., 1953), p. 202; and Charles Thomas Samuels, *The Ambiguity of Henry James* (Urbana: University of Illinois Press, 1971), p. 106.

11. William Rounseville Alger, *The Friendships of Women* (Boston: Roberts Brothers, 1885), p. 364.

12. *Louisa May Alcott: Her Life, Letters, and Journals*, ed. Ednah D. Cheyney (Boston: Roberts Brothers, 1890), p. 165.

13. Louisa May Alcott, *Little Women* (New York: Grosset & Dunlap, 1947), p. 204.

14. June 5, 1855; quoted in A. B. Hopkins, *Elizabeth Gaskell: Her Life and Work* (London: John Lehmann, 1952), pp. 225-226.

15. *The Nation*, 2 (Oct. 22, 1866), 246.

16. See John Henry Raleigh, *Matthew Arnold and American Culture* (Berkeley and Los Angeles: University of California Press, 1961), p. 42: "Both [Arnold and James] were convinced that the future was in the hands of America."

17. Quoted in Judith Becker Ranlett, "Sorority and Community:

Women's Answer to a Changing Massachusetts, 1865-1895," Ph.D. diss., Brandeis, 1974, p. 72.

18. Leon Edel, *Henry James, The Middle Years: 1882-1895* (Philadelphia and New York: J. B. Lippincott Co., 1962), p. 144.

19. February 9, 1882, and March 19, 1905; *The Notebooks of Henry James*, ed. F. O. Matthiessen and Kenneth B. Murdock (New York: Oxford University Press, 1947), pp. 41, 320-321.

20. Quoted in Ranlett, p. 160.

21. Van Wyck Brooks, *New England: Indian Summer, 1865-1915* (New York: E. P. Dutton & Co., 1940), p. 469.

22. Henry James, *The American Scene* (Bloomington and London: Indiana University Press, 1968), pp. 102, 105. Future references to this edition will appear in the text.

23. Maria J. McIntosh, *Woman in America: Her Work and Her Reward* (New York: D. Appleton & Co., 1850), p. 57.

24. *The Complete Tales of Henry James*, ed. Leon Edel, 6 vols. (London: Rupert Hart-Davis, 1963), V, 396.

25. Oct. 8, 1879; Cheyney, p. 322. See also Ranlett, ch. 3; Sicherman, p. 476; and Estelle B. Freedman, "Their Sisters' Keepers: An Historical Perspective on Female Correctional Institutions in the United States: 1870-1900," *Feminist Studies*, 2 (1974), 77-95. A depressing reminder of how far we have or have not come from Alcott's exuberant "salvation for all" is Rose Giallombardo's *Society of Women: A Study of a Women's Prison* (New York and London: John Wiley & Sons, 1966). According to Giallombardo, the total desolation of these women without men is less sexual than social; deprived of their sole means of attaining status, the women have evolved an elaborate masquerade in which some of them strut about in elaborate drag, even at times assuming the role of a strict, respectable paterfamilias, and order the others about. Life is thus tolerable and familiar once more because it holds at least the charade of salvation through a man. "The hardest part of living in a prison is to live with other women," says one; all seem to agree that a world without men is an anti-communal jungle (pp. 99-100).

26. See Irving Howe's introduction to the Modern Library College Edition of the novel p. xvi: "while Basil Ransom is ready to talk about the proper place of women, who are for him the solacing and decorative sex, James is far too much of a realist to suggest that they can or ever will again assume this place: even Ransom's lady relatives in Mississippi, deprived of their darkies, have been reduced to hard work." Howe's exposure of Basil's inadequacies is a good antidote to Lionel Trilling's erection of his sadism into a cultural norm, though Howe and Basil are oddly at one in their detestation of Boston's feminists.

27. In *The American Scene*, pp. 414-417, James ironically corroborates Basil's sexual vision of history in his portrait of the South as an analogue of Boston, "a sick lioness," overrun by women.

28. See, among many, Howe, p. xxiii; Samuels, pp. 97-99; Theodore C. Miller, "The Muddled Politics of Henry James' *The Bostonians*," *Georgia Review*, 26 (Fall 1972), 336-346; and Robert C. McLean, "*The Bostonians*: New England Pastoral," *Papers on Language and Literature*, 7 (Fall 1971), 374-381.

29. See R. Laurence Moore, "The Spiritualist Medium: A Study of Female Professionalism in Victorian America," *American Quarterly*, 27 (May 1975), 200-221, for the historical links between spiritualism, feminism, and the theater. For Moore, spiritualism was one of the few avenues by which women could take center stage, while being able to deny responsibility for their entranced assumption of public power.

30. This concept of "performance" is an important indication of the changing presentations of female communities. In *Jane Austen's Novels: The Fabric of Dialogue* (Athens: Ohio University Press, 1962), pp. 113-144, Howard S. Babb discusses the welcome disappearance of the word "performance" from the dialogue of *Pride and Prejudice*, when Elizabeth and Darcy come to understand each other; and see Chapter 2 for an examination of this welcoming privacy into which the female community triumphantly propels Elizabeth. But the goal of the women in *The Bostonians* is the achievement of, not the escape from, performance in the widest sense of the word.

31. David Donald Stone, *Novelists in a Changing World: Meredith, James, and the Transformation of English Fiction in the 1880's* (Cambridge, Mass.: Harvard University Press, 1972), pp. 84, 306.

32. Henry James, *The Princess Casamassima* (1886; rpt. New York: Harper & Row, 1968), p. 35. Future references to this edition will appear in the text.

33. For Princess Ida and Madame Beck see Chapter 3; Stone, pp. 302-303, discusses some similarities between Olive and Christina, and innumerable critics have linked the forbidding spinster to such lovable Jamesian creations as Isabel Archer, Julia Dallow, and Milly Theale, as well as to her more seemingly wholesome antagonist, Basil Ransom.

34. Henry James, *The Tragic Muse* (1889-90; rpt. New York: Harper & Brothers, 1960), p. 212. Future references to this edition will appear in the text.

35. D. J. Gordon and John Stokes, "The Reference of *The Tragic Muse*," in *The Air of Reality: New Essays on Henry James*, ed. John Goode (London: Methuen & Co., 1972), p. 92; and David Howard, "*The Bostonians*," ibid., p. 71.

36. See Edel, *Middle Years*, p. 81; and Leon Edel, *Henry James*,

The Treacherous Years: 1895-1901 (Philadelphia and New York: J. B. Lippincott Co., 1969), p. 153.

37. March 25, 1889; *Notebooks*, p. 97. On p. 98, the editors quote some remarks by Du Maurier corroborating James's account, with Du Maurier's significant addition: " 'Well,' I said, 'you may have the idea and work it out to your own satisfaction.' "

38. Howard, in Goode, p. 67.

39. Compare Florimond's similar extended soliloquy in "A New England Winter" (1884), which begins: "He felt at moments that he was in a city of women, in a country of women" (*Tales*, VI, 142). Florimond's diagnosis is correct, but his dismay is called into question by the flimsy and pretentious nature of his career as "an impressionist." In the final analysis, the women who pass him back and forth among them represent less a sinister sexual conspiracy than the force of greatest integrity.

40. See, for instance, Elizabeth Schultz, "The Bostonians: The Contagion of Romantic Illusion," *Genre*, 4 (March 1971), 45-59; and Graham Burns, "The Bostonians," *The Critical Review*, 12 (1969), 45-60.

41. Henry James, *The Turn of the Screw* (New York: W. W. Norton & Co., 1966), p. 16.

42. Quoted in Leon Edel, *Henry James, The Master: 1901-1916* (Philadelphia and New York: J. B. Lippincott Co., 1972), p. 383.

43. See Sharon Hartman Strom, "Leadership and Tactics in the American Woman Suffrage Movement: A New Perspective from Massachusetts," *The Journal of American History*, 62 (September 1975), 296-315.

44. Lionel Trilling, "The Bostonians," in *The Opposing Self* (New York: The Viking Press, 1955), pp. 109-119.

45. Edel, *Treacherous Years*, p. 79; my italics.

46. Ranlett, p. 120.

47. George Moore, *A Drama in Muslin: A Realistic Novel* (1886; rpt. London: Walter Scott, n.d.), p. 170. Future references to this edition will appear in the text.

48. Gissing, *The Odd Women*, p. 35.

49. Gillian Tindall, *George Gissing: The Born Exile* (New York and London: Harcourt, Brace, Jovanovich, 1974), p. 264.

50. George Gissing, *In the Year of Jubilee* (London: Lawrence & Bullen, 1894), p. 44.

51. Tindall, p. 255.

52. See Chapter 1. See, too, its final waning appearance in Arnold Bennett's *The Old Wives' Tale* (1908), where the only sisterhood that links Constance and Sophia Baines is their common deterioration before death, which frees them from the aspirations that separated them in girlhood.

53. George Gissing, *New Grub Street* (1891; rpt. Boston: Houghton Mifflin Company, 1962), p. 298; hereafter cited in the text as *NGS*.

54. Korg, p. 54.

55. George Gissing, *Charles Dickens: A Critical Study* (1898; rpt. New York: Haskell House, 1974), p. 241.

56. In *James Joyce*, Ellmann discusses at length the influence of George Moore on "The Dead," but adds: "Moore said nothing about snow, however [in his *Vain Fortune*]. No one can know how Joyce conceived the joining of Gabriel's final experience with snow"; Richard Ellmann, *James Joyce* (1959; rpt. New York and London: Oxford University Press, 1974), p. 260. But the snow in Moore's *Drama in Muslin* seems a likely source for Gabriel's culminating vision of Irish sterility and sleep.

57. Tindall, pp. 203-205, turns over every pebble to find it.

58. Quoted in Korg, p. 52.

5. A World at War: One Big Miss Brodie

1. Aristophanes, *Lysistrata*, trans. Jack Lindsay, in *The Complete Plays of Aristophanes*, ed. and with an introduction by Moses Hadas (New York: Bantam Books, 1962), pp. 287, 294, 302.

2. Mary A. Livermore, "Coöperative Womanhood in the State," *The North American Review*, 153 (September 1891), 284, 295.

3. Harriot Stanton Blatch, *The Mobilization of Woman-Power* (1918); quoted in William L. O'Neill, *Everyone Was Brave: A History of Feminism in America* (Chicago: Quadrangle Books, 1971), p. 187.

4. *The Forerunner: A Monthly Magazine*, 6 (January 1915), 17.

5. Ibid., 6 (August 1915), 212.

6. Ibid., 7 (February 1916), 43.

7. Ibid., 6 (January 1915), 26.

8. "Their Answer," ibid., 7 (July 1916), 177.

9. See her "When it Changed," in *Again, Dangerous Visions*, ed. Harlan Ellison (New York: New American Library, 1972), pp. 271-281; and *The Female Man* (New York: Bantam Books, 1975).

10. E. M. Forster, *Howards End* (1910; rpt. New York: Vintage Books, 1921), pp. 290, 28.

11. For a more detailed discussion of the contradictions that underlie Dorothy Sayers' self-sustaining women, see Nina Auerbach, "Dorothy Sayers and the Amazons," *Feminist Studies*, 3 (Fall 1975), 54-62.

12. Virginia Woolf, *Three Guineas* (1938; rpt. New York: Harcourt, Brace & World, 1966), p. 74. Future references to this edition will appear in the text.

13. Muriel Spark, *The Abbess of Crewe* (New York: The Viking

Press, 1974), p. 12. Future references to this edition will appear in the text abbreviated as *Ab. Crewe.*

14. Muriel Spark, *The Prime of Miss Jean Brodie* (1961; rpt. New York: Dell Books, 1966), pp. 34-35. Future references to this edition will appear in the text. John Updike, "Between a Wedding and a Funeral," *The New Yorker* (Sept. 14, 1963), p. 192, sees *The Prime of Miss Jean Brodie* and *The Girls of Slender Means* as Spark's turn to "history and autobiography"; for her, they seem to be identical genres.

15. David Lodge, "The Uses and Abuses of Omniscience: Method and Meaning in Muriel Spark's *The Prime of Miss Jean Brodie,*" *Critical Quarterly,* 12 (Autumn 1970), 248-249.

16. Frederick R. Karl, *A Reader's Guide to the Contemporary English Novel,* rev. ed. (London: Thames and Hudson, 1972), pp. 324-325.

17. Lodge, p. 250.

18. Muriel Spark and Derek Stanford, *Emily Brontë: Her Life and Work* (London: Peter Owen, 1953), pp. 11-12.

19. Muriel Spark, *The Bachelors* (London: Macmillan and Co., 1960), p. 63.

20. Thomas Hughes, *Tom Brown's Schooldays,* Everyman's Library (1857; rpt. London and Toronto: J. M. Dent & Sons, 1924), p. 265.

21. John Erskine, *The Influence of Women and its Cure* (New York: The Bobbs-Merrill Co., 1936), pp. 11, 64.

22. Muriel Spark, *The Girls of Slender Means* (New York: Alfred A. Knopf, 1963), p. 6. Future references to this edition will appear in the text.

23. Frank Kermode, *Continuities* (London: Routledge and Kegan Paul, 1968), p. 209.

24. Muriel Spark, *The Driver's Seat* (1970; rpt. New York: Bantam Books, 1975), p. 97. Future references to this edition will appear in the text.

25. Muriel Spark, "The First Year of my Life," *The New Yorker* (June 2, 1975), p. 37. Future references will appear in the text.

26. See *Literary Women* (New York: Doubleday & Co., 1976), pp. 106-107.

27. See, for instance, Susan Gubar, "Sane Jane and the Critics: 'Professions and Falsehoods,' " *Novel: A Forum in Fiction,* 8 (Spring 1975), 259: "The comedy of Austen's novels explores the tensions between the freedom of her art and the dependency of her characters. While they proclaim and profess, while they stutter and sputter and lapse into silence and even hasten to perfect felicity, she attains a woman's language that is magnificently duplicitous"; and Malcolm

Bradbury, "Muriel Spark's Fingernails," *Critical Quarterly,* 14 (Autumn 1972), 243: "Muriel Spark senses a necessity, a need for wholeness and coherence . . . [which] makes her novels a teleological or, as we are learning to say, an end-directed economy which makes them into very exact, very formal and very duplicitous objects."

28. Simone de Beauvoir, *The Second Sex,* trans. and ed. H. M. Parshley (American ed. 1953; rpt. New York: Bantam Books, 1961), p. 562.

29. See, for instance, Lois Gould, "Creating a Woman's World," *The New York Times Magazine* (Jan. 2, 1977). Gould discusses the self-conscious unease among the members of Daughters, Inc., a woman-staffed and "woman-identified" publishing house, as they claim to eschew the concern for money and power of their male competitors from whom they are trying to withdraw.

30. Djuna Barnes, *Nightwood* (1936; rpt. New York: New Directions Books, 1961), p. 136. Future references in the text will be to this edition.

31. Monique Wittig, *Les Guérillères,* trans. David Le Vay (1969; rpt. New York: Avon Books, 1973), p. 14. Future references to this edition will appear in the text.

32. Ti-Grace Atkinson, *Amazon Odyssey* (New York: Links Books, 1974), p. 138. Future references to this edition will appear in the text.

Index

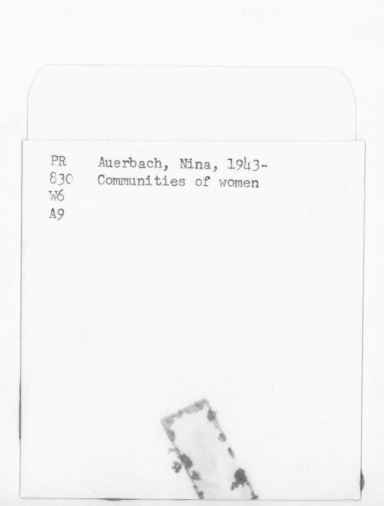